ND A LEVEL

SOCIOLOGY
DEALING WITH DATA

Shaun Best
Graham Harris
Ian Marsh

Janis Griffiths
Tanya Hope
Keith Trobe

Pearson Education Limited
Edinburgh Gate,
Harlow,
Essex CM20 2JE, England.

ISBN 0582 299306

First published 1999
Printed in Singapore

The Publisher's policy is to use paper manufactured from sustainable forests.

Contents

Preface

The aim of this book is to help you to write more effective answers to data-response questions in A-level Sociology.

Skills-based sociology at A-level was introduced in the new AEB examination syllabus in 1991. This syllabus placed a far greater emphasis than before on the skills dimension in A-level Sociology. It identified three skills which students would be expected to display in their answers to Paper 1 (data-response questions) and Paper 2 (essay questions). These skills are:

- knowledge and understanding;
- interpretation and application;
- evaluation.

Since then the emphasis on a skills-based approach has become firmly established within other examination syllabuses – most notably the IBS (Interboard Sociology). This approach has not been unique to sociology and the SCAA has produced syllabus cores which include the knowledge, skills and assessment objectives for all major A-level subjects.

The 1998 AEB A-level syllabus has maintained this emphasis on skills across all of the six papers (including the coursework element – Paper 4) that are available to candidates. Indeed, it has tied in the three 'skill domains' more closely with the assessment objectives of the different examinations. The 1998 syllabus has many similarities with its predecessor, particularly in terms of the assessment objectives. The major changes relate to the introduction of various different routes (or papers) to an A-level qualification. The AEB has responded to the government requirement that quality of language (QOL) should be assessed in all A-level syllabuses by including QOL in all the assessment criteria, rather than allocating specific marks to it.

The IBS A-level syllabus (a coalition which has replaced a number of separate A-level Sociology syllabuses – including the Cambridge, Oxford and Welsh Joint papers), which was examined for the first time in 1995, includes very similar assessment objectives to the AEB – knowledge and understanding; interpretation and analysis (to all intents and purposes the same as application); evaluation; and communication and presentation.

When marking examination answers, examiners look to see how effectively students have displayed their skills in the domain areas. The data-response questions and essay questions are framed so as to allow these skills to be displayed when answering them.

Chapter 1 starts by identifying the characteristics of data-response questions and the skill domains examined in this kind of question. It then looks at the ways in which students can exhibit these skills in their answers to stimulus response questions.

The other six chapters focus on the six areas of Sociology covered by Paper 1 of the AEB A-level Sociology syllabus – the paper which all AEB A-level and AS-level students have to take. Each of the chapters follows a similar format and looks at how the skills needed to produce effective answers to stimulus-response questions can be developed and enhanced through each of the six areas:

- Theory and Methods;
- Family;
- Education;
- Work, Organisations and Leisure;
- Social Stratification and Differentiation;
- Culture and Identity.

The chapters start by considering the skill domain of knowledge and understanding and the sort of questions that are asked to identify these skills. They then move on to the other skill domains of interpretation and application and evaluation.

Each of these chapters ends with two full, examination-style, data-response questions. A model answer is provided for the first question, along with a brief commentary on how that answer addresses the different skill areas. A detailed mark scheme is provided with the second question, to enable you to think about how examiners go about marking data-response questions.

This book is not a conventional sociology text-book of the kind that introduces and examines all the main areas of A-level syllabuses and covers the full range of sociological theories and findings. It is not a knowledge-based textbook. The focus here is on the interpretation, application and evaluation of the sociological knowledge you already have as a sociology student and which you will continue to gain from other texts and sources. However, each chapter includes useful material that will provide you with relevant sociological knowledge.

Chapter 1

Key Skills

Introduction

This chapter will try to answer the following questions about the skills needed to produce effective answers to data-response questions in A-level Sociology:

- Why are skills so important?
- What are the key skills?
- How can I recognise these skills in examination questions?
- How can I apply these skills in my answers?
- How can I analyse and use data items in my answers?

Why are skills so important?

In the same way that simply knowing how the controls on a car work and having read the *Highway Code* do not necessarily make you a good driver, having a good knowledge of sociological theory and research does not necessarily mean you will get a top grade in an A-level Sociology exam. Of course, knowledge is very important in whatever you do, but equally as important, if not more so, is the ability to use and apply that knowledge. This book is not intended to help you extend your knowledge of sociology – there are many excellent textbooks which will do that – but to show you some of the ways in which you can use your knowledge to the best effect in an exam. This first section demonstrates and discusses the skills involved in doing this.

Skills and exams

Although the exam syllabuses that you are likely to be following will change periodically, something which is likely to be considered very important for some considerable time to come is the emphasis on skills. Although these are sometimes worded differently, essentially they boil down to three key skill areas:

Knowledge and understanding

This covers what you know about sociological theory and research. Most A-level courses and textbooks focus on outlining and explaining what sociology is and what has been discovered by sociological research and writing.

Interpretation and application

This is mainly to do with selecting sociological theory and research that are relevant to a particular question and using this knowledge in a way which answers the question.

Interpretation requires you to select and show you understand the meaning of various sorts of data included in the stimulus material for the question, for example extracts from studies, tables, charts and graphs. **Application** requires you to use your sociological knowledge and understanding in responding to the question by drawing on your knowledge of sociological ideas, explanations and arguments and linking this to the question.

Evaluation

Ultimately, the only point in having any knowledge of anything is being able to use it to make a judgement about a claim. Was that a good football match or concert that you watched? In sociology, as in life, we don't just go around describing things; we also evaluate how good or bad they are.

As well as talking about skills, examination syllabuses also talk about the **marks** awarded. Virtually all students are concerned about the marks they get – so what do you get marks for? If you read the exam syllabus that you are following, you'll see that you get marks for each of the skill areas. Generally speaking, the proportion of marks given to each skill area is the same – so you get about one-third of your marks for your sociological knowledge, another third for how you apply that knowledge and a further third for how well you use that knowledge to evaluate a claim.

Have a look at some **mark schemes**. When a chief examiner writes an exam question, he or she also writes a mark scheme. This is intended as a guide to the examiners who will be marking candidates' answers, and every examiner is expected to become very familiar with what is in the mark scheme. In every one of these mark schemes – and each of the following chapters will give you examples – words like 'evaluate', 'apply', 'balanced accounts', 'relevant studies', appear with great frequency. In order to achieve top mark bands and get a top grade, it is vital that you display more than simply your knowledge of sociology.

Furthermore, the style of the **questions** used in exam papers shows very clearly that you are expected to display a full range of skills in your answers. Questions usually ask you explicitly to evaluate a claim, often using words and phrases like 'assess the claim that ...' or 'how far is it true to say that ...'. These **action words** require you to do much more than just display your knowledge and understanding. They want you to use them to gauge how accurate a particular claim is.

So, from the exam syllabuses, papers, mark schemes and types of questions asked, it is clear that in order to produce effective answers to stimulus-response questions, you need to show that you understand and can employ a full range of skills.

What are the key skills?

Here we will look in greater detail at the three key skills areas in A-level Sociology. Although they are interconnected, we will treat them separately at first, although your final answers should draw all three together in a truly 'skilled answer'!

Knowledge and understanding

When answering any data-response question you will need to be able to show that you know and understand sociological material, in the form of theories, concepts, methods, and also evidence, in the form of research studies. Where are you to find this? Although the data items in the question will include some information, this is likely to be fairly minimal and intended to act as prompts or clues to what knowledge is likely to be relevant. You cannot simply rely on the data items to provide the necessary amount of information so you will need to bring to the question a well-developed **knowledge** of sociology if you are to produce a thorough answer. Much of the course you have been following is likely to focus on 'getting through' the material necessary to deal with this skill area in the examination. As it is not the purpose of this book to take the place of existing textbooks, we will assume that you have built a good 'knowledge base' ready to be allied to the other two skills areas. The focus of our examination of the different areas of the syllabus in Chapters 2 to 7 will be on the skills of interpretation, application and evaluation.

Interpretation and application

To gain marks for interpretation and application you have to demonstrate that you have interpreted the stimulus material and data and that you have applied them to the question. First, you have to interpret the question. Exactly what issues does it refer to? Unless you 'de-code' the question properly, you are likely to produce a general, 'catch-all' answer rather than one which really focuses on the specific issues stated in the question. Once you have interpreted the question, you then need to employ sociological theory and evidence which are relevant to that particular question. The key word here is **relevance**. If you include sociological knowledge which is not relevant to the question, you are penalising yourself by wasting precious time because an examiner will simply ignore any inappropriate sections.

To demonstrate your skills of **interpretation** (and to gain marks for this) you must use the information that is provided in the stimulus material (fortunately, the particular questions usually direct you to the appropriate item!). To gain **application** marks you have to apply sociological knowledge that is relevant to the question being asked.

Evaluation

Evaluation involves the **testing** of a statement or claim against sociological theory and research findings. Most stimulus-response questions set up a claim and then ask you to reach a judgement about its accuracy by examining sociological arguments and research evidence which might be relevant to that claim. Here you have to do more than just display your sociological understanding – you have to use it to reach an informed conclusion about the claim made in the question.

Examiner's comment

All examiners see many examples of candidates' answers which show good sociological knowledge but which fail to get into the top mark bands because the knowledge is not applied well or there is little or no evaluation. In each of the chapters in this book there are example questions with exemplar answers from two or more candidates. Often both of these answers will use the same sociological knowledge but only one will apply it in an evaluative manner. We have deliberately constructed these kinds of answers so that you can see the importance (in terms of marks) of interpreting, applying and evaluating sociological knowledge.

These are the sort of questions students and teachers might think about when considering how well equipped they are to demonstrate the different skills:

Knowledge and understanding

- Do I know the main points of view and arguments for this issue?
- Do I know the major sociologists who have contributed to this debate?
- Do I have an understanding of the historical context of this debate?
- Do I know the main points of their writings/studies?
- Are there any concepts or ideas I am unsure of?

Interpretation and application

- Have I practised interpreting appropriate statistical data in this area?
- Have I used/can I find any newspaper/journal articles which can be applied to debates in this area?
- What evidence can be used in examining the issues in this area?
- Can I use studies to support or undermine particular points of view?

Evaluation

- How many sides to the debate can I identify in this area?
- What are the strengths and weaknesses of the evidence and ideas in this area?
- Which evidence and arguments are most convincing and why?
- Which of the opposing viewpoints is most 'true to life'?

How can I recognise these skills in examination questions?

The wording of questions will indicate the skills being tested and you will find it very useful to learn how to de-code questions to uncover the particular skills that are being examined. Your answers, of course, should reflect these skills. Particular key words or key phrases are associated with particular skills. Some of the action words ('action' because they define what you should be doing) draw on more than one skill but, in general, they can be categorised in relation to one or other of the skill domain areas.

Below we give some of the action words that are most commonly associated with the skills of knowledge and understanding, interpretation, application and evaluation. These are only examples and it is important to realise that other words and phrases can be used in examination questions. Remember also that there are dangers in being too rigid in linking a particular 'command phrase' with one particular skill domain.

Knowledge and understanding

The following words and phrases provide information on how you are expected to answer the question:

- 'State ...'
- 'Name ...'
- 'List ...'
- 'Which perspective ...'

Interpretation and application

These key words and phrases encourage you to use your sociological knowledge and understanding to interrogate and analyse both the data items and the question itself. This requires explanation rather than description (although some description of theories and studies is inevitable and necessary) so you will need to identify possible reasons for trends and patterns shown in the extracts. Although we have included separate lists for interpretation and application, some of the words and phrases relate to both skill areas.

Interpretation: key words and phrases

- 'Identify ...'
- 'What sociological perspective is illustrated by Item A ...'
- What trends and/or patterns are indicated in Item A ...'
- 'Using information from the items ...'
- 'What do you understand by ...'
- 'What is meant by ...'
- 'Define ...
- 'According to Item A ...'

Application: key words and phrases

- 'Identify ...'
- 'What sociological perspective is illustrated by Item A ...'
- 'Suggest reasons why ...'
- 'What explanations have been offered for the patterns ...'
- 'What are the implications of ...'
- 'What reasons can be given ...'
- 'Provide examples to support Item A's claim that ...'
- 'Using material from the items and elsewhere ...'

Evaluation

Key command phrases like these focus on the idea of testing a claim and reaching a judgement about its accuracy.

- 'Evaluate ...'
- 'Assess ...'
- 'To what extent is it true ...'
- 'How useful ...'
- 'Critically assess ...'
- 'How valid is the claim that ...'
- 'Suggest arguments for and against ...'
- 'How far is ... supported by sociological evidence ...'
- 'Assess the usefulness ...'
- 'Assess the strengths and weaknesses of ...'
- 'Compare and contrast ...'

Example of a data-response question

Figure 1.2

a) When carrying out research, what do sociologists mean by the term 'population'? (Item A) *(1 mark)*

You need to **apply** knowledge of the sociological use of the term 'population'. You need to give only a brief description.

b) Identify and briefly describe two types of samples commonly used in sociological research other than the form of sampling referred to in Item A. *(4 marks)*

This asks you to **apply** your **knowledge** of types of samples. You should ensure you identify two different types of samples and give a description of each type.

It is very important to read and **interpret** Item A and identify the form of sampling mentioned so that you exclude it from your answer.

c) Item B states that 'there is no sociological value in using an unrepresentative sample'. How far do you agree with this claim? *(4 marks)*

The reference to Item B directs you to read and **interpret** this piece of data. What does it have to say about the issue of representativeness and sampling?

What is meant by an 'unrepresentative sample'? You need to **interpret** this term and **apply** your **knowledge** of samples in terms of the concept of representativeness.

This is a clear instruction to **evaluate** a claim. Remember to give a **balanced** assessment putting arguments both for and against the claim.

d) Assess the strengths and weaknesses of postal questionnaires in sociological research. *(8 marks)*

Another common example of an **evaluation** instruction. Try to get a good **balance** between strengths and weaknesses.

You need to **apply** your **knowledge** of the strengths and weaknesses of this research technique. Avoid lengthy descriptions and maintain a **focus** on its uses and problems.

What is meant by the term 'postal questionnaires'? Be careful not to just notice the 'questionnaires' part – you need to focus on the 'postal' dimension as well to provide a full answer. You should **interpret** both elements in the term and **apply** your sociological **knowledge**.

e) Using information from the Items as well as from your own studies, evaluate the claim that 'there is little difference between sociological understanding and everyday, commonsense knowledge'. (Item C)
(8 marks)

This directs you to read and **interpret** all the data items – check through them for evidence and argument relevant to this particular claim.

A very clear example of an instruction to **evaluate**! Again, remember the importance of producing a **balanced** response arguing both for and against the claim. Finish off your answer with a final evaluation paragraph.

Interpret this claim from the data item. Item C is likely to at least partially explain this view of sociological and commonsense knowledge. Some of this may be of use in your answer.

Figure 1.2 (*cont'd*)

It may well seem fairly straightforward to analyse these questions, identifying the skills indicated above. However, under examination pressure it is very easy to miss some of this 'de-coding'. Some common errors – and their likely consequences – might have been:

i) In question (b) identifying and describing a type of sampling in Item A – with the loss of two marks.

ii) In question (b) only identifying and not describing two kinds of samples – again with the chance of losing two marks.

iii) Forgetting the need to present a balanced answer to question (c) and only arguing that there is no sociological value in using an 'unrepresentative sample'. By agreeing with the claim rather than testing it – again a loss of two marks.

iv) Most students will have a prepared 'list' of the advantages and disadvantages of questionnaires – but question (d) asks for an assessment of **postal** questionnaires – a loss of between one or three marks could result.

v) Just presenting a 'list' answer to either or both of questions (d) and (e) would not meet the demands of an **evaluation** instruction. Therefore knowledge is not enough – you need to **apply** it to get into the top mark band.

vi) A difficult question (e) and many candidates would not have a prepared answer for it. This is where a few marks at least can be earned by interpreting the data items carefully.

A quick examination of these pitfalls shows just how easy it can be to lose marks. Conversely, a good understanding of what the skills are and how to spot them is **worth** marks!

How can I apply these skills in my answers?

Having introduced the key skills and discussed how to recognise them in data-response questions, the rest of this introduction will focus on putting the skills into action in answering different styles of questions – from 1–2-mark questions, to short paragraph answers, to the mini-essay answers that a stimulus-response question can require.

Producing a focused answer (or how to avoid writing down all you know about the subject without answering the question!)

One of the commonest faults in answering data-response questions is not addressing the question being asked and, instead, writing down as much information as possible in the time available. To avoid this and produce a good answer involves using the skills of application and interpretation. In essence, these skills involve the de-coding of the question, working out exactly what it requires of you and then selecting from your knowledge only that which is relevant to the specific question.

Another way of thinking about this skill is to consider the idea of a '**focused answer**'. To try to understand what a focused answer is, let's start by working out what the purpose is of any kind of question, whether sociological or not.

The purpose of questions

Examination questions are similar in certain ways to the questions we deal with in everyday life. One way to develop the skills necessary to deal with such questions is to start with the lessons we have all learned about how to handle normal day-to-day questions and then to apply this understanding to examination questions.

A common everyday question is 'What kind of day have you had?' If you respond by giving a minute-by-minute account of the day's events, this would not be seen as an appropriate answer.

Briefly explain why this is not an appropriate response.

One of the comedian Rik Mayall's early inventions was a character called Kevin Turvey who used to respond to everyday questions in a fairly unconventional manner. Kevin Turvey would reply to questions in a truly unfocused way, describing in enormous detail the minutiae of his day, at times giving not just a minute-by-minute account, but a second-by-second description.

The logic of enquiry – response

A question such as 'What kind of a day have you had?' usually sets out an issue, a problem or a task of some kind to which you have to respond. Appropriate responses usually do the following things:

- Identify the task/problem in the question. This is sometimes shown in the way we may begin our reply by repeating the question in some form, for instance by saying, 'What kind of a day have I had? I'll tell you what kind of a day I've had ...'
- Identify the issue raised in the question. Any problems of definition or possible misunderstandings may be raised in our reply. We may ask, 'What do you mean, what *kind* of a day have I had?'
- Provide a direct answer to the question. For example, stating that: 'Today has been great/terrible/boring/indifferent, etc.'
- Finally, explain why this is our evaluation of the day. We may put forward evidence or arguments to justify the judgement we have made. So we may say, 'This morning was an absolute disaster because ...'. Then we may alter or moderate our initial judgement by saying, 'Mind you, this afternoon got distinctly better when ...'.

If we do not de-code the question properly in the first place, then the whole process of response falls apart. This is true not just of everyday questions and responses, but also of academic questions. So how do you go about de-coding the questions?

De-coding data-response questions and extracting the issues

If you are to produce focused answers, you will need to understand the question and extract from it the issues, problems and questions it raises. Only then will you be in a position to create an answer which is focused on the question. This section describes some common errors and misreadings of questions and indicates some of the skills involved in writing focused answers.

These are examples of typical questions and some of the common errors made in answering them, plus suggestions for more focused ways of dealing with them. Read these examples carefully so that you can begin to recognise what the questions are really asking you to do.

1 How far do you agree with the claim that science is a systematic method?

Common errors

- only arguing that science is or is not a systematic method;
- including all kinds of research as 'science';
- not defining what 'systematic' means.

Response required
- arguments and evidence both for and against science being systematic;
- recognising the ambiguous nature of both words, 'science' and 'systematic'.

2 To what extent have sociologists agreed that parents are a critical factor in pupils' achievements?

Common errors
- simply listing the studies which connect pupil achievement and home background;
- commonsense descriptions of pupils' home backgrounds;
- presenting a summary of all studies of differential educational achievement.

Response required
- identifying the range of ways in which parental influence may affect achievement;
- an evaluation of the effects of home background relative to other influences (such as school);
- an evaluation of the strengths and weaknesses of research examining parental influence.

Producing a balanced answer (or how to avoid agreeing with the question!)

Candidates need to present a 'balanced' answer, particularly in dealing with the parts of data-response questions which carry six or more marks. A 'balanced answer' recognises the need to examine all sides of an issue or claim and to reach a conclusion about the claim on the basis of the evidence and argument. One problem which candidates often experience under examination pressure is that the wording of questions may emphasise one aspect of an issue and, as a result, they are often drawn towards dealing only with that one aspect. Often the result is an answer which seems to agree with the claim rather than one which has tested it. Always remember that the question is asking you to evaluate the relevance or accuracy of a claim and this means you must examine alternative claims and how far sociological research and theory support them.

Let's look at two examples which illustrate this point.

1 Assess the view that ethnic minority pupils are discriminated against in schools.

The wording of this question places a clear emphasis on schools discriminating against ethnic minority students. This may lead some candidates to write only about how schools discriminate against ethnic minority pupils. However, what the question wants you to do is to *assess* this claim. To do this you have to look at other aspects of this issue. Is it teachers who discriminate? Is it the whole school system? Is it a product of societal racism? How prevalent is discrimination? Do schools operate deliberate anti-racist policies of a kind which prevent discrimination? Do all ethnic minorities face discrimination or does it vary from group to group? How can we measure discrimination? What problems are there in defining and measuring discrimination and its effects? How recent is the research in this area? Once you start to follow lines of enquiry like these, your answer will achieve greater balance and will begin to evaluate the claim in the question much more effectively.

2 Discuss and assess the relative merits of Marxist and functionalist views about the functions of the family.

Many candidates might respond to this question by outlining whichever view of the family they were most familiar with, or by writing all they knew about these two views of the family in general. This does not meet the demands of the question. The question is about the *functions* of the family, so the answer should not deal with the family *in general*. The wording also asks for a discussion and evaluation of the relative merits of the two perspectives and this means that a candidate has to carry out several sub-tasks if he or she is to produce a complete and balanced answer. The question can be broken down into the following sub-tasks:

- identifying the key elements in Marxist views of family functions;
- the advantages (merits) and disadvantages of the Marxist view;
- identifying the key elements in a functionalist view of family functions;
- the advantages and disadvantages of the functionalist view of family functions;
- a conclusion as to the relative merits of the two perspectives.

An answer could take the form of the structure suggested above or it could equally well be constructed in a way which integrated these tasks, producing a more sophisticated response. Whichever form the answer does take, the key point to note is that these tasks have to be covered if the candidate is to produce a balanced answer.

Creating balanced answers

The key to creating balanced answers is to consider **alternatives** to the claim or parts of the claim in the question. This requires you to think logically and to use your sociological knowledge to draw out alternative ideas. These alternatives may also give you part of the structure of your answer and in an exam it is worth taking a minute or two to consider them before starting to write.

For example, let's look at the following question and then try to think of alternatives.

How far is it true that, in most societies, the two people who produce a child are responsible for its upbringing?

How can we analyse this question? The claim in the question is that, in most societies, the natural parents are expected to raise and socialise their offspring. You can no doubt immediately think of evidence which supports this claim as, after all, this is the usual pattern in our society. However, the question wants you to judge whether this is generally the case throughout society and in all societies. So the thing to do is to think of alternative child-rearing arrangements that exist in our society and in other societies.

What alternative arrangements are there for child rearing? Write down as many as you can think of.

You may have come up with some of the following alternative arrangements:

- both natural parents have responsibility for their children;
- adoption;
- only one parent is the primary carer;
- there may be collective responsibility, as in the kibbutz system.

If you have identified three or more alternatives, then you have 'cracked' this question – it is about *variety* of family/childcare arrangements. This is not immediately clear from the wording of the question as it specifies only one arrangement, but by analysing the question logically you will not only produce a balanced answer, but will create a structure for your answer.

Activity Identifying alternative claims and ideas

For each of the following questions carry out this two-stage process:

i Identify the claim being made by rewriting it in your own words.
ii List the alternatives to the claim

1 **To what extent have sociologists agreed with the assertion that parents are the crucial influence on pupils' educational achievement?**

2 **Assess the argument that work has little influence on leisure.**

3 **Evaluate the usefulness of the concept of an 'underclass' as a description of the position of women in the class structure.**

You may not have covered these topics before, but that is not the point. The aim of this exercise is to think of alternatives to the statement put forward in the question so that you do not fall into the trap of simply agreeing with the question but, instead, produce a balanced response.

Creating evaluative answers (or how to present a critically argued response)

We have seen just how important the skill of evaluation is in answering stimulus-response questions in sociology. It carries one-third of the marks and most part-questions carrying large marks have standard evaluation command words or phrases in them.

There are *two* elements to creating responses which are fully evaluative:

i) putting your answer into an **evaluative structure**;
ii) using **evaluative words and phrases** throughout your answer.

The evaluative structure

As with any answer, it is important that your response is structured, that it has a pattern and is organised appropriately. There is a very simple format which, if applied correctly, will create an evaluative answer. Bear in mind that the whole purpose of evaluation is to test the claim in the question. Logically, this means that you should *first* identify what the claim is. Then, *second*, you should examine the sociological arguments and evidence which appear to support that claim. The next logical *third* step is to outline and review sociological evidence which appears to disagree with the claim. *Finally*, having done all of this, you will be in a position to reach an informed and evaluative conclusion about the claim.

Your answer should therefore fall into *four* sections.

1 Identifying the claim in the question

- what are the key characteristics of the statement/claim?
- which sociological perspectives/theories have put forward this view?
- what sociological debate or issue is this statement/claim part of?
- are there any problems in defining the key ideas/concepts in the question?
- in what different ways can this issue be measured?

2 Sociological research evidence and theoretical arguments in support of the claim

- briefly identify the main theoretical arguments which support the claim;
- what research has been done on this issue?
- what have been the main conclusions reached from research evidence?
- you could also include in this section any criticisms of these studies;
- is there anything in the data items which seems to support the claim?

3 Sociological research evidence and theoretical arguments critical of the claim

- identify the main theoretical arguments which partly or fully contradict the claim – what alternative claims have been put forward?
- what are the main points of any research which does not support the claim or which supports another claim?
- what criticisms can be made of these arguments and studies?
- is there anything in the data items which partly or fully contradicts the claim?

4 Conclusion/evaluation

- which of the arguments and evidence in sections 2 and 3 are the strongest and most convincing?
- in the light of the evidence you have examined, is the claim correct/partly correct/appropriate only to some societies at certain times/incorrect/inconclusive?
- does the evidence point to an alternative conclusion?
- make sure you justify whatever conclusion you reach – always give reasons for your judgement.

As you present your answer it is important for you to continue to link the evidence and theory to the specific claim you are testing. The section on page

13 takes you through some of the words and phrases you can use to make these links.

You may also notice how the other skills fall in with this structure.

This format has **balance** in terms of looking at both theoretical arguments and at research evidence. Similarly, by examining evidence and arguments both for and against the claim being evaluated, a balanced assessment will emerge. It is also important to keep the for and against sections as even as your knowledge and understanding will allow – again, this makes for good evaluation. Such an answer will also be balanced through having an introduction which de-codes the question and which then returns for a final concluding evaluation at the end.

The structure outlined above also provides the basis for a **focused** answer. By using the introduction to examine the claim in the question, you will get off to a good start by immediately relating your answer to the precise wording of the question. This is also very helpful to you when working under exam pressure as it will help to get your mind fully focused on the question right from the start. You are then far less likely to wander off the point in the rest of your answer. Similarly, by returning to the issue in a final evaluative section, you will remain focused on the specific content of the question.

This format also gives you lots of opportunities to put good **interpretation** and **application** of knowledge into your answer. There is an element of interpretation in the opening section as you de-code the question. The middle two sections will only work if you select theory and evidence which are relevant to the particular claim being assessed. In addition, you can interpret the data items, applying evidence from them within the whole format.

Helpful hints in applying this structure

- This is a basic framework. A more sophisticated approach would probably evaluate the evidence in sections 2 and 3 as you go through them, linking research and theory to the claim being tested. In this way you would be creating a 'running evaluation' which would help to make your final conclusion all the more valid. However, it is very important to remember that even if you do create a 'running evaluation' you still need a separate evaluating section at the end of your response. Mark schemes often specifically identify this final evaluation as being worthy of reward – so include one!
- Some research or theory will not fit easily into either the 'for' or 'against' categories. In this case, do not try to force it to fit in where it does not go, but explain that the evidence here is ambiguous or that the issue is more complex than the evidence seems to allow for. It is perfectly reasonable to point out in an answer that some research or theory can be interpreted or used in different ways. Candidates who do this where it is relevant increase the sophistication of their answers and gain higher marks.
- The claims made in stimulus-response questions should be familiar to you from your sociology course. Think about the context in which you will have come across them. Which major issues and debates do they seem to be concerned with? Often the claim will have been extracted from a data item on the exam paper. Read this item carefully. What clues does it give about the claim you are being asked to test?
- Read the claim in the question very carefully. What is the *precise wording* of the claim? Does it say 'contemporary society' or just 'society'? If it is the former, then you must confine your content to recent social developments and if, in your answer, you refer to historical studies then you will be penalising yourself by including material not relevant to that specific question.

Evaluative words and phrases

It is also very important constantly to employ words, phrases and sentences which give your answers an *evaluative feel*. Your answers will then move from being knowledge-driven to having a real cutting edge about them. These words and phrases also give your responses a dynamic feel. They convert summaries of sociological knowledge into material which is being well applied to the question. They also fulfil the function of creating links between your knowledge and the specific claim under examination.

Evaluatives linking words and phrases

Words and phrases which help to generate a good evaluative feel to an answer can be usefully categorised into:

- those giving a critical edge;
- wording supportive of a claim;
- useful phrasing in a final evaluation paragraph.

Of course, it would be wrong to see these as being completely separate groupings as many of these wordings overlap and can be used to good effect at various points in an answer.

Words and phrases giving a critical edge to an answer

'On the other hand ...'
'Alternatively ...'
'Other sociologists ...'
'Some research appears to contradict ...'
'A's work is methodologically suspect ...'
'However ...'
'Not all sociologists have agreed that ...'
'B places more stress on ...'
'C emphasises different aspects ...'
'Rather than ...'
'D denies that this is the case ...'
'Nevertheless ...'
'E has been critical of ...'
'F has been criticised from a number of different perspectives ...'
'Perhaps the strongest attack comes from ...'
'Other research attaches little importance to ...'

All these words and phrases suggest either weaknesses/criticisms or alternatives to the claim being tested.

Words and phrases which give a supportive tone to part of an answer

'Other sociologists have agreed with ...'
'Further research appears to confirm ...'
'Investigations which support this claim include ...'
'A number of sociologists have accepted that ...'
'The weight of the evidence suggests that this claim is generally accurate ...'
'A's research provides supporting evidence that ...'
'B has reached very similar conclusions ...'
'Furthermore, most sociologists agree ...'
'C's research does seem to show ...'
'A major strength of ...'

Using phrases such as these helps to create the feeling that a candidate is applying knowledge and prevents answers from turning into lists of sociological information. These forms of words highlight the strengths and advantages of particular arguments and evidence.

Words and phrases that are useful in a final evaluation paragraph

'These differing explanations are not necessarily mutually exclusive ...'
'A definitive answer has yet to be reached ...'
'The weight of the evidence appears to suggest ...'
'Most sociologists tend to ...'
'Part of the explanation may lie in ...'
'The evidence is far from conclusive ...'
'It seems likely that ...'
'There seem to be no grounds for arguing that ...'
'The evidence seems very ambiguous ...'

The aim of a closing paragraph is to make overall sense of an answer by offering a reasoned and justified evaluation of the claim being analysed by the candidate.

Activity

Read the following question and a candidate's answer to it.

i See how it follows the suggested format of the four sections set out on page 11.

ii Using a highlighter or different-coloured pen, identify the words or phrases which provide instances of linking, evaluative words, phrases and sentences.

iii After doing this, look back to the example of everyday questions and responses given above (page 8) and you will be able to see the similarities – and one important difference – between everyday and academic enquiry-response patterns.

Assess sociological evidence concerning the extent to which ethnic minorities in Britain are absorbed into the majority culture.

Answer

The location of ethnic minorities in the British stratification system has been the focus of a great deal of sociological research and theoretical argument. How far are ethnic minorities absorbed into the general culture and how far are they excluded or marginalised? Early sociological research in Britain during the 1950s argued strongly that, after the initial impact on the host society of the arrival of an immigrant group, hostility would subside and the newcomers would be gradually absorbed into the host culture. This approach to race relations, typified by Patterson's 'Dark Strangers' study, can be located in a broadly functionalist perspective, emphasising the way in which the disequilibrium created by the arrival of a new cultural group is coped with and social equilibrium restored. The assumption underlying this model is that the new group has to amend its cultural norms to those of the host society. According to this approach, given that most primary immigration into Britain ceased a generation ago, ethnic minorities should be well on their way to being fully integrated into the majority culture.

Some sociological research indicates that absorption is underway, if not complete. Certain ethnic minorities – particularly non-white groups – have achieved a certain degree of acceptance. For Asian and Afro-Caribbean British people, the picture is less clear. In housing, the initial settlement of predominantly male workers in inner-city areas in overcrowded, poor-quality shared housing, has given way to family settlement and a gradual movement out into higher-quality housing. In employment, the high degree of Asian self-employment suggests that some individuals at least have moved out of unskilled and semi-skilled manual work. In education, Asian students as a group now have a performance profile which is broadly similar to that of white students and this has enhanced their occupational opportunities. Changes in the legal framework and the development of equal opportunities policies have assisted the process of acceptance and it could be argued that a degree of absorption into the majority culture has been achieved.

However, there is a great deal of evidence which suggests that this has been a limited and very partial process, if indeed it has occurred at all. Research carried out by the PEP/PSI, the CRE and other sociologists over the past 25 years reveals a picture of continuing prejudice, discrimination and disadvantage on a large scale. In housing, despite an improvement in the quality of housing as a whole, the degree of disadvantage between ethnic minorities and whites has been maintained. In particular, Afro-Caribbeans and Bangladeshis continue to experience a high level of disadvantage in terms of both housing tenure and housing quality. Afro-Caribbeans have a comparatively low owner-occupation rate and although Asians as a group have a high owner-occupation rate, they are concentrated in the poorest quality housing. Within the general 'Asian' group there are substantial variations in housing experience and Bangladeshis in particular occupy probably the weakest position of all. In terms of employment, all the survey data suggest that non-white British people are disproportionately represented in the lowest-paid, lowest-status jobs, working more anti-social hours and shift work and having been pressurised into self-employment as an attempt to escape discrimination. Surveys of attitudes towards black British people also indicate a continuing high rate of prejudice against black people and the expectation that this will continue.

Although there is considerable variation in the experiences of ethnic minorities in Britain, it is highly debatable whether they have been absorbed into mainstream society. There may be greater acceptance than there was 30 years ago, but racial prejudice, racial discrimination and racial disadvantage typify their day-to-day experiences. Furthermore, some sociologists have questioned the assumptions behind the notion of absorption. This is not a necessary process and the possibility of a multi-cultural society which emphasises the benefits of many different cultural practices is one which some would see as a preferable outcome.

Activity

In this activity two example answers are given to the same question. One is clearly of a higher standard than the other because of the way the student has employed evaluation skills.

Look at the mark scheme and then read through both answers. Suggest the mark that you feel each merits and give a brief reason for your mark. (NB: highlight the evaluative elements in the stronger answer.)

Assess the contribution of historical approaches to our understanding of the family. *(8 marks)*

Mark scheme

0 marks — No relevant points.

1–2 marks — Candidates will be unsure of the distinctive contribution to our understanding of the family, but may merely describe a few studies of historical approaches.

3–5 marks — The range of historical approaches used will be fair and accurately reproduced. Moreover, they will be used to discuss the contribution of historical approaches to the sociology of the family, though not always in a discrete fashion.

6–8 marks — A good coverage of historical approaches will be linked to a good evaluation of their contribution. Conclusions as to the value of these approaches may be drawn in a separate part of the response.

Candidate A's answer

Laslett and Anderson are two historians of the family who have conducted research into the development of the family.

Laslett looked at family size in pre-industrial Britain, looking at the period 1500 to 1820. Only about 10% of households contained kin beyond the nuclear family. He found few 'extended families' of the sort usually associated with pre-industrial societies and this he believed reflected early mortality and short life expectancy. In addition to his own research, Laslett looked at the results of similar investigations into family size elsewhere in Europe before industrialisation. He found that the typical family in pre-industrial Europe was basically nuclear in size, average 4.75 persons per household. So the image of agrarian extended families of three generations all living and working together was proved wrong by Laslett's work.

Anderson examined the household composition of Preston in 1851 after industrialisation had occurred. He found from the census data that 23% of families were 'extended' in form and this was the result of the pressure of industrialisation. Living with kin was an economic necessity. Just to survive, to be supported and looked after in the hard world of an industrialised town meant that the extended family was necessary.

Both these studies have their methodological problems. Laslett's data is 'unofficial', coming from quasi-censuses and both his and Anderson's evidence is such that it is hard to distinguish between 'household size' and 'family size'.

Nevertheless, the contribution of these two historians to our understanding of the family has been important, as no longer do we see pre-industrial societies as having extended families and industrial families as having nuclear families.

Your mark: /8

Explanation of your mark

....

....

....

....

....

....

Candidate B's answer

Historical approaches have made an important contribution to the study of the family, in particular in respect to the issues of the relationship between industrialisation and family structure, and the process of social change and the family.

Before the 1960s, the sociology of the family was dominated by functionalism. This approach argued that there was a 'fit' between family structure and society. Parsons claimed that there was a functional fit between the large, co-residential family and pre-industrial society, whilst the nuclear family isolated from kin met the prerequisites of industrial society. The process of social change, argued Parsons, occurred through the dynamics of structural differentiation. As a society industrialised, the family met the needs of industrialisation through changing from an extended to a nuclear structure.

Functionalist claims about the relationship of family form to society went largely unchallenged for a long time until the validity of this claim was more or less assumed. Laslett's first historical demographic study of the British family (1965) and Anderson's (1971) study of families in the recently industrialised town of Preston in 1851 examined the very foundations of functionalist claims about the family and industrialisation. Laslett's analysis of the British family form between 1500 and 1821 found that only 10% of households contained kin beyond the nuclear family. Few extended families existed in agrarian, pre-industrial Britain and Laslett's further research into European family life produced additional evidence about the lack of extended families in pre-industrial times. The typical pre-industrial family was not the extended form that Parsons claimed 'fitted' the needs of agrarian society, but the nuclear family which, according to Laslett's figures, averaged 4.75 persons per household.

Anderson's study of Preston using the 1851 census data questioned whether industrialisation produced a nuclear family structure. If functionalist arguments were correct, then Anderson should have found that there were few extended families in newly industrialised Preston in 1851. In fact, Anderson found that 23% of households were extended in structure. He also argued that they took an extended form because of the economic pressures of industrialisation. Living with kin was an economic necessity in the harsh world of newly industrialised Britain. Therefore, not only was there no straightforward 'fit' between nuclear family structure and industrialisation as Parsons claimed, but industrialisation actually created extended families.

The work of historical demography has had a major impact on this area of the sociology of the family. Their findings have largely disproved the previously taken for granted assumption made by functionalist writers that there is a 'fit' between family structure and the economic structure. Their work has also opened up the debate about the relationship between social change and family form as well as forming part of a wider challenge to the position of functionalism as a perspective on the family. On a cautionary note, their contribution has been limited to these two aspects of the sociology of the family and both Anderson and Laslett have been criticised for their methodological confusion of 'family' and 'household'.

Your mark: /8

Explanation of your mark

....

....

....

....

....

....

Commentary

The aim of this activity is to illustrate the difference between focused and unfocused answers.

It should be clear from your reading of these two answers that candidate B's response is of a better standard than candidate A's answer. The important aspect of this exercise is for you to understand why this is the case. Why is the second answer of a higher quality than the first?

To help you recognise the difference, carry out this task.

Using a highlighter pen, identify those elements in each answer which you think are 'knowledge'. This is when information about the studies is being presented.

Now, in a different colour, highlight the aspects of each answer which are 'focusing' the answer to the question. These are the linking sentences which tie evidence and knowledge into an argument.

Compare the two answers. You should notice that each candidate has about the same knowledge, but that candidate B uses it much more effectively. Candidate B also uses much more argument.

From this exercise you should recognise the importance of the key 'action' element in the question. Candidates are not being asked to describe or list historical approaches to the study of the family but to assess their contribution to the study of the family. What issues have been raised by historical approaches? What questions have they asked? Is their work criticisable?

Because assessing – which is the evaluation skill – is a difficult task, many candidates avoid it and substitute the 'write all you know' type of answer. This is a strategy based on wishful thinking and will result in low marks. The only way to achieve higher grades is by confronting this problem.

How can I analyse and use data items in my answers?

Data-response questions offer you several data items (usually three or four) around which are built several questions. Most of the data items are written text items but a few contain graphs or tabulated information. Whatever the questions ask you to do with the data items, it is vital that you understand them before attempting your answers. The aim of this section is to help you to develop the basic techniques of analysing data.

Analysing written text

The first step towards understanding any form of written text is to recognise that it has a **structure**. This does not mean that it contains sentences and paragraphs, but that it should have an underlying logic. The content of the text will follow a pattern. This may take the form of an argument, or it may be a list of points which, together, create a definition, or it may be a summary of a theory/piece of research. Whichever it is, there is likely to be a list of points which, taken together, create the argument/theory/summary. It is very useful to practise drawing out the points in an extract to see how they connect together. This sequence of points and the way they connect form the logical structure of a data item.

It is very likely that you will then be able to use this structure as the starting point – and in some cases, the framework – for your answer.

To see how this works in practice, read through the following example:

The underclass

A definition of underclass: This term is sometimes used to identify those social groups which do not enjoy full participation in society. Members of these groups perform the least desirable jobs and receive the lowest rewards. Their jobs are also insecure, resulting in periods of unemployment, and have few fringe benefits and no pension rights. The jobs they occupy are those found in the 'secondary sector' of the 'dual labour market'. They also do not have the same basic legal, political and social rights as the rest of society. As a result they are 'marginalised' in that they are largely excluded from mainstream social activities. Several groups are sometimes considered to form part of the underclass – migrant workers, the poor, the unemployed and women.

How useful is the idea of an underclass as a description of the position of women in the class structure? *(9 marks)*

This is quite a demanding question. The idea of women possibly forming an underclass is not one which is mentioned in any detail by the main A-level textbooks so candidates are unlikely to have a prepared answer to this question. In this circumstance, a sound analysis of the data item is vital to create a structure for your answer. By establishing a clear idea of what underclass means, you would then be able to muster your knowledge about the occupational and class position of women in Britain and to see if it fits this concept.

Summary of the main points in the text:

- underclass groups are in the poorest paid, worst jobs;
- these jobs are in the secondary sector of the dual labour market;
- they are often unemployed, no pensions;
- they have fewer political, social, legal rights than mainstream society.

One way to tackle this question would be to take the information and evidence you have about the position of women in the occupational structure and use them to test whether they support or deny each of the elements in the definition of under class given in the data item. Are women often unemployed? Do women occupy the least desirable and worst rewarded jobs? Are women confined to the secondary labour sector? Do they have fewer social, legal and political rights than men? Do they, on balance, therefore form an underclass?

What many candidates would have done with this question would be to describe various theories of the class position of women or offer a series of unconnected points about women and the occupational structure. Such answers are unlikely to result in anything other than a low mark.

By analysing the data item, you would have provided yourself with a framework for answering the question in a focused way. This type of answer is far more likely to produce a higher grade.

Activity Analysing text in data items

Now try to analyse the next two examples of text. In each case, follow this procedure:

- **Read the data item through in a careful way.**
- **Can you see its structure? What is it about? What points are being made?**
- **Using a highlighter or an ordinary pen, identify the main points in the text.**
- **Make a brief note of these points.**

The experiment

The experiment is the classic research method of the natural sciences. The laboratory experiment enables the scientist to identify and control all the factors which might influence the outcome of an interaction, and to measure this outcome. This process allows the scientist to expose the cause and effect relationships between variables and to generate theories which predict future behaviour. The element of control and the accurate description of the experiment allow other scientists to repeat the investigation in an exact way in order to check the initial results. This process of replication enables the original results to be verified. Scientists therefore claim that the experimental techniques generate data which is valid, verifiable, accurate and which enables them to test hypotheses.

Summary of main points:

■

■

Functionalist theory

The functionalist analysis of social stratification begins with the recognition that all known societies have some form of social inequality. This leads them to conclude that the universality of inequality means that it is both inevitable and positively functional for society. Davis and Moore argued that certain positions in society are more functionally important than others and required particular skills in their performance. As only a limited number of people have the necessary talents, and as the time taken to train these talents into the skills required involves them in sacrifices of one kind or another, these people have to be enticed into undergoing training. This is achieved by offering them greater future rewards (in the form of higher status, better pay, more fringe benefits, etc). Therefore, social inequality acts as a motivating force to attract the most talented members of society into the functionally most important positions. It is therefore a necessary part of society.

Summary of main points:

■

■

The skills involved in analysing an item of written data are very similar to those you would use in your note-making. You can easily practise the analysis of data items by taking a paragraph or two of text from an A-level textbook and trying to work out its structure.

Analysing tables of data

Some stimulus-response questions relate to data presented in tabulated form. Although these tables will be very simple statistics it is still very easy to misread them or to misunderstand the questions asked in relation to them. There are several useful points to note about reading tabulated data and these will be summarised after this worked example.

Item A

Look at the data in the table below (Figure 1.3) and read the two questions which were asked about it.

Figure 1.3

16–18-year-olds participating in education and training schemes

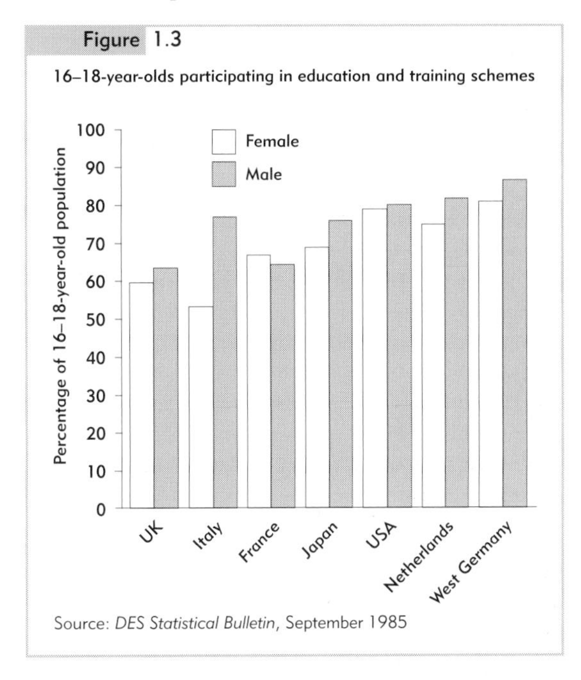

Source: *DES Statistical Bulletin*, September 1985

1 In which country is the gap between males and females participating in education and training schemes the largest? *(1 mark)*

2 How might sociologists explain the patterns of participation in education and training schemes shown in Item A? *(6 marks)*

Although question 1 is fairly straightforward, involving the reading and interpretation of the table, question 2 has a number of possible pitfalls which a candidate needs to be wary of.
First read candidate A's answer to question 2.
Now read candidate B's answer.

Candidate A's answer

There is a clear gender gap shown by the data in Item B. In all the countries except France, a greater proportion of males was in education or on training schemes after the age of 16. There are many sociological explanations why this might be the case. Sociologists have rejected psychological and biological explanations of gender differences in achievement, and have instead highlighted the social basis of educational differences. Some have pointed to the way in which early socialisation in the family provides females and males with different expectations about education and work through, for example, the different toys they are given. Stanworth has shown how teachers' expectations of male and female students are different. She found that teachers held stereotypical views about them and their likely educational achievement. As a result, girls had lower expectations of their likely performance and career aspirations. The classroom is therefore a place where a sexual hierarchy is firmly in place. Dale Spender has further supported this view in her studies which show how males get more attention than females and how males are allowed to dominate the classroom.

Therefore, it is easy to see how there are fewer women on education and training courses.

Candidate A's mark = 3/6

Candidate B's answer

The data shows that in all countries in the data, there is a gender division. In France, more women than men are in education between the ages of 16 and 18. In the other countries, it is the other way round. In Germany, about 90% of boys are on training courses and 83% of women are. In the USA, there is little difference between the sexes. In Italy, there is a very large gap between men and women. This might be because there are more women than men in this age bracket.

Candidate B's mark = 1/6

Commentary

Now let us see why these candidates' answers received the marks they did.

Candidate A seems to have written quite a sound answer but only received 3/6. Why is this the case? What is missing from this answer?

It is useful to re-read the question and the data. The question asks you to do two things. First, you have to identify the trends shown in the data. Candidate A successfully identifies one trend, that of a gender divide, but there are other trends which should also be drawn out. Because question 1 drew attention to the gender divide, many candidates would have simply examined that aspect of the data. But the question states 'trends' not 'a trend', so candidates who read this question properly would recognise that there is more than one trend in the data. A complete answer would have to deal with the other trend(s) as well as the gender divide. Look back to the data item and pick out the other trends in the data (there is certainly one trend to be seen, and perhaps another could be drawn out).

Candidate B has produced quite a weak answer. It is essentially just a list of the trends shown in the data with one attempted explanation which is inaccurate. The question clearly asks candidates to offer sociological explanations of these trends so a simple list will not get any real reward. Furthermore, as the table relates to percentages of males and females, it is inaccurate to argue that there might be more females than males in the age group.

Both candidates misread or misunderstood the question and in each case the result was a loss of marks.

Points to remember when reading tables of data

- Read the title of the data carefully. This might give you some clues as to how to go about your answer. For example, the item above is about both education and training schemes for 16–18-year-olds. You may be able to discuss whether it is appropriate to group education and training together in statistics like these.

- Are the figures in percentages or are they raw numbers? If they are raw numbers, check at the top of the column of numbers whether they refer to '00s, '000s, 0.000s, or greater.
- Check the area covered by the figures. Is it England and Wales, Britain, a region or another country?
- If the figures relate to a period of time, which years are included? Are the gaps between the years quoted the same, or are they irregular intervals?
- Look at the figures for major differences between groups.
- Look at the figures for trends over time. Note that if the question asks for more than one trend, then there will be more than one trend in the data. Search for it.
- Are the trends steady changes over time or are there sudden jumps and falls? How great are the changes – minor or substantial?
- Does the question ask you to describe trends and patterns or to explain them. If it is to describe the trends, then a short and precise written description and interpretation of the data is required. An explanation, on the other hand, requires the presentation of a number of reasons why the trends and patterns take the form they do. In this case, a simple list of trends will not do.
- Finally, as with any type of data, take time to read the data carefully in order to avoid making costly errors.

Checklist for answering data-response questions

The following chapters provide plenty of examples of data-response questions in different areas of sociology. They also consider how you can go about using the skills of knowledge and understanding, interpretation and application and evaluation in answering such questions.

Before you start to answer any data-response questions, we suggest that you should consider the following checklist:

- Have you identified the 'action word/s' correctly?
- Have you interpreted the title accurately?
- Are you able to apply information across different topic areas in sociology?
- Do you have relevant and up-to-date examples to bring into your answers?
- Have you planned your answers to the higher mark questions?
- Have you worked out the approximate time you should spend on each part of the question?
- Have you used the allocation of marks as a guide to the length/detail of your answer?

If you answer 'no' to any of the above questions, you may not be able to fulfil all the skill requirements and will therefore risk losing marks.

Chapter 2

Sociological Theory and Methods

Introduction

Key concepts in sociological research
The relationship between methodological and theoretical issues

Knowledge and understanding

Typical quotions

Interpretation and application

How to 'read' data items for useful knowledge
The 'coat and hook' method of linking data items and knowledge

Evaluation

An overview
How to write evaluative conclusions
Bringing 'balance' into answers

Practice data-response questions

Introduction

Sociological theory and methods are the core elements of most, if not all, introductory courses in sociology. Their key importance is reflected in A-level syllabuses and the prominence given to them in sociology textbooks. The purpose of this chapter is to help you to answer data-response questions on this area, rather than to provide you with 'knowledge' of sociological theory and methods. To provide coherence, the focus of the questions in this chapter is on sociological research and the link between research methods and theory, rather than on sociological theory by itself.

Key concepts in sociological research:

- validity;
- reliability;
- representativeness;
- quantitative data;
- qualitative data.

These are all key parts of the sociological knowledge you will need for answering questions in this area. You will find definitions of them in textbooks and it would be a useful exercise to look up and compare the definitions given in different texts. As regards these definitions, you should note that candidates often do not distinguish carefully between reliability and validity. These terms mean very different things in sociology so you are well advised to have a fairly precise understanding of them. The full exam questions on pages 36–44 shows you just how important it is to know what these concepts mean.

A range of different research methods is available to sociologists and these methods are usually categorised according to whether the technique is a **primary** or **secondary** research method and whether it generates primarily **quantitative** or **qualitative** data. The main methods can be expressed as shown in the diagram below (Figure 2.1).

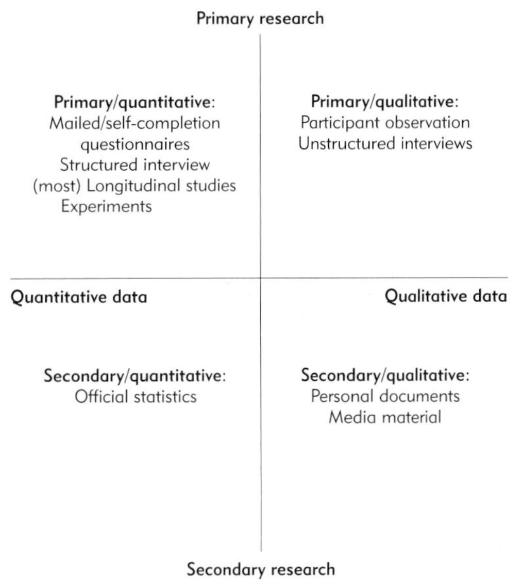

Most questions ask you to evaluate the usefulness

Figure 2.1

	Primary research	
Quantitative data	**Primary/quantitative:** Mailed/self-completion questionnaires Structured interview (most) Longitudinal studies Experiments	**Primary/qualitative:** Participant observation Unstructured interviews
	Secondary/quantitative: Official statistics	**Secondary/qualitative:** Personal documents Media material
	Secondary research	Qualitative data

of one or more of these methods in sociological research. To do this you need to have a good understanding of the strengths and weaknesses of each method. You should recognise that whether a method is seen as being useful often greatly depends upon which key concept – validity or reliability – and which methodological approach – quantitative or qualitative – is seen as most important. It is a very good idea to relate weaknesses and strengths to notions of validity and reliability rather than just present them as 'lists' of advantages and disadvantages.

The relationship between methodological and theoretical issues

Some of the major methodological issues within sociology occur where sociological theory meets research methods. You need to have a good understanding of these issues which include:

- the link between structuralist sociology and quantitative research methods;

- the link between interpretivist sociology and qualitative research methods;
- how far sociology can be considered to be scientific;
- whether or not values should and can be kept out of research;
- how far it is true to say that there is a distinctive feminist methodology;
- the influences on choice of research method.

In the rest of this chapter we will be looking at how the different skill domains can be applied to theory and methods issues including sampling, official statistics, longitudinal studies, personal documents, interviewing, participant observation and values in research.

Knowledge and understanding

Sometimes a part-question, carrying only a limited number of marks, asks you to define, comment on or criticise some aspect of research methodology. Although these are sometimes thought of as being relatively straightforward questions, with the marks almost 'in the bag' before you have even started your answer, a sensible candidate treats them with respect. You need to answer these as carefully as any other question. This section shows you a number of typical part-questions of this kind. Some have mark schemes and exemplar answers attached; others leave it to you to attempt your own answers.

Typical questions

Example 1

Briefly explain what is meant by the term 'representative sample'. *(2 marks)*

Mark scheme

1 mark for a brief explanation of 'sample'.
1 mark for a brief explanation of 'representative'.

Candidate A's answer

A representative sample is a small group – part of the whole population being studied – used in research. If chosen properly, it will represent the whole group.

Candidate B's answer

Researchers usually cannot interview or survey all members of a group they want to study so they research a small section of it. They usually try to make sure that the sample is a cross-section of the larger group with the same proportion of males, females, elderly, young, etc. In this way the sample will represent the whole group.

Candidate C's answer

Sociologists have to use samples in their research. A sample is a small part of the whole group they are studying.

Commentary

This seems a fairly accessible question which only requires a brief definition. However, even in this two-mark question there should be an element of 'balance'. To get full marks you need to explain both 'sample' and 'representative'. The most likely danger here is that candidates will only define the 'sample' aspect. If you look at the three exemplar answers, candidate C does not convey any meaning of 'representativeness' and so loses one mark.

The other danger with this question is how to define 'representative' without using the words 'representative' or 'represent'. You need to find some alternative word or explanatory phrase and avoid just recycling the term in the question. Candidate A falls into this trap and also loses one of the two available marks.

Example 2

Give three reasons why the data produced by quantitative surveys can be fairly easily compared. *(3 marks)*

Mark scheme

One mark for each distinct reason relating social surveys to the generation of comparable data. These may include:

- all respondents being asked the same questions;
- questions being asked in the same order;
- fixed category/closed responses;
- ease of computer coding of responses;
- often limited numbers of questions asked;
- replicability at a later date for longitudinal comparisons.

Candidate A's answer

The data produced by surveys is mainly quantitative. It is expressed in numbers and statistics, and these are easier to compare than the often wordy qualitative data from interviews or observation. In a survey, people are asked the same questions so their answers can then be compared. Because they are asked the same questions, the responses will be the same.

Candidate B's answer

1 Social surveys use closed questions so, as this limits the range of responses given, the data from a number of respondents can be easily compared. Usually, these responses are coded on computer and this makes comparisons very quick and easy to carry out.

2 Because respondents often will not be comfortable answering long questionnaires, the sociologist often keeps the social survey fairly short. This means that the data is quick to encode and compare.

3 ?

Commentary

The first candidate nearly gets all three marks but is restricted to just two because the final point is not made sufficiently separate to the second point in the answer. It is not quite true to claim that if respondents are asked the same questions then the responses will be the same – it all depends upon the type of questions used and that is where the third and final mark can be gained.

Candidate B, despite apparently only offering two points, does gain all three marks. The response makes three points – the use of closed questions, the application of computers, and keeping the survey brief. The lesson to be taken from this response is that it is probably not appropriate to break up your answer into clearly identified points in case the examiner misses where you have made two scoring points but have put them together as one.

Now try to create your own answers to these similarly brief questions:

1 **Explain what sociologists mean by 'interviewer bias'.** *(2 marks)*

2 **Name two problems sociologists are likely to encounter when using closed questions.** *(2 marks)*

3 **Briefly outline one advantage and one disadvantage of 'triangulation'.** *(2 marks)*

Interpretation and application

How to 'read' data items for useful knowledge

It is very important that you do not simply turn stimulus-response questions into a comprehension exercise. Simply repeating the content of the data items will not create an effective answer. You can use elements in the data items but you must bring in a substantial amount of your own sociological knowledge and understanding. A good answer will tie in your own knowledge with the content of the data items. One way to do this is to employ the 'coat and hook' method.

The 'coat and hook' method of linking data items and knowledge

One way to get the right balance between data items and your own knowledge is to look at it in the same way as the relationship between a coat-hook and a coat. You should aim to use the contents of data items as 'hooks' on which to hang your sociological knowledge. The data items offer a starting point for at least part of your answer. You can then attach your own knowledge to these elements and bring in further points not specifically referred to in the data items.

Of course, the relationship between the content of the data items and your own knowledge can be more complex than this, but the 'coat and hook method' gives you the basic technique.

Item A

The advantages of longitudinal studies are that they make it possible to study change over time, through a series of snapshots rather than as a continuous process.

There are several difficulties with longitudinal studies, in addition to the usual problems of sample-based research. It may be difficult to recruit a sample of people who know that they are taking on a very long-term commitment. Generally, people are rather flattered at the thought of being so important, but this may in turn create the problem that they become untypical because they know they will be questioned regularly about their lives, activities and attitudes.

Then there is the problem of keeping in touch with the sample. Members will die, move away, emigrate and perhaps change their minds about being included. Small children may have no choice about being included but could develop strong feelings about being involved as they grow up.

With reference to Item A, and from your own knowledge, identify and give examples of the advantages and disadvantages of longitudinal studies. *(10 marks)*

First let us identify the 'hooks' in this item.

The opening sentence identifies a 'hook' when it refers to an advantage of longitudinal studies being that they '... make it possible to study change over time ...'.

A further 'hook' can be found in the second paragraph where it talks about members of the sample '... being untypical because they know that they are in the sample ...'

A final 'hook' occurs when the item identifies '... the problem of keeping in touch with the sample'.

This is quite a useful data item which identifies three clear 'hooks' and, because it mentions both disadvantages and an advantage, it reminds you of the need to present a balanced assessment of longitudinal studies.

Attaching your own 'knowledge coats' to the data item 'hooks'

All three of the 'hooks' we have identified in this item are fairly incomplete statements – none of them really makes a full point about longitudinal approaches. So you have a great opportunity to add your knowledge to them. Let's see how this could be done by examining the student response and commentary on page 27.

In addition to the student response shown, you should also make sustained reference to your other knowledge of longitudinal studies. You cannot rely simply on the three points made in the data item; you should include all the other advantages and disadvantages of this approach as well as creating a final evaluation section. Don't just restrict yourself to using the 'hooks' in the data item. Bring in everything you think is relevant to the question you are dealing with.

Student answer and commentary

Candidate's answer

The opening sentence identifies the 'hook', noting its origin in the data item.

The second sentence amplifies the 'hook', putting longitudinal studies into the context of most research. This amplification is based on the second part of the opening sentence in the data item – but is rewritten in the candidate's own words.

As the author of Item A indicates, the great advantage of longitudinal studies lies in the way they make it possible to study change over a period of time. Most sociological research consists of 'one-off studies' of groups to which the researcher never – or very rarely – returns. Longitudinal studies therefore make it possible for the sociologist to compare the attitudes and behaviour of the same group of people, looking for changes and continuities over time. It is this ability to make comparisons which marks off the longitudinal approach from most other research.

The rest of the paragraph then explains why studying changes over time is an advantage, making the further point about longitudinal studies enabling researchers to compare data.

The opening sentence identifies one important characteristic of many longitudinal studies and provides an introduction to the second 'hook'.

The next sentence identifies the second 'hook'.

A longitudinal study usually tries to keep the same sample for the whole period of the research. As Item A says, this produces the problem of how far the sample can be considered to be typical. Knowing they are involved in a research programme may affect the responses of members of the sample. They may try to give responses which they think the researchers want to hear or, if they are no longer committed to the research project, deliberately give misleading or unhelpful responses. This adversely affects the validity and usefulness of the data generated.

The rest of the paragraph then goes on to explain what problems may arise from using a panel sample, relating them to issues of the validity and usefulness of data.

The third 'hook' is identified in the opening sentence but it is expressed in a different form of words–compare this opening sentence with Lines 15–16 in the data item.

The third sentence offers an example to illustrate the 'hook' – a good way to tie in your own sociological knowledge and understanding.

A further problem occurs when the researcher tries to maintain contact with the sample. Because members of the sample die, move away and become disinterested in the research, the sample size is likely to diminish over time. For example, the National Child Development Study began in 1958 with 17,000 children but by 1981 this had reduced to 12,000 connectable respondents. The result of this 'sample attrition' is to reduce the likely representativeness of the study. The whole point of including everybody born in a particular week was to ensure that the sample was as representative as possible. With the example above, there is no way of knowing which groups became under and over represented by 1981.

The rest of the paragraph then explains why this aspect of longitudinal studies can be problematic, linking the 'hook' to a specific example.

Activity

Here are three data items. Take each in turn, read the question attached to it and try to identify the 'hooks' in the item. Then, using your class notes or any major sociology textbook, design a model answer to each of the questions in a similar manner to the answer structure outlined above.

Item B

Many statistics about church membership and attendance are collected by the religious organisations themselves, and may not be directly comparable. The criteria for membership may vary both between and within churches. Is a member of the Church of England someone who, when asked which church they belong to, replies 'C. of E.', or is it someone who is on the church electoral roll or else attends regularly? Not only have methods of church statistics varied over time, but the apparent decline of church attendance on a Sunday may simply reflect that less people go, not that the total number of attenders has declined.

Source: adapted from I. Thompson, *Sociology in Focus: Religion*, Longman: Harlow 1986

Using the evidence of Item B, and knowledge gained from your own studies, what reasons can be given to support the claim that official statistics are of little use to the sociologist. *(6 marks)*

Item C

Personal documents have many uses in sociological research. A personal document gives a participant's own view of particular experiences. Such sources are used in sociology to represent the opinions and meanings of actors involved in given social situations. However, personal documents, particularly those produced at the request of a sociologist, are not merely a way of putting human flesh on statistical bones. They can serve as a check on or, at least, provide another viewpoint to statistically-based findings.

Source: adapted from M. O'Donnell, *Introduction to Sociology*, 4th edition, p. 37, Nelson: London 1997

Using Item C and your own knowledge, what evidence is there for the claim that 'personal documents have many uses in sociological research? *(6 marks)*

Item D

The quickest and most effective way for a sociologist to obtain a large amount of information from a wide range of people is the mailed questionnaire. Whereas many research studies are limited to interviewing or observing a limited number of individuals, the mailed questionnaire can be sent to literally thousands of people. However, once the questionnaire passes out of the researcher's control several problems can arise which limit its usefulness in sociological research.

Using your own knowledge and the information in Item D, identify and describe the advantages and disadvantages of mailed questionnaires in sociological research. *(6 marks)*

Evaluation

The focus of this section is the skill of evaluation. It is organised in three stages:

- first, a quick review of what evaluation means and how to show it in an answer to a typical question on theory and methods, in this case concerning types of interviews;
- next, how to create evaluative conclusions, using the example of a question on interviews;
- finally, how to make sure your answer is balanced, using the example of a question on sampling.

An overview

The two key elements in creating an evaluative answer are:

- evaluative structure;
- evaluative language.

An **evaluative structure** involves constructing an answer which contains:

- a section identifying the claim in a question;

- sections examining the argument and evidence for and against the claim;
- a final evaluative conclusion.

Throughout, it is important to use **evaluative language**. Look back at the section in Chapter 1 which identifies these two elements of evaluation. Remember that important aspects of evaluation also include making sure your answer is **focused** and **balanced**. Before working through the rest of this chapter, re-read pages 7–10.

Having refreshed your memory about the vital skill of evaluation, now read this worked example of two answers to a question on types of interviews.

Item E

Interviewing has a strong claim to being the most widely used method of collecting primary data for sociological purposes. Interviews do not all follow the same process and the normal way of differentiating types of interview is by the degree of structure imposed on its format.

In the **standardised structured interview** the wording of questions and the order in which they are asked is the same from one interview to another. The piece of paper the interviewer uses is called the '**interview schedule**' and that word schedule seems to suggest how formal this kind of interview is.

At the other end of the scale is the non-standardised interview which is also called an **unstructured** or **focused** interview. Here interviewers simply have a list of topics which they want the respondent to talk about, but they are free to phrase the questions as they wish and to ask them in any order that seems sensible at the time. The bit of paper the interviewer holds in this interview is called an 'interview guide' and the word 'guide' indicates the less formal nature of the interview, with interviewers taking their own path within certain guidelines.

Source: adapted from N. Fielding, 'Interviewing' in N. Gilbert (ed.) *Researching Social Life*, Sage: London 1993

With reference to Item E and elsewhere, evaluate the strengths and weaknesses of the two different types of interviews that are identified. *(8 marks)*

Mark scheme

0 marks — No relevant points.

1–2 marks — Answers in this mark band may rely heavily on the information in the items. Any additional knowledge of either type of interview will be limited and descriptive. Any evaluation will tend to be commonsensical and/or assertion. Answers which treat the two different types of interviews as one research technique will remain in this mark band.

In this band, candidates' answers are likely to be characterised by poor logical expression of ideas and the use of a limited range of conceptual terms, perhaps often used imprecisely and/or inaccurately. Spelling, punctuation and grammar may show serious deficiencies and frequent errors, perhaps impairing the intelligibility of significant parts of the answer.

3–5 marks — Responses will deal with both types of interviews but will be imbalanced in their coverage. Examples will be applied and not simply described. Evaluation is likely to be limited to the juxtaposition of the strengths and weaknesses of both types of interviews. In the middle of this mark band there may be lengthy answers which present a list of the strengths and weaknesses of both types of interview.

In this band, candidates' answers are likely to be characterised by a fair to good logical expression of ideas and the competent use of a reasonable range of conceptual terms.

Spelling, punctuation and grammar will be of a reasonable standard. Commonly used words and sociological terms will generally be spelt correctly. There may be minor errors of punctuation and grammar, but these will not seriously impair the intelligibility of the answer.

6–8 marks In this mark band, there will be a balanced account of both types of interview, which is accurate, substantial and supported by well-applied examples. Responses may recognise that interviews are not easily placed in these two simple categories. Answers will be presented in an evaluative framework. Towards the top of this mark band, methodological and theoretical issues will be clearly identified and examined.

In this band, candidates' answers are likely to be characterised by a very good to excellent expression of ideas and the precise use of a broad range of conceptual terms.

Spelling, punctuation and grammar will be of a very good to excellent standard. Commonly and less commonly used words will always be spelt correctly. Punctuation and grammar will be used correctly throughout to facilitate the intelligibility of the answer.

Student answers and commentary

Candidate A's answer

No introduction of any kind. One brief sentence which really just restates the question.

In Sociology, there is two main types of interview. These being unstructured and structured. Structured interviews are primarily concerned with gathering formal information about a respondent such of age, gender, religion. They are used because they have a high response rate meaning a wide variety of people will answer the set questions. The questions are a lot of the time 'closed' questions meaning that the research only obtains quantifiable data which is distinct/specific to the questions. Structured interviews are beneficial not only to the researcher but also to the interview. The interviewer can openly explain the purpose of the interviews and can receive distinct but yet more in-depth information. In relation to the respondent, unlike in unstructured interviews, structured allows people who cannot read or write to take part in such interviews. However, this particular interview technique does have less than advantageous aspect.

A new paragraph with the opening sentence being indented is a clear sign to the examiner that the candidate has begun a section on the advantages of structured interviews.

'… high response rate …' compared to which other method(s)?

'… openly explain …' is not really an accurate statement about structured interviews.

Again '… in-depth information' is not an accurate statement of the structured interview technique.

Usually the interviewer involved is paid to undertake the interview meaning the process can be fairly expensive to perform. In addition, general cost can increase if the interview becomes more widespread and involves more respondents. Finally, there is an increased rate of interviewer bias. The questions may prompt answers from respondents which have been devised from the interviewers specific point of view.

Again, not an accurate statement, all interviews have this characteristic – it is not specific to structured interviews.

A more clearly made point. Interviewer bias is identified and partly explained – but not really applied to structured interviews.

'Unstructured' interviews are much more 'informal' and are used to obtain information through informal conversation. They are more beneficial to use in an interview situation with 'sensitive' groups of people. Personal feelings of hostility and untrusting are all possible feelings which are allayed through the use of

A much stronger section. A whole cluster of advantages is explained and a good illustration is offered.

unstructured interviews and can help to develop a rapport and trust between interviewer and respondent creating a comfortable atmosphere in which a respondent is more likely to submit real feelings and opinions. In this way, in-depth information is obtained. In addition 'sensitive' subjects are more likely to be discussed openly in an information environment reflected in a study by Dobash and Dobash (1949) into marital violence. The found 'information; was much more in-depth using this particular process.

There are also disadvantages. Interviewers bias can affect how interviewees react and what they say. Interviewed people may give answers that are socially desirable but which are not really what they think. There is also the problem of knowing whether the interviewees responses are strictly true. Finally, the data from unstructured interviewers cannot be turned into figures and therefore cannot be compared.

Candidate B's answer

Strong introduction, the candidate 'deconstructs' the question, gives clear indication of understanding the task and recognises the dimensions of the question.

Good organisational skills. An introductory paragraph followed by paragraphs on advantages and disadvantages.

Collecting data via face-to-face interviewing of research subjects is a major sociological research tool. Interviews can take any forms from those which basically deliver a questionnaire in an interview format to those which have a degree of informality verging on participant observation. Although interviews are often classified into either 'structured' or 'unstructured' for the sake of analysing styles of interview, in reality an interview can employ a combination of both styles.

Sophisticated point, recognising that the two types of interviews may not, in reality, be so separate.

Structured interviews are as the item suggests, a more formal method with a set structure the same questions are asked in the same structure to all interviewees. This means the format is easy to compare results and produce quantifiable data – useful for statistics such as gender, age and occupation. There is likely to be little interview bias involved using structured interviews as the respondent is less aware of the interviewers characteristics and views on the subject. This makes the results more valid and reliable. Generalisation may also be formed as the results may be comparable.

Applies important methodological concepts. Links characteristics of structured interviews to the methodological concepts of reliability, validity, etc.

There are however disadvantages to structured interviews and cases where structured interviews are more appropriate to use. Structured interviews formal style may stifle some peoples answers as they do not want to open up. Unstructured interviews are more informal and appear like conversations between the interviewer and respondent. This makes unstructured interviews good to use when tackling sensitive subjects – this may be highlighted through the qualitative data produced by Dobash and Dobash's study of marital violence. Sensitive groups are more likely to respond to the interviewer through unstructured interviews. Fielding discovered that in the case of the frail and elderly for example, many would not respond to a postal survey as they felt vulnerable and threatened – they were suspicious of the survey.

Another well-applied example.

Example of a study applied clearly and well. The study is used to illustrate the point about sensitivity.

Unstructured interviews also allow the interviewee to express their own personal viewpoint on the matter. Respondents can guide the interview into areas they feel have significant importance and meaning. This produces research which is colourful, vivid and in depth. If a structured interview had been used in this case, results would not be exactly as each individual had meant.

The meanings and attitudes of respondents may therefore be explored more in the structured interview. As there are shades of meaning and attitudes are not as simple with cut and dried answers, unstructured interviews get a fuller picture and view of what the respondent is trying to express – as they are saying in their own chosen words, rather than the words of the interviewer.

The validity and depth produced by the unstructured interview may prove to be of great use to the researcher as they achieve a clear understanding of the respondent and what they mean. The study by Haralambos, for example, of the meanings attached to Blues and Soul music in America shows the great depth of emotion the music creates, and what exactly it means to the black people of the time.

Application skills. Another appropriate example applied well.

There are however disadvantages concerned with unstructured interviews. The results produced often widen the scope of the interview and therefore results may not be comparable or quantifiable. Generalisations should be avoided as different people mean different things.

There is also the question of the validity of the data – people may lie or deny the bad aspects and exaggerate their good traits just to be socially desirable. For example, people lie about attending church and their voting opinions. Also, O'Connell Davidson found people lie when recounting their sexual activity to the interviewer.

Use of an important concept linked to characteristics of unstructured interviews.

There is also a great deal of interview bias – people are affected by social and psychological characteristics of the interviewer. J. A. Williams found that the greater the social difference, the less people opened up. His study found that black Americans in the 1960's were more likely to admit to civil rights demonstrations if the interviewer was black.

A good example of how to make and explain a point in a brief but effective manner.

Overall, there are many disadvantages and advantages of both structured and unstructured interviews. It merely depends on the data required e.g. qualitative, quantitative, comparable, incomparable as to the best method.

A comparatively weak finish. A couple of weak points hastily made but not really evaluated.

Summary

Candidate A:

Overall Not a strong response but still enough points made to score 4/8.

Strengths One good section which clearly identifies the advantages of unstructured interviews. Some other accurate points are made elsewhere in the answer. The candidate does consider both advantages and disadvantages of the two types of interview.

Weaknesses No introduction or conclusion. The answer 'loses shape' and lacks an evaluative structure, becoming more of a 'list' answer offering a number of advantages and disadvantages. There is some element of balance but for both types of interview there is more about advantages than disadvantages.

Candidate B:

Overall A good effective answer which would have earned at least 6/8 if not 7/8.

Strengths This is a well-balanced answer. The four main paragraphs following the introduction are of equal length, and cover each of the advantages and disadvantages of the two types of interview.

The material presented is accurate and fairly comprehensive. In a large topic area like 'interviews' there is a great deal of material which could be used. For an 8–10 mark part-question a candidate does not need to cover absolutely everything.

Weaknesses The weakest part of the answer is the conclusion. It is not a full evaluation but briefly states one or two points.

How to write evaluative conclusions

You will have noticed that both candidates A and B in the preceding example failed to produce an effective, evaluative paragraph. This section will attempt to show you how this fault can be rectified.

Although it is vital to the success of your answer that you show evaluation skills throughout the answer, it is also very important to complete your response with a final evaluative section. An evaluative conclusion increases your chances of gaining a higher grade because:

- it confirms a clear focus on the issue in the question;
- it contributes to the overall balance of your answer;
- all questions demand an answer – this is where you offer your final, considered decision;
- it helps an examiner to see how you have deployed some of your evaluation skills.

What is an 'evaluative conclusion'?

We can start to understand what constitutes a good evaluative conclusion by looking at examples of final paragraphs which do not really offer an effective evaluative end to an answer. It is fairly easy to see why neither candidate A nor candidate B created a conclusion which 'works'. One is non-existent; the other ineffective. In the case of candidate B, the poor end to their response might well prevent them from gaining the top grade that the rest of their answer deserves.

Another typical weak conclusion is a final paragraph which simply summarises the main points already made in the answer – this is basically a list and will almost always lack any evaluative considerations.

In constructing an effective evaluative conclusion you might consider the following issues.

1 What possible judgements could be made about the claim you are dealing with? You could:
   - agree with the claim;
   - disagree with the claim;
   - partly agree/disagree with the claim;
   - view it as being accurate in parts;
   - be critical of the question/claim itself.

2 Are you providing a justified answer? It is not enough to offer what could be described as a 'simple judgement'. Just making a decision is insufficient. You need to be able to justify your judgement, presenting reasons why your overall conclusion is an appropriate one.

   In theory and methods questions it is useful to employ some of the key concepts of validity, representativeness, reliability, replicability, positivism, etc. in your conclusion (and in the rest of your answer!). How useful a particular method can be judged to be often depends upon how it matches up to the notions of validity and reliability. By using these and other concepts you will have something to evaluate a method against. This takes you away from some form of personal judgement or from bland statements like: 'This method has both weaknesses and strengths'.

How can these ideas be applied?

If we applied some of these considerations to the question on interviews (page 29), a conclusion like this might emerge:

Answer

The usefulness or otherwise of each style of interviewing depends to a great extent upon what the researcher wants the data to do. If the researcher wants to create a large representative sample from which to generalise their research findings, then a structured form of interviewing is necessary. Similarly, a structured approach is appropriate for any research which places greatest emphasis on generating statistical evidence. The usefulness of these two different interviewing techniques also depends on the research issue, the research subjects and the opportunities for research. More sensitive issues are possibly best approached through an informal style of interviewing.

To some extent the division of interviews into 'structured' and 'unstructured' is a little artificial. Some interviews are not easily slotted into either category; some use elements of structure and more open-ended techniques. For example, in the Dobash study of marital violence the bulk of the interview was carried out in an informal manner but some structured questions were also introduced to create quantitative as well as qualitative data. This combination of the two styles of interviewing was a genuine and successful attempt at triangulation.

This evaluative conclusion has made a judgement on the basis of the different criteria for 'usefulness' employed by different sociologists, and has challenged the questions' simplistic separation of interviewing into two techniques.

It is important to note that these are high level skills which, if displayed in an A-level answer, are likely to create an excellent impression on an examiner.

Bringing 'balance' into answers

As Chapter 1 pointed out, it is very easy to throw marks away simply by not producing a balanced answer. Remember that this is partly because there is an almost natural temptation to agree with the claim made in a question and, under exam pressure, it is understandable if candidates forget the need to put alternative arguments and claims.

Let's see how this might be applied to a question on sampling.

Item F

One of the key stages in any social survey is the selection of the group to be studied or interviewed. Because of cost and time, most surveys are limited to interviewing a sample – and it is vital that the sample selected should be as representative as possible.

Source: M. Slattery, *The ABC of Sociology*, p. 94, Nelson: London 1992

How far do sociologists agree that samples 'should be as representative as possible'? *(5 marks)*

Mark scheme

0 marks	No relevant points.
1–3 marks	A brief outline of one or two reasons why samples should or should not be representative. In this band the answer is likely to present an imbalanced response – usually one which only argues that samples should be representative.
4–5 marks	A more balanced response in which the candidate indicates reasons why samples should not be representative as well as presenting arguments why they should be representative.

Candidate A's answer

Sociologists stress the importance of their samples being representative because if a sample is not representative of the whole group being studied then the sample's data cannot be generalised to the whole group. If a sample is representative then what is true for the sample will also be true for the whole group. The data will be reliable.

Candidate B's answer

Sociologists agree samples should be representative because if it is, then the results of the interviews will be also true of the whole group. The data will therefore be unbiased and reliable. Sometimes however it is not possible to get a representative sample as you may not know the make-up of the whole group you are studying.

Candidate C's answer

Some sociologists believe that samples need to be representative. The results from a representative sample can be generalised to the whole population. If a sample was unrepresentative then the data would only be true of the sample and not true of the whole group. This fits in with the positivist emphasis on research being objective and scientific.

This is not always possible to achieve in practice as sometimes it is impossible to find the characteristics of the whole population and therefore the sociologist cannot form a representative sample. Interpretivists also do not believe that representativeness is either possible or necessarily desirable as it is validity that they are after. So getting a representative sample for them is not at all vital.

Commentary

Candidate A's answer falls into the trap of not producing a balanced answer and only states the case for samples being representative – agreeing with the claim in the question rather than testing it. Nevertheless, the answer deals with reasons why samples should be representative well enough to earn two marks. However, it cannot get into the top mark band without at least some consideration of the opposite case.

Candidate B does rather better simple by suggesting one additional reason why samples may not necessarily need to be representative – even though they begin with the contradictory claim that: 'All sociologists agree that ...'!

Candidate C goes the whole hog and earns full marks because they meet the challenge of producing a balanced answer, clearly putting arguments both for and against the claim.

A final comment

The key skill illustrated in this example is that of balance and the wording of the question makes the need to display this skill very clear.

The command phrase, 'How far do sociologists agree ...', is a major clue here. If one thing in life is certain it is that sociologists do not agree! So neither should you in your answer! The wording of the question invites you to respond in terms of '... some sociologists agree that ...' and then '... some sociologists disagree that ...', with you filling in the reasons why they agree or disagree.

Practice data-response questions

We finish this chapter with two full data-response questions of the type asked at A-level. Question 2.1, on sociological research, is followed by a mark scheme and two complete student responses. Each response is commented on in terms of how it demonstrates the key skill domains and therefore what marks it would merit according to the mark scheme. Question 2.2 includes questions that relate sociological research to sociological theory. A mark scheme is provided and it is suggested that you have a go at this question in light of the material and ideas discussed in this chapter.

Question 2.1

Item G

Ken Pryce carried out covert participant observation of an Afro-Caribbean church congregation in Bristol:

The situation was made even more awkward by the fact that there was no way in which I could even take notes on the spot. I found I needed to take notes most during my first encounters with church members when I was getting to know them.

In addition to these strains, I found the church services – which were generally whole day affairs – too wearisome and physically exhausting. Each church service always left me groggy and somewhat mentally incapacitated, and this further interfered with my note-taking.

Source: adapted from K. Pryce, *Endless Pressure*, Penguin: Harmondsworth, 1979

Item H

In the preface to his ethnographic study on a mental institution, Goffman described some of the ways in which his work could be biased:

My method has other limits too. To describe the patients' situation faithfully is necessarily to present a one-sided view. (For this last bias I partly excuse myself by arguing that the imbalance is at least on the right side of the scale, since almost all professional literature on mental patients is written from the point of view of the psychiatrist, and he, socially speaking, is on the other side.)

Further, I want to warn that my view is probably too much that of a middle-class male; perhaps I was overly sympathetic to the conditions that lower-class patients experienced. Finally, unlike some patients, I came to the hospital with no great respect for psychiatry.

Source: adapted from E. Goffman, *Asylums*, Penguin: Harmondsworth, 1968

Item I

If a method of collecting evidence is reliable, it means that anyone else using this method, or the same person using it at another time, would come up with the same results. The research could be repeated, and the same results would be obtained. For example, an experiment in a chemistry lesson should always 'work'. It should always produce the result that is expected, whoever is doing it, at whatever time, provided that the proper procedures are followed.

Some methods in sociology are regarded as being more reliable than others. Any method that involves a lone researcher in a situation that cannot be repeated, like much participant observation research, is always in danger of being thought unreliable.

Source: P. McNeill, *Research Methods*, p.14, Routledge: London 1985

1 Apart from the problems mentioned in Item G, give two further difficulties likely to be experienced when carrying out covert research. *(2 marks)*

2 Explain why the experimental method (Item I) is rarely used by sociologists. *(5 marks)*

3 Using the items and your own knowledge, examine the claim that participant observation achieves a high degree of validity but lacks reliability. *(9 marks)*

4 With reference to the items and elsewhere, evaluate the view that it is impossible to keep values out of sociological research. *(9 marks)*

Mark scheme

1 One mark for each of two problems experienced in covert research other than observer exhaustion and recording field notes; the problems have to relate to the covert aspect of research and may include:

- creating or finding a suitable 'cover' role within a group;
- sustaining that role over a substantial time period;
- avoiding discovery of researcher identity;
- being unable to ask questions in an overt manner;
- the ethics of maintaining a false identity;
- not being able to fully penetrate a group which may have an 'inner core' of members.

2 1–2 marks Candidates' answers will be confined to one or two reasons, probably not fully explained, why experiments are rarely used by sociologists. The suggested reasons must be accurate, although they may be explained in a common-sense rather than a fully academic manner.

3–5 marks Candidates will offer a good range of appropriate reasons and these will be explained in a more precise manner. Towards the top of this band, candidates will offer either a limited number of reasons which are then accurately explained in some detail, or they will give a full list of reasons, not all of which may be explained in great detail.

3 0 marks No relevant points.

1–3 marks Candidates' responses will be based on a confused and/or inaccurate understanding of validity and reliability. Generally, in this mark band candidates will not distinguish between the two concepts Candidates will rely either on a few points culled from the items or upon a description of a study using participant observation.

4–6 marks Towards the bottom of this band answers will tend to present a list of advantages and disadvantages of participant observation, with little specific reference to the notions of validity and reliability. Towards the top of this mark band candidates will relate their understanding of the advantages and disadvantages associated with participant observation to the concepts of reliability and validity. At the top of this band, candidates may identify some of the theoretical dimensions of this question.

7–9 marks In this band, candidates will make explicit links between the advantages and disadvantages of participant observation and the concepts of validity and reliability. Responses are likely to be contained in a framework based on these two concepts. Examples of participant observation studies will be specifically related to validity and reliability. Towards the top of this band, candidates may be critical of the usual claim that participant observation achieves a high degree of validity.

4 0 marks No relevant points.

1–3 marks Candidates in this band may rely upon a description of some sociological studies, with some passing relation to the way values may affect the research process, or may simply recycle elements from the Items. Responses will express little or no understanding of the theoretical aspects of this issue.

4–6 marks Towards the bottom of this band candidates will present an imbalanced response, arguing either that it is possible or impossible to keep values out of the research process. At this level, candidates will express a limited number of arguments for the position they advocate. There will also tend to be a focus on the practical problems involved in keeping values out of research. Towards the top of the band there will be at least some understanding of theoretical concerns and issues.

7–9 marks In this band candidates will have a clear focus on the theoretical dimensions of this question. They may express this in terms of competing theoretical positions or in terms of the 'sociology and science' debate. Towards the top of this band the practical issues concerning values and research may be placed in a theoretical context.

Candidate A's answer

1 If the identity of the observer is known to the group, then this will affect their behaviour. It is also very difficult to maintain a secret identity during research, the researcher may be found out.

Commentary: 1/2 marks

This candidate has identified one difficulty with covert research – the second point made in the answer. But the first point is neither clearly explained nor relevant to covert research. Under exam conditions, it is easy to miss critical wording – in this case, the focus on 'covert'.

2 Sociologists do not often use experiments because they do not work very well outside of the laboratory. Social behaviour is very complex and a simple experiment probably cannot measure what really happens in social life. For example, if you try to measure how superstitious people are by putting a ladder against a wall and watching to see how many people avoid walking under it, you still do not know why they did so. Some might avoid going under a ladder because they are superstitious but others might be afraid of things being dropped on their head.

Experimenting on people is usually seen as being wrong. Even if they do not come to any physical harm, people might be affected in other ways by being part of an experiment. Also, if they know they are involved in an experiment, this will affect how they behave.

For these reasons, sociologists do not usually use experiments, although sometimes they do use field experiments when a normal social situation is converted into an experiment, as for example in dressing the same actor as a working class and a middle class person and having them ask for directions to see whether their class affected people's responses.

Commentary: 3/5

The candidate makes some points about why the experiment is not often used in sociology. Their explanations are put in a fairly commonsense way but they are generally accurate. Had the answer stopped after the first paragraph, they would probably have had their mark limited to 2/5. By making a point that the experiment can be used in certain circumstances, the candidate just scrapes into the next mark band.

3 It is usually interactionist sociologists who use participant observation as a way of researching groups. This can take two forms, covert and overt research. With covert observation the people being studied do not know they are being studied whilst with overt observation, they know the observer is a researcher. There are several reasons why participant observation is considered valid. It allows the research subjects to be observed in their normal social settings. This makes the data accurate and a true reflection of a group's behaviour. Being part of a group means that a researcher can 'get the inside story'. Group members are more likely to 'open up' and show what they really think if the observation is covert. By joining a group a sociologist can uncover what they believe and this is what validity is all about. This is particularly true if the research is covert because the observer will not influence the way the group acts.

Some sociologists believe that participant observation is not a very reliable research method. This is a very subjective approach, it is only the observer's interpretation of events and this is their opinion. There is no way of checking whether they have made the correct interpretation or not. Participant observation is not a very scientific approach and it does not produce statistical data which can be analysed and checked. These studies cannot be replicated as a different observer might reach different conclusions. This approach is also unreliable because the presence of a stranger (the researcher) in the group may alter their behaviour, making the observer's interpretations inaccurate.

So the claim in the question is basically correct, participant observation studies might be more valid but they are not very reliable ways of collecting information.

Commentary: 4/9

Although this answer has some sociological knowledge, this is not always accurate and is not well-applied to the question. Neither 'validity' nor 'reliability' are clearly defined and there is some confusion about their apparent meaning as applied by the candidate. The response also fairly uncritically accepts the claim about participant observation. The answer is also rather weak in structure, coming across as being fairly disjointed.

4 It is very difficult to keep values out of the research process as there are all kinds of values in society so some bias is inevitable. The writer of Item B makes it clear that he is biased because he is a middle class male and also not on the side of psychiatry. This means that his research will favour patients. Sociologists such as Becker argue that values are always present in society so they will always affect research.

What the sociologist chooses to study is one way in which values come into research. Some sociologists will want to only study those things which they think are important and this is a personal judgement. When they are actually doing the research it is likely that they will see things in the way they want to. The Glasgow Group read certain ideas into television news bulletins that other people might not have done. When they choose which method they will use, that is also an example of how values can affect research.

Functionalists however, believe that it is possible to be unbiased in sociology. They argue that research should be like the natural sciences and as much like the laboratory experiment as possible. The laboratory experiment is the best way to keep values out of research. However, even functionalists see that this might not be possible when looking at how people act in society.

Commentary: 4/9

This is a poorly structured response but makes just enough points and has just enough balance to struggle into the middle mark band. With a stronger structure putting the 'for' and 'against' cases in clearly separate sections, it would move up the middle mark band. It also needs much more sociological knowledge, especially of the theoretical positions relevant to this issue.

Candidate B's answer

1 If the identity of a researcher is uncovered as they carry out covert observation, they will probably find they cannot keep the research going. When joining a group the researcher will have to find some role to occupy in the group which they can use as a 'cover'. This may not be easy.

Commentary: 2/2

No problems here. The candidate identifies two problems specifically relating to the covert research. They are not textbook definitions, but that is not required to gain both marks.

2 Experiments – particularly laboratory experiments – are not often used in sociology. Although Positivists advocate the use of methods which allow researchers to measure behaviour, and although the laboratory experiment is usually seen as the most 'scientific' research technique, it is difficult to apply to the study of social behaviour for several reasons.

The laboratory is a very artificial setting compared to the social world. What may be true in the laboratory may not be simply transferable to the real social world. The aim of an experiment is to control all the variables that affect behaviour and in social interaction, this is not easy to do. The variables which affect how individuals behave in social life are so numerous and complex that it is doubtful whether it is possible to identify let alone control them. One very important variable which will affect how someone behaves is the fact that they know they are part of an experiment. This shows that experiments are difficult to use because the essence of social behaviour is 'meaning' and simple experiments cannot measure this.

Experiments have also been criticised on ethical grounds. Many experiments mislead those involved in them in order to avoid their knowledge of the experiment influencing their actions. This may be necessary to keep the research process reliable but how ethically sound is it to actively mislead research subjects? Research by Bandura and others into the relationship between violent media stimuli and behaviour has often involved children as young as four years of age. Again, there must be doubts on moral grounds of the appropriateness of such an approach.

As it is, sociologists do not always ignore the experimental approach. Although the laboratory experiment is largely ignored, sociologists do use field experiments at times. This involves creating an experiment out of an existing social activity or creating a situation which is readily believable. For example, research into racial discrimination has used the field experiment. Actors representing a range of ethnic identities applied for the same job all with similar qualifications and experience. How often they were summoned for interview gave an indication of the extent of discrimination. Although useful, this approach does not meet all the scientific criteria for the laboratory experiment and may not be considered to be an experiment by Positivists.

Commentary: 5/5

Although this is not a 'perfect' answer, it does all that is necessary for a five mark question. A good range of reasons why experiments tend not to be used in sociological research is accompanied by explanation in some depth and an element of balance is provided in the final paragraph.

3 Participant observation involves a researcher joining a group and either covertly or overtly observing their activities. Interpretivists claim that this approach produces data which is high in validity for several reasons. By validity, most sociologists mean that the data generated is an accurate statement of the meanings a social group or individual hold. The information produced by participant observation meets the demands of validity partly because the method allows the researcher to see what a group does rather than, as with interviews, hear what it claims to do. By sharing the experiences of a group, the observer can uncover the meanings people attach to events. This is an insight which formal methods of investigation do not produce. If the research is covert, it is also true that the observer's presence will not greatly affect how the group behaves, it will not disturb their natural setting. The researcher is likely to come across things they would otherwise not have thought to ask about, again adding to the validity of their data.

However, this claim to be high in validity can be challenged. The observer will be interpreting the behaviour of the group – in other words, putting their views onto what they see and hear. So what results might not be an accurate view of the group, it depends how good the observer is. If the study is overt, then knowing they are being studied is even more likely to alter the way people behave.

It is more accurate to claim that participant observation is not a very reliable method. Sociologists who carry out participant observation do not claim to be using a reliable method. Reliability involves carrying out research in a clearly defined way, with others being able to repeat it in the same way and being able to check the results. This is a very scientific concept and participant observation falls well short of this demand. A different observer might follow a very different course and make very different interpretations. No-one can check the observations made to see if they are accurate. Observation also does not produce statistical data so the results cannot be analysed for patterns and causes and effects.

Overall, it seems that participant observation produces information which has some validity but which also might have problems with its validity. It is unlikely that participant observation ever can be seen as reliable because it is such a loosely structured way to go about research.

Commentary: 7/9

This answer has many strengths. It has a clear focus on the question but does not simply accept the claim in the question at face value. The answer has a good structure in that there is a section on validity, one critical of the validity claim and a third section concerned with the issue of reliability. The conclusion is a reasoned one and directly relates to the arguments preceding it. It does lack any application of examples and it could be more comprehensive in the coverage of the characteristics of participant observation.

4 Values are probably an inescapable part of social life and this has led some sociologists to suggest that it is impossible to keep values out of sociological research. There are so many kinds of values – personal, religious, academic, political – that these sociologists may well be correct in their claims. Others however, have claimed that sociology should attempt to be objective and keep values from affecting the research process. Indeed, there may be two separate questions here, whether sociologists should keep values out of research and whether this can be achieved in actual research.

Howard Becker argued from an interactionist perspective that it is impossible to carry out value-free research. He said that as the essence of social interaction is the communication of meanings, then as meanings are often value judgements, then social life is constructed of values. As sociological research is itself a social process, then values must be part of it. Becker believed that the researcher should therefore explain his values to the reader, as Goffman is apparently doing in Item B. Any reader will then be able to recognise any bias in the research. The difficulty with this claim is that even sociologists are not always aware of their own bias and it is also hard for a reader to spot when a researcher is being biased.

Gouldner is very critical of any idea that sociology can be free from values. He believes that values should play an important part in sociological research. A radical, Gouldner claims that sociology should be based on radical values and employ its knowledge and understanding to help the weakest groups in society. Gouldner also points out that functionalists – who claim to keep values out of research – are not neutral but usually take a point of view which supports the status quo. The problem here is that few sociologists would represent themselves as taking such an openly radical stance.

It is also clear that values can affect many stages in the research process. It is impossible for the sociologist to escape from the time and place in which they are writing. We are all social beings so what is going on in society as we work will be bound to have some effect on what we research. Personal values will affect what the sociologist chooses to research. This can be seen in the work of many feminist sociologists who have focused their research primarily on issues concerning women. Similarly, the choice of methods involves something of a value judgement. Whether quantitative or qualitative data is required is a decision which will be made reflecting the beliefs of the sociologists concerned. Once the data is collected, then it has to be interpreted by the researcher. The whole notion of 'interpretation' is concerned with selecting the meanings to be drawn from data and this is a matter of judgement and values. Research into bias in media messages by the Glasgow Media Group has often been criticised for being their interpretation of the media messages. Other researchers may have reached different conclusions.

It is the case that some sociologists, particularly Positivists, have claimed that sociology should try to be free of values. They see the sociologist as the 'neutral technician' of society acting as objectively as the natural scientist, following strict rules of investigation.

Commentary: 6/9

This answer begins very promisingly and the candidate displays a good understanding of both theoretical and practical reasons why it is very difficult to keep values out of research. The response is limited, however, by the imbalanced coverage it offers. There is very little concerning the alternative view that values can and should be kept out of research. A little more along this line would have moved the answer into the top mark band.

Question 2.2

Item J

Source: N. Jorgensen *et al.*, *Sociology: An Interactionist Approach*, Collins Educational: London 1997

Item K

Theoretical and methodological approaches play a large role in decisions about which particular research technique or method to use. The methodological debate between structural and interpretivist sociologists frames the choice of method. Structuralists have traditionally been inclined to methods which produce qualitative data while interpretivists have been more inclined to methods which generate qualitative data.

Source: adapted from M. Kirby *et al.*, *Sociology in Perspective*, p. 84, Heinemann: Oxford 1997.

Item L

Shere Hite based her report on family life on a sample of 3,208 returned questionnaires – a far larger sample than most sociological research can stretch to. She sent out 100,000 copies of her questionnaire via magazines such as *Penthouse* and *Women Against Fundamentalism.* She claimed that a sample of over 3,000 makes for an effective study. In fact, sample size matters far less than sampling methods. Few methods are more suspect than those that involve self-selection – Hite's technique. Her statistics come from the 3% who responded and neither Hite nor anyone else knows how representative such a sample is.

Source: adapted from P. Taylor *et al.*, *Sociology in Focus*, pp. 613–14, Causeway Press: Ormskirk 1995.

1 **Identify and briefly explain two problems sociologists may have in using official statistics such as those in Item J.** *(4 marks)*

2 **Give one example of a type of secondary data other than official statistics.** *(1 mark)*

3 **Give one example of a primary research method.** *(1 mark)*

4 **Evaluate the usefulness of postal questionnaires as a sociological research technique.** *(8 marks)*

5 **How far is it the case that 'structuralists have traditionally been inclined to methods which produce quantitative data while interpretivists have been more inclined to methods which generate qualitative data'?** *(11 marks)*

Mark scheme

1 One mark each for two appropriately identified problems that sociologists encounter with official statistics. These do not have to be specifically associated with suicide statistics. One further mark in each case when the candidate extends or amplifies the problem initially identified.

2 One mark for any suitable type of secondary data including personal records, media reports, existing sociological research, etc.

3 One mark for any appropriately identified primary research method including participant observation, structured observation, experiments, structured interviews, unstructured interviews, self-completion questionnaires, etc.

4 1–2 marks Candidates' responses will identify only one or two specific characteristics of postal questionnaires, probably based on the items. The response will be very descriptive in style and content.

3–5 marks Towards the bottom of this mark band answers will tend to list advantages and disadvantages of postal questionnaires but in a limited way. At this level, evaluation will be limited to perceived weaknesses and strengths. Towards the top of this mark band candidates will begin to place strengths and weaknesses in a theoretical context, relating them to concepts of reliability and validity. There must be some focus on the postal element of this technique to get to the top of this band.

6–8 marks Candidates will present a full account of the strengths and weaknesses of this approach, with a clear focus on the postal dimension. Evaluation will be explicit and based on an appropriate understanding of the theoretical context. Claims will be treated in a critical manner and examples will be well contextualised.

5 1–3 marks Responses in this mark band will be unclear as to the methodological issue considered by this question. Candidates are likely to repeat elements from the data items in an uncritical manner or in a form which indicates minimal understanding. Responses are likely to be clouded by long, poorly expressed descriptive passages.

4–7 marks In this band, candidates will have a understanding of the issue. Nevertheless, particularly at the lower end of this band, responses will be imbalanced in their coverage, probably producing arguments and evidence in support of the claim. Towards the top of this band, answers will demonstrate awareness that the claim may not be entirely accurate.

8–11 marks In this band, candidates will exhibit a clear understanding of the issue. This understanding will be reasonably thorough. The response will present a balanced appreciation of the issue and the claim will be thoroughly examined in a critical manner.

Chapter 3

The Family

Introduction

Perspectives on the family

Knowledge and understanding

Take control of your own learning

Interpretation and application

Ideology in historical materials
Differentiating between feminism and Marxism
Cues within a text will help you analyse it
Interpretation of texts
Creating an answer
Analysing statistical data
Taking information from a variety of stimulus materials

Evaluation

The significance of evidence in evaluation
What should an evaluation answer look like?
Ideology and evaluation answers

Practice data-response questions

Introduction

In order to gain a full understanding of any piece of sociological writing that you read, it is important to be aware of the theoretical and ideological position taken by the writer. In sociological language we use the term 'perspective' to refer to differing theoretical and ideological positions. The ability to identify perspective is an enormously useful skill in almost any serious study and should be practised on any pieces of writing or media texts that you look at.

Before you begin a really detailed analysis of the piece of writing, you should look for certain key features, terms, words and ideas which will tell you the sociological perspective of the author. As you work your way through sociology texts, and this chapter in particular, see if you can identify other terms and features of each perspective which have not been suggested below.

Perspectives on the family

- In very simplistic terms, **functionalist perspectives** and those of the '**New Right**' will tend to express satisfaction with the family as a social institution, and concern at the 'decline' of family structures and, perhaps more important, family values.
- The perspective a sociologist holds informs the sort of research questions she or he will examine and **feminism** tends to be identifiable by its insistence on considering the notion of gender and how gender roles translate into social roles.
- **Marxist theoretical perspectives** can usually be identified by their emphasis on economic constraints and their considerations of the ideology of the family.
- Early **British empirical** writers can be identified by their tendency to look for trends and patterns and their desire to quantify social behaviours.

As a final note, be cautious about rigidly allocating a piece of stimulus material to a particular perspective as there are debates within perspectives and not all stimulus materials will necessarily be sociological in intent. The first four extracts in this chapter are taken from very different perspectives and illustrate the points made above.

Questions asking you to identify the perspective of a piece of writing are looking for the skills of interpretation and application. They will usually appear at the start of the questioning and it is sometimes a useful exercise to go through a past paper identifying the skill domains of the various questions on each topic. These answers carry few marks, usually only one or two, but they are relatively easy marks to gain.

Knowledge and understanding

Knowledge is a complex area and deserves a little discussion with relation to the family.

What should you know? First, there is the technical language of family analysis and household form. This can be acquired from any good sociological dictionary and/or textbook. Second, you should have a clear knowledge of the main perspectives, especially their similarities and differences. If you do not already keep a vocabulary book or list of key terms in your notes, you are well advised to start doing so because sociology is a subject that deals in concepts and you need to express yourself in a clear but precise language.

It is very important to use knowledge to support all of your answers to questions, especially those requiring evaluation. Here the knowledge takes the form of supporting evidence and it should reflect the sociological reading that you have done and the understanding that you have gathered from the sociology that you have studied.

Take control of your own learning

It is not the role of the teacher or lecturer to provide you with all this further knowledge, it is your own task to acquire the additional understanding and information which you will use to support your evaluations and judgements. Your teacher or lecturer may suggest areas of further reading and the examination boards produce booklists for you to use as the basic 'tools of the trade' of sociology. You could also use the extracts in this chapter and in other texts as a guide to further reading.

Understanding shows a slightly higher level skill because it implies rather more than the reiteration of class notes. Here, too, you can improve your understanding of social perspectives and ideologies by looking in newspapers and periodicals. Recent publications can also give you a view of what people's concerns are and an idea of the type of questions that could be asked on families. Look at the vocabulary and facts that you have learned and see how they are used by practising academics, writers and thinkers.

Interpretation and application

While no one would ever undervalue the acquisition of knowledge about sociology, many excellent texts are available. The focus of this text is to help you to practise the higher level skills of interpretation, application and evaluation. While there will be an emphasis on the family section of the A-level examination in this chapter, examination success alone should not be the only reason for acquiring these skills. They are your keys to understanding sociology as an academic discipline.

Before looking at the first extract and question, it is important to remember that a very clear and careful reading of questions and extracts is essential. You are advised to read questions with a pencil in your hand, marking clearly the verb which indicates what the question asks you to do, and underlining the actual sociological terms and words which should be discussed. Many revision texts will show you how to do this and will also analyse the meaning of various formal wordings of questions. In the case of Item A, you are asked to identify a perspective and any other discussion will be irrelevant and will gain you no credit.

Item A

Whether or not leisure activities are a <u>compensation</u> to people who do not fulfil themselves in their work, the <u>family certainly is</u>. As a multi-purpose institution (although not to anything like the same extent the all-purpose one of Stage 1) it can provide some <u>sense of wholeness</u> and <u>permanence</u> to set against the more restricted and transitory roles imposed by the specialized institutions which have flourished outside the home. The upshot is that, as the disadvantages of the new industrial and impersonal society have become more pronounced, so has the <u>family become more prized</u> for its power to counteract them.

Source: M. Young and P. Willmott, *The Symmetrical Family: A Study of Work and Leisure in the London Region*, p. 269, Routledge and Kegan Paul: London, 1973

What sociological perspective on the family is illustrated in Item A?

Young and Willmott's work was of enormous significance in the 1970s and is often used in textbooks of the time without query or criticism. It described changes in the family based on research in the Thames Basin through the 1950s, 60s and 70s. The Stage 1 family referred to in the extract is described by Young and Willmott as being pre-industrial. Families were said to exist as part of a mutually supportive economic and emotional system. This theorising has been seriously criticised by historians such as Laslett and Anderson, among other writers, who should be well covered by knowledge-based texts.

The key terms and expressions which identify the perspective are underlined for you in Item A. You will see that they describe the family in very positive terms – as a 'compensation', and 'prized'. Your answer should suggest functionalist, though the reference to 'Stage 1' would allow you 'British empiricist' if you were also aware that Young and

Willmott are British writers rather than two of the American writers who tend to dominate the functionalist tradition.

Ideology in historical materials

If you look at the historical text (Item B), dating to the period of the Second World War, you will see a similar perspective in a non-sociological text. In the strip designed for Peak Frean's steak pies you will see that the role of the female is to make her husband happy and it is her task to reconcile this aim with her civic duties.

Item B

Figure 3.1

What role is identified as being most significant for a woman in the cartoon? *(1 mark)*

The next extract offers a very different and extremely strongly argued view of family dynamics.

Item C

Yet, how fundamental a change has there really been? A gross asymmetry in heterosexual relations remains, despite these improvements. Men still seek and are willing to pay for the services of prostitutes, often asking for the fulfilment of the most bizarre fantasies and fetishes. They pour huge sums of money into the burgeoning trade of pornographic magazines, pictures, films and video-tapes which represent women as objects of male desire. Clubs, pubs and conferences of business-men and union men are routinely entertained with girly strip-shows. Men still rape women. Fathers still commit incest with their daughters. It is practically never the other way round. This asymmetry in sex is still as great as it ever was, much greater than in many supposedly primitive societies. Women are no longer expected to be chaste, but sex is still on men's terms. It is almost as if women's obvious sexual enjoyment were just another thing that men can demand of them. A far cry from the feminist dream of autonomy, it turns out that a 'liberated' lady is more fun in bed – for the man. ... This sexual asymmetry is social rather than natural in its origins. It is part of the pattern of courtship and of marriage.

Source: M. Barrett and M. McIntosh, *The Anti-Social Family*, p. 74, Verso Editions: London 1982

1. **Identify the perspective offered in the extract in item C.** *(1 mark)*
2. **What suggestions are made in the passage to suggest that males use sexuality as a form of power relationship rather than as an expression of love?** *(2 marks)*

The key feminist terms and language of item C have been identified for you by underlining. Recognise the force of the language, the references to male violence and the concern with gender roles and socialisation. There is also a clear and total rejection in the final sentence of biological definitions of gender and the theorising of writers such as Morris, or Tiger and Fox who were often cited in arguments against the emergent feminist movements of the early 1970s.

Differentiating between feminism and Marxism

The next passage (Item D) appears superficially similar to the feminist perspective, but read it carefully as there are a number of clues which should make it clear to you that this is, in fact, a Marxist perspective. You may already know that Engels was a close friend of Marx and that they co-operated on much writing in the late nineteenth century. The date in the source refers to the date of publication of a particular edition of the text. This analysis was actually written after the death of Marx.

Your answer, however, should centre upon the clues given in the text, that the real subject of the passage is not just the family but a consideration of the family as a microcosm of wider society. For your own benefit, you should underline all of the references to power relationships and economics. You will then see clearly that the real issues being considered are ones of inequalities of power and economic dependence rather than the issues of gender relationships.

Item D

The modern individual family is based on the open or disguised domestic enslavement of the woman; and modern society is a mass composed solely of individual families as its molecules. Today, in the great majority of cases, the man has to be the earner, the bread-winner of the family, at least among the propertied classes, and this gives him a dominating position which requires no special legal privileges. In the family, he is the bourgeois; the wife represents the proletariat. ... the peculiar character of man's domination over woman in the modern family, and the necessity, as well as the manner, of establishing real social equality between the two, will be brought out into full relief only when both are completely equal before the law. It will then become evident that the first premise for the emancipation of women is the reintroduction of the entire female sex into public industry; and this again demands that the quality possessed by the individual family of being the economic unit of society be abolished.

Source: Frederick Engels, 'The Origin of Family, Private Property and State' in *Marx and Engels, Selected Works in One Volume*, Lawrence and Wishart: New York 1968

1. **What does the author of the passage suggest gives men their dominant role in the family?** *(2 marks)*
2. **How does the author feel that women can achieve power in the family?** *(2 marks)*
3. **What do the terms 'bourgeois' and 'proletariat' mean in the context of the extract?** *(2 marks)*

Question 3 in Item D and questions 1 and 3 in Item E ask you to apply your knowledge of sociological terminology. It is fully expected that you should understand what is meant by certain sociological terms related to your area of study.

Cues within a text will help you to analyse it

Use the next extract as an example of how to look for cues within the text or the questions which can help you to find an appropriate answer.

Item E

There is clear evidence that cohabitation is becoming an established alternative to marriage in a number of European societies. In Sweden and Denmark, more children are raised by cohabiting parents than married ones. The evidence on the comparative stability of marriage to cohabitation is still unclear, but it seems clear that parents with children have a sense of long term commitment. The debates surrounding the 1996 Divorce Bill legislation in Britain have included concerns about the possible weakening of marriage but historical trends in divorce inexorably move towards liberalization. Whether this is arrested depends on how influential New Right politicians are in exerting their wishes to strengthen marriage and family life. Such issues are obviously irrelevant to the growing numbers of cohabiting couples.

Source: N. Jorgensen *et al.*, *Sociology: An Interactive Approach*, p. 120, Collins Educational: London 1997

1 **Explain the meaning of cohabitation.** *(1 mark)*

2 **What ideology of the family is typical of politicians of the 'New Right'?** *(2 marks)*

3 **In what ways does marriage differ from cohabitation? Offer a simple sociological explanation of the differences between the two social arrangements.** *(2 marks)*

Item E offers you a number of possible choices for knowledge questions. You should be aware that cohabitation is when people live together without having a legal contract of marriage. However, if you did not know this, you can guess, because pair couples are being discussed and cohabitation is offered as an alternative social arrangement to marriage. It is the legal status of marriage which should be drawn upon to answer questions 1 and 3. Marriage confers legal rights and responsibilities on partners which do not exist for co-habitees. It is these legal rights and distinctions which make the issue of homosexual marriage of such significance for gay partners in long-standing relationships.

To gain the two marks in question 2, item E, you are advised not simply to repeat the words of the sentence. You should demonstrate knowledge of the 'New Right' which is typical of the kind of up dated but traditional thinking popular among supporters of Mrs Thatcher and the Conservative Party of the 1980s. However, bear in mind that lengthy explanations will not gain any bonus points and you are under serious time pressure in this examination!

Interpretation of texts

Item F

The average child in Britain will have cost its parents £50,000 in food, clothing and leisure by the age of 17, according to a report commissioned by the Joseph Rowntree Foundation and based on the living standards of more than 1,200 children and their parents.

It shows that there is little difference in the overall average spending on children from rich and poor families and from two or one parent households.

Sue Middleton, one of the report's authors, said that the findings demonstrated to what extent parents – particularly poor parents – are prepared to make sacrifices rather than see their children go without. 'Children in one-parent families get only 10 per cent less spent on them than those in two-parent families,' she said.

Source: A. Frean, 'Why Parents are £50,000 out of pocket', *The Times*, 10 July 1997

1 **Who commissioned the report on the average cost of child rearing in Britain today?** *(1 mark)*

2 **Look at the above extract. What do the authors of the report suggest is the reason for the low percentage differences between the amount spent by rich parents and by poor parents in modern Britain?** *(2 marks)*

Question 2, item F, and the extract itself, provide a good illustration of the skill domain of interpretation. Interpretation is your ability to draw information out of a piece of text or data and then to comment upon it. The author of the extract suggests that poor people buy luxuries for their children by depriving themselves of basic necessities. She has taken a basic statistical finding about spending among a sample of 1,200 children and their families and offered an interpretation of that data, a suggestion as to why poorer people and richer people appear to be spending broadly similar amounts of money on their children. Were you to be required to evaluate the passage, the question would ask you to make a judgement on the conclusions that the authors of the report have drawn. However, evaluation is to be covered later in this chapter and the next extract offers a slightly different interpretative challenge.

Item G

One of the unwritten laws of contemporary morality, the strictest and best respected of all, requires adults to avoid any reference, above all any humorous reference, to sexual matters in the presence of children. This notion was entirely foreign to the society of old. The modern reader of the diary in which Henri IV's physician, Heroard, recorded the details of the young Louis XIII's life is astonished by the liberties which people took with children by the coarseness of the jokes they made, and by the indecency of gestures made in public which shocked nobody and which were regarded as perfectly natural. No other document can give us a better idea of the non-existence of the modern idea of childhood at the beginning of the seventeenth century.

Source: P. Aries, *Centuries of Childhood*, p. 100, Jonathan Cape: London 1962

What evidence does Aries provide to suggest that childhood is a social construct? *(4 marks)*

Creating an answer

In your answer to the above question you will need to do a little more than simply draw information from the passage. You should perhaps show that you are aware that a social construct is a specific and technical term used in social action theories. It is necessary to define the term to prove that childhood can indeed be seen as a social construct. There is space here for some degree of comment on the evidence that Ariès uses. For instance, 'Ariès uses as his evidence the report of a single writer who described the upbringing of a royal child in the court of the French king, Henri IV. The behaviours which were acceptable to people of that place and era would no longer be considered acceptable today ...' and continue with your analysis which should include reference to **place**, **time** and **cultural beliefs** in defining acceptable social behaviours.

If you are working at speed, it is advisable to pay particular attention to the final paragraphs of chapters and the final sentences of paragraphs as they act as a summative conclusion to what has gone before. In Item G, the concluding sentence is the one that offers the fullest clue to an understanding of the question. While the rest of the passage is a report, the phrase which has been underlined in the extract is a conclusion to the piece and this should draw your eye to an appreciation of what the subsequent question is asking. This does not always happen, however, and the following extract shows just how important a careful reading of the text can be.

Item H

Family violence is greater in poor and minority households, but it occurs in families at all socio-economic levels. Research has shown the incidence of family violence to be highest among urban lower-class families. It is high among families with more than four children and in those in which the husband is unemployed. Families in which child abuse occurs tend to be socially isolated, living in crowded and otherwise inadequate housing. Research on family violence has tended to focus on lower socio-economic groups, but scattered data from school counselors and mental health agencies suggest that family violence is also a serious problem among America's more affluent households.

Children who are victims of abuse are more likely to be abusive as adults than children who did not experience family violence. Research shows that about 30 per cent of adults who were abused as children are abusive to their own children.

Source: H. I. Tischler, *Introduction to Sociology*, p. 367, Harcourt Brace: Fort Worth TX 1996

To what extent is family violence linked with poverty and low socio-economic status in America, according to Tischler? *(4 marks)*

Interpretation and analysis questions should challenge you to think in a critical way about the data presented in the question. In item H, violence within the family is seen as being related to poor socio-economic background and the temptation will be to accept uncritically the basic premise of the question as it fits known stereotypes of violence in the family. Logic also suggests that incidences of violence within families may be increased by the experience of poverty, disempowerment, and stress. Poorer answers will tend simply to reiterate the passage with no interpretative skills being employed.

A clue is given to you in the wording of the question, 'To what extent ...?' This is a clear indication that you should test the accuracy of a claim. The trick with this passage is not to be dragged into a consideration of the causes of violence but to look within the extract at the reliability of the methodologies discussed. Your answer should stress that if only poor families have been studied, then the data is not completely trustworthy; and that violence within wealthier families is being ignored by American sociologists. Another factor offered within the extract to account for violence is previous childhood experience of violence.

Analysing statistical data

Statistical extracts need special skills of interpretation and you are advised to use a clear ruler in the examination to read graphs and tables with accuracy.

Statistics are often used to 'prove' a case. They are increasingly quoted to make a point of view valid and you have already seen them used with reference to family research and knowledge in Item G.

In statistics there are serious issues for any sociologist to consider:

- Who created the data?
- Are the statistics reliable and/or valid?
- Can statistics offer a real understanding of a problem, or are they simply descriptive of a pattern of behaviours?

In simple terms, these questions raise the issue of trust. Do you trust the information? Commonsense alone tells you that the author of any data has a case to prove in terms of perspective or ideology, or has some significant vested interest in the value of the data. Look at the source of the information carefully. It will always be provided and can tell you a lot about the material. By way of illustration, would a legal firm have the same view of divorce statistics as a charity representing the causes of abused wives? Again, data may not give you meanings. You may see your aged mother on a daily basis and be supporting her. However, you may deeply resent the burden that she represents to you and your family.

Reliability and validity in sociological data

When asked to interpret statistics, these issues should be at the forefront of your analysis. Indeed, questions of reliability and validity have already been raised in the consideration of Item H.

Remember that reliability in terms of sociological analysis refers to the degree of trust that you can place in the accuracy of the data gathered. This can only really be determined through a consideration of the methods used to collect and analyse the materials.

Validity asks you to consider the appropriateness of the methods used to gain the data. Questions of reliability and validity are difficult to make judgements on without a fairly clear understanding of methodology, which is why the theory and methods sections of most syllabuses for sociology are so heavily emphasised.

Item I

See Figure 3.2 on page 53.

1 **What percentage of births were outside marriage in 1971?** *(1 mark)*

2 **What percentage of births took place outside marriage in 1995?** *(1 mark)*

3 **What changes have taken place in the number of births registered to one parent only between 1971 and 1995?** *(2 marks)*

4 **To what extent do the figures for births outside marriage support the view that there has been a decline in family values in our society?** *(4 marks)*

The key skill needed for answering questions 3 and 4 is to take the data and then do something positive with it. It is tempting to rehash the information

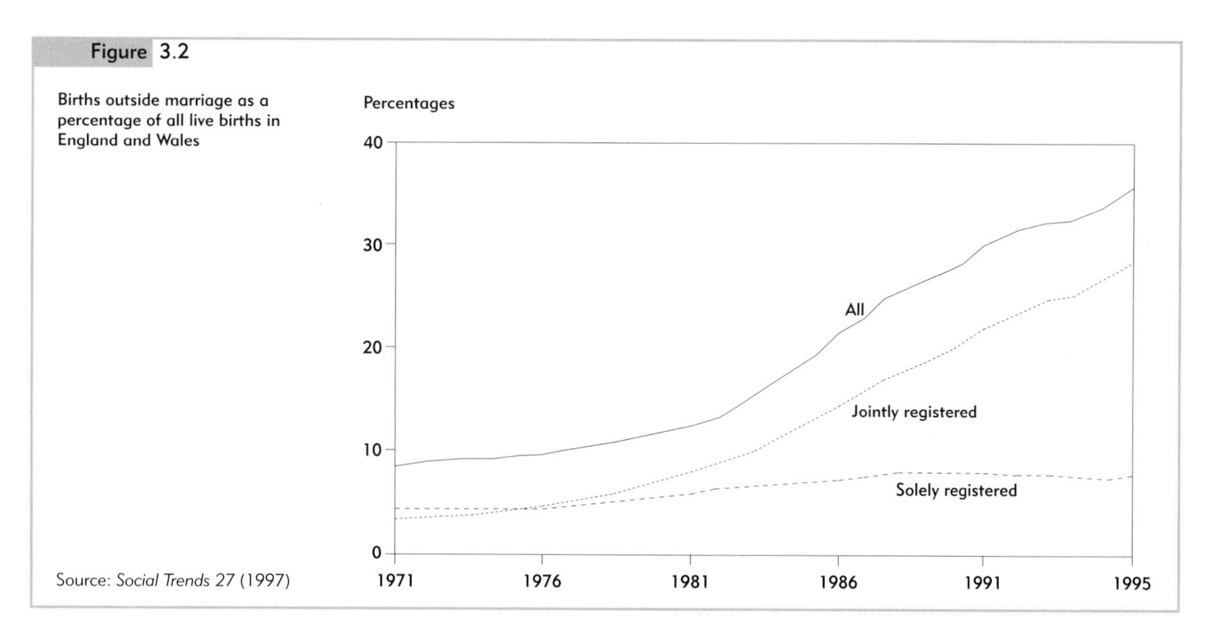

Figure 3.2

Births outside marriage as a percentage of all live births in England and Wales

Source: *Social Trends 27* (1997)

provided in the data and simply to rephrase what is offered in statistical form as a series of words. Any question based on interpretative skills will require additional thought to explain the data or the application of theoretical material and research evidence to develop it in some way.

For example, the graph shows that there has been a rise of something close to 20 per cent in the number of births outside marriage in the period 1971 to 1995. Taken as raw data, this could provoke a degree of moral panic as it implies a very significant rise in the number of single parents. However, a closer look at the graph shows that the number of mothers registering births without naming a father has remained remarkably static at about 6 per cent of all live births. The significant change has come in the number of couples who have chosen not to marry before the births of their children. Refer back to Item E and you will see that the pattern shown in the graph in Item I is common to much of Western Europe. There is a strong argument to support the view that family structure is not being rejected by people, although the institution of marriage itself has lost some of its previous social significance.

Item J

Figure 3.3 Patients aged 16–64 consulting doctors by legal marital status

Cause of consultation	gender	married	divorced
diseases of blood	m	97	135
	f	104	98
mental disorders	m	83	190
	f	91	151
symptoms, signs and ill defined conditions	m	97	129
	f	98	120

Source: adapted from Fiona McAllister, *Marital Breakdown and the Health of the Nation*, 2nd edition, p. 8, One Plus One Charity 1995

What protection does marriage appear to offer against mental health problems? *(4 marks)*

Model answer

In general, those who are married are healthier than those who have been widowed or divorced. However, widowed people are also likely to be slightly older in the sample and therefore more susceptible to complaints of ill health. There are gender differences apparent in the table and males are more likely to experience ill health if they are divorced or widowed than females. The rate of mental ill-health is very much higher for males than females and for divorced or widowed males than for divorced or widowed females. Marriage would therefore seem to protect males from mental ill-health more than it protects females. It protects people of both genders however.

Commentary on the model answer

This answer does not reproduce data that can be read from the table. It offers an overview of the trends indicated and raises questions about the validity of the table. A general conclusion is offered in the last two sentences. The temptation to draw overreaching conclusions based on unprocessed data has been avoided.

Taking information from a variety of stimulus materials

One of the following three extracts is taken from a piece of A-level coursework, one from a standard text and one from a historical text. All of them cover the issue of domestic labour and the relationships between men and women in the home. A variety of possible questions are given.

The first extract, Item K, looks at domestic labour, but some subtle relationship data is being presented as to how husbands and wives negotiate their relationship as well as the allocation of domestic labour. This data very much echoes the second passage, in Item L, from a feminist text where women are seen as passive but manipulative in their acceptance of low status. The final extract, Item M, is taken from a classic text where Roberts describes family and social life in a slum (an area of desperate working class poverty) in Salford at the beginning of the century. It offers a contrasting historical perspective to the more recent examples of the modern texts.

Item K

The male respondents qualified their unequal lack of participation in domestic labour by a number of excuses. Respondent 10 thought that he only ironed the large sheets and towels because he was taller than his wife who couldn't manage such a large expanse of material. It was interesting to note that his much smaller wife took the responsibility for hanging wall paper by using a step ladder, but he thought her incapable of managing to iron a large sheet. Other excuses for not doing as much work were the fact that the men worked longer hours and that women were more suited for delicate housework (respondent 36). The men were not willing to take on any more work or swap jobs with their wives. The old adage of housework being women's work seems to be lingering in Barry.

The results from the questionnaires show that women claim responsibility for the greater amount of housework and the male response backs this up. There were discrepancies in the questionnaires between husband and wife in the jobs that the man claimed they shared and that the woman claimed that she did alone. An example is provided in the interview of respondents 9 and 10 mentioned above where the female claimed that she did all the ironing as she irons all the clothes. The male partner irons the sheets and towels. <u>He thinks that his wife is too proud to admit that her height restricts her from ironing effectively. She claims that she lets him do those items that do not matter if they are creased. The truth will never be known as neither partner will admit the truth to each other. While this is an amusing insight into the behaviour of married couples, it does not help the investigator decide</u>

whether or not they view ironing as a shared activity and therefore neither male nor female.

Source: K. Nicholas, 'Does the New Man Exist in the South Wales Community of Barry', p. 35, unpublished A-level research project, 1997

Item L

The experience of many women has also proved that even when two partners in a marriage bring in similar incomes the man retains his domination in all sorts of non-economic ways. The structures of domination and submission go far beyond the material facts of providing and dependence, into the unconscious, into sexuality, into all the rituals of love, cosiness, deference, cajoling, leadership that go to make up the daily interactions between wives and husbands. The practice of consciousness raising in the Women's Liberation Movement has uncovered many subtle, taken-for-granted ways in which men dominate and women submit. Some of the most disturbing of these are the forms of collusion in our own oppression that we all adopt. Women's guilt, lack of self-confidence, willingness to get something by charm if they can't get it as of right, all play into the hands of men's power.

Source: M. Barrett and M. McIntosh, *The Anti-Social Family*, p. 70, Verso Editions: London 1982

Item M

Men in the lower working class, aping their social betters, displayed virility by never performing any task in or about the home which was considered by tradition to be women's work. Some wives encouraged their partners in this and proudly boasted they would never allow the 'man of the house' to do a 'hand's turn'. Derisive names like 'mop rag' and 'diddy man' were used for those who did help. Nevertheless, kindlier husbands, especially when their wives were near exhaustion at the end of a day or in the last stages of a pregnancy, would willingly do housework, cooking, washing the children or scrubbing a floor, provided doors remained locked and neighbours uninformed. Bolder spirits would even go out and shake rugs, bring in clothes and clothes lines and swill flags (wash the pavement outside the home), always at the risk of scoffing onlookers.

Source: R. Robert Roberts, *The Classic Slum*, p. 54, Pelican Books: Harmondsworth 1973

1 What sociological evidence is there to support the view that women collude in their own domination by men? *(7 marks)*

2 How might sociologists assess the claim that men are taking an increasingly active role in domestic work? *(6 marks)*

3 What explanations have been offered by sociologists for the increasing participation of men in domestic labour? *(6 marks)*

4 Using information from the extracts, assess the view that there has been little change in the relationships between married partners over the past 100 years. *(8 marks)*

The questions ask you to develop your interpretation and application skills. You do not need to make a judgement on the accuracy of any claim, as that would be evaluation. You do need to look at the data on offer in the extracts and explain, in the light of your knowledge, what you think is happening to society. This is an area where you will be required to refer to ideas and information in the extracts and to your own knowledge and understanding.

The sociological evidence that is required to answer questions 1 and 4 should be drawn from feminist and Marxist analysis in the first place. All the extracts suggest that women allow men to dominate them and collude (help or participate) in their own domination. However, the first two passages imply a degree of manipulation of their partners by the women in order to gain what they require from men. These two passages clearly illustrate the difficulty of analysing any complex relationship between people. The most relevant sections have been underlined for you.

Questions 2 and 3 require some thought and analysis of the views of functionalist sociologists such as Young and Willmott who thought that couples were becoming more equal in the domestic sphere. These should be contrasted with writers such as Hannah Gavron, Sue Sharpe and Ann Oakley who suggest that while there has been some change in domestic labour arrangements, in reality, women take the major burden. Information that you can take from the extracts themselves centres on the way that Roberts describes a situation in which men would seriously compromise their masculinity by participating in domestic labour at the turn of the century. By the time Nicholas studied families in Barry in 1996/7, a man could actively boast of his participation in ironing heavy articles of linen. However, the male respondent cited can only allow himself to take on these female domestic roles because he is more masculine than his petite wife and therefore she is dependent on him. His wife presents the task allocation as a sop to his vanity.

Evaluation

Evaluation is probably the hardest task that can be asked of a student. The education system, and social life in general, train us to provide the 'required' or 'acceptable' answer to questions. Sociology requires you to provide your own answers irrespective of whether this makes other people uncomfortable with what you have to say. This responsibility often makes less confident students uneasy with the subject and the temptation is to try and learn facts without really reflecting on them. However, in sociology you are often required to make your own considered judgements on arguments and/or research findings. This is, essentially, the key skill of evaluation

The significance of evidence in evaluation

The above point must also be qualified with a clear warning. If you offer a view without regard to some sociological knowledge or supporting evidence, then you are simply being opinionated. Such responses will be penalised severely under examination conditions as being a 'commonsense' answer. Any good sociologist knows that such an answer is simply a cover-up for ignorance and is trained to recognise the difference between groping for an answer and a clear direct attempt to evaluate material.

Before attempting any detailed analysis of evaluation questions, attempt this practice exercise by:

1. Writing a one-sentence judgement on each of the following propositions.
2. Listing as many relevant authors or studies that you can think of to refer to when evaluating these propositions.

- Parents are less of a significant agency of socialisation of their children than the mass media.
- The isolated nuclear family is a myth.
- Male domestic violence is symptomatic of the patriarchy of society.
- The 'new man' is a middle class concept.
- Gay families are not real families in any sociological sense of the word.
- The 'cereal packet' family no longer describes the reality of modern British household structure.

What should an evaluation answer look like?

There are three possible conclusions to any question which asks you to evaluate a question.

1. You can agree with the terms of the question.
2. You can disagree with the terms of the question.
3. You feel that, on the whole, there is good supportive evidence which can be tempered by many serious criticisms!

Item N

[The Cowley car plant closed.] Within a single generation a major tradition of employment, political alignment, income and identity for working-class men, indeed a tradition that formed cultures of masculinity was all but extinguished. In 1991 there were two hundred and seventy young men aged between seventeen and twenty nine without a job in Blackbird Leys alone. A Youth Service Report to Oxford City Council in 1991 noted that throughout the city there were only ten vacancies for eighteen-year-olds.

Source: B. Campbell, *Goliath: Britain's Dangerous Places*, p. 32, Methuen: London 1993

Item O

It portrays a mode of masculinity which is pre-social: it has no manners, it is not house-trained or domesticated, it has no social skills of negotiation and conciliation. It belongs nowhere because neighbourhood and home are places that real men *leave*. The moral centre of *Robocop* is agnostic. It is mobile and promiscuous because it responds to provocation and it is moved only by *force*. Robocop is neither good nor bad; he is freed from any ethical problem because he is only an enforcer.

Source: B. Campbell, *Goliath: Britain's Dangerous Places*, p. 276, Methuen: London 1993

1. **Suggest two possible ways, according to Beatrix Campbell, in which males gain their notions of masculinity.** *(4 marks)*
2. **Using the items above and your own sociological knowledge, to what extent do you agree that notions of masculinity are undergoing a significant change in modern Britain?** *(8 marks)*

As mentioned above, the possible answers to question 2 are:

a) Notions of masculinity are undergoing a significant change.
b) Notions of masculinity are not undergoing a significant change.
c) There are strong arguments to suggest that some change in notions of masculinity is taking place, but equally there are good arguments against this view as well.

Unless your answer takes one of the above positions in relation to the question then you have not answered the question. You are advised to decide on a final sentence before you even begin writing a word on your answer paper. In that way you can signal your intentions and understanding to the examiner from the start. He or she will probably skim-read much of your answer so it is important that your first sentences hit the correct note and make the right signals. A poorly written first paragraph will receive much more attention and then errors in the full text are perhaps more likely to be noticed.

The safest answer and the one that allows you the widest range of sociological discussion is always the third because then you can show that you are able to understand opposing points of view and draw a measured and balanced conclusion. You are also able to make use of a wider range of evidence than if you simply apply one perspective to any question. As a basic principle, if you feel confident and sure of your views, then it is wise to challenge the assumptions of any question simply because so many other people who answer the question will not. Your answer will be different, and therefore more interesting from the start. As we have implied already, 'first impressions count'!

What issues should you raise? Point out that Campbell is a feminist. You know this because she is asking questions about the notion of gender. She is discussing notions of gender among working class men. Is there a class dimension to this issue? How real is the 'new man'? Campbell also refers to work and occupation as defining characteristics of notions of gender. Perhaps changes in the occupational structure of Britain need some discussion in your answer. Campbell also refers to media constructions of the notion of masculinity. If you feel unhappy with the previous ideas, then you could take your answer into a discussion of male stereotypes and role models. The possibilities are open. Whatever your final choice as to the nature of the discussion, you should, however, end with one of the three conclusions offered to you and it should be apparent all the way through your discussion what your final sentence is likely to be.

Item P

In France, pro-family policies, which have the underlying aim of promoting population growth, have been widely accepted for over fifty years. Financial support for families, beginning with grants at birth, is received by a wide cross-section of society, without stigma, and enjoy high levels of take-up. The original intention was to compensate for the absence of a family wage by providing a universal benefit, the *Complèment Familiale*, for all families with children. The system has now become more complex, with many categories and income tests, but still provides over 10 per cent of the average production worker's weekly wage for the family with two dependent children. Housing benefits are available and assessed annually, and family taxation is low. The main thrust of family support is based on means and the presence of children. The ideology is that earned income is the main component of income, but that families with children will need a supplement to the income they can earn. There is no built-in conflict between receipt of earned income and the receipt of state supplementary income to help with the cost of raising children. The policy has not had a significant effect on the raising of birth rates, but has led to a high degree of successful sharing of the costs of childcare within society.

There is only one benefit specifically targeted at lone parents, the API, which is set at a generous level but only for a short period, usually one year. This benefit has aroused criticism as the level of discretion is thought to encourage fraud. But the benefit, although an important component of the income perhaps for those (usually young never-married mothers) who receive it, is only a tiny part of the package of benefits available as a right to French families. The success of this benefit system in offering support to working mothers is borne out by the increasing proportion of French lone parents in employment.

Source: M. Maclean, *Surviving Divorce*, p. 38, Macmillan: London 1991

Item Q

For a variety of reasons, living at home can prove problematic for (single) young mothers and their children. In Britain an increasing proportion of pregnant school girls are taken into care each year due to intolerable family circumstances. Girls under 16 are not eligible to apply for local authority accommodation; they may, however find themselves in bed and breakfast accommodation at public expense if home life has proved impossible for whatever reason; when the baby is due they may have the opportunity to stay in a Mother and Baby Home for a short period, though this sort of accommodation is less and less available in Britain and the US, as the **social stigma** of unmarried pregnancy and motherhood wanes. Just-16-year-old mothers may find themselves in severely inadequate bed and breakfast accommodation with their babies, lonely and isolated, on their way to substandard housing in a run-down area often on the edge of town with all the related problems that invariably ensue from such a move. For a young single mother on welfare benefits, the prospect is bleak indeed.

Source: F. Hudson and B. Ineichen, *Taking It Lying Down*: Sexuality and Teenage Motherhood, p. 118, Macmillan: London 1991

Item R
BBC World Service
DECLINE IN MARRIAGE

There is prominent coverage of what the papers say is a revealing picture into the way family life is changing in Britain. Figures just out show that divorce has reached record levels, while the number of people getting married is at a 50 year low. Under the headline, 'the end of family life in Britain', the *Daily Express* says that the average marriage now lasts less than ten years. The paper says the situation is being compounded by what it calls the scandal of young girls choosing to have children but not to marry in order to get state-benefits and subsidised housing. Britain, the *Express* says on its editorial page, has an unprecedented crisis in human relations on its hands. The *Daily Telegraph*, in its editorial, agrees, arguing that marriage is still the best context for raising children. The fact, the paper says, that more and more children are being brought up outside it has wide public consequences.

Source: Media Review WebPage, 23 August 1995

1 **Explain the meaning of 'social stigma'.** *(1 mark)*

2 **Evaluate the suggestion that many young women choose to become single mothers in order to acquire housing benefits.** *(10 marks)*

3. **Evaluate the suggestion that the family is in decline in Britain.** *(12 marks)*

In the above extracts (Items Q and R) you have very different and opposing viewpoints as to the situation of young unmarried women. Item Q suggests a life of desperation and hopelessness, while Item R offers a view of the young mother as a cause of social ills because she is state-dependent and manipulative. This is in direct contrast to Item P which considers the position of the single mother in France. You will have your own views as to which is the most accurate view of the situation. It may even be tempting to become political about this issue because it does arouse strong feelings. However, your possible answers to question 2 remain:

- Young women do choose to become single mothers for benefits.
- They do not become single mothers to receive benefits; there are more complex factors at work.
- Some young women may believe that becoming pregnant will improve their circumstances but others who become pregnant do not.

Attempt conclusions to question 3 on your own.

Remember, evaluation questions do not always use the word 'evaluate' in them, as in the examples above. Those questions have been clearly signposted for you. Other words and phrases that indicate evaluation is required include: assess, compare and contrast, or critically examine. (See page 7, Chapter 1 for other examples.)

Ideology and evaluation answers

After reading the questions above you may have begun to realise that you will need to consider some broader issues when attempting to evaluate positions held by many commentators on the family.

- Family ideologies can translate into social debates and perspectives. Ideologies may influence family policy and governmental actions and so have very real significance in people's daily lives.
- Many people genuinely hold the view that changes in family structure herald the breakdown of our society.
- Definitions of family and kinship held within broader society are influenced by a range of factors that, broadly speaking, relate to **social differentiation**. Such factors could include gender, culture, class, age and ethnicity.
- Although post modernism tends to minimise social class as a factor determining social constructions of the family, modern feminists such as Bea Campbell do link social class and concepts of gender construction closely.
- Some analyses of the family can be emotional because this is such an intimate area of experience, touching on religious, moral and political belief and also sexual behaviours. This is an area where people can be both hypocritical and illogical in their analyses. It is your role as a sociologist to be very even handed and objective in your own analysis of the family.

Try to recognise some of these points in the following extract.

Item S

The term 'career woman' has unfortunately come to imply in many minds a 'hard' woman devoid of all feminine characteristics.

But Rose Heilbron and many more have shown only too well that capability and charm can go together.

Why have so few women in recent years risen to the top of the professions? One reason may be that so many have cut short their careers when they marry. In my view this is a great pity.

For it is possible to carry on working, taking a short leave of absence when families arrive, and returning later. In this way gifts and talents that would otherwise be wasted are developed to the benefit of the community.

The idea that the family suffers is I believe, quite mistaken. To carry on with a career stimulates the mind, provides a refreshing contact with the world outside – and so means that a wife can be a much better companion at home.

Source: M. Thatcher, 'Wake up Women', The *Sunday Graphic*, 17 February 1952

1 What ideology of the family can you recognise in the above extract? (Look at the final sentence expressing reasons why women should work.) ***(2 marks)***

2 The writer of the extract became the first female prime minister of Britain in 1979. Evaluate her suggestion that women fail to reach the top of their chosen professions because they do not work after marriage. ***(2 marks)***

You should look at all of the information that you are offered in a question. The temptation is to read the text alone, but looking at the title and date of publication of a text gives you many valuable cues as to what the questioner has in mind. For instance, any text describing families which was published in the 1970s has had a quarter of a century to become out of date. If you subscribe to the Marxist view that society is in a constant state of change, then you will certainly appreciate the significance of the point that the people described in those studies as having small children will almost certainly be grandparents by now. Item S, for example was published in 1952. This is close to half a century ago and babies born at that time are certainly now middle aged and probably beginning to look towards retirement.

Opening out your discussion from the original stimulus material

Your answer to this and other questions should show awareness that when the above extract was written, many middle class women failed to work after marriage because they were expected to give up their careers. This is an accurate analysis by the author. However, at the time of writing her article Mrs Thatcher was the wife of an extremely wealthy man and had no children. There were a variety of reasons for the failure of married women to work after marriage other than simple lack of will. Many women would have felt that it implied that the husband earned too little to support a family. Others were actually forced to leave their jobs on marriage, including teachers and nurses. Working class women have always worked and few have had careers. Modern reasons for women failing to reach the top of professional trees include: the glass ceiling, maternity breaks, unacknowledged prejudice by employers and preferential treatment of male careers in a marriage partnership. You may think of other reasons why women still do not appear at the top of career structures. Interestingly, Mrs Thatcher herself was not well known for promoting women and, famously, there were few long-standing women MPs in her Cabinets

Families and the elderly in society

Item T

Research into the physiological aspects of ageing is clearly important for the light that can be shed on physical and mental performance. The general conclusion seems to be that while performance in certain ways, e.g. physical strength, does decline with age, yet chronological age is by no means an accurate indicator of capacity to perform a task. Psychological evidence is just as important because the way in which both prospective employee and employer view the older worker will affect their attitudes. There is evidence that stereotypes are common about ageing and that these influence the behaviour of people in the employment market. These beliefs can affect recruitment, transfer, training and redundancy polices.

Source: A. Tinker, *The Elderly in Modern Society*, p. 55, Longman: Harlow 1981

Item U

A popular myth about families is that family members have moved away from each other, and have little contact. In a recent British study 32% of respondents said they lived under an hour away. Only 9% reported they were more than 5 hours away. Contact is also fairly frequent. Mothers were seen daily by 11% and 58% said they phoned or wrote at least once a week. A recent survey of older people found that 69% of older people in the UK have contact with family at least once a week.

The ageing of the population has significant implications for the families and the care of older people. There are now more three and four generation families. Many children will know not only their grand parents but also their great-grand-parents – something quite unthinkable in the past.

The 1990 GHS Carer's Report revealed that 10% of adults were caring for their parents or parents in law. Older people are particularly important members of the extended family, providing child-care for their working daughters and often caring for their own elderly parents. Statistics on Northern Ireland show that a very small proportion of families with children consist of just grandparents and their children (0.3%) but we know nothing more about these types of families.

Source: A. Condy, 'International Year of the Family: Factsheet 1', p. 4, United Nations IVY: London 1994

Item V

Yet the family ideal makes everything else seem pale and unsatisfactory. Those who live alone often suffer from loneliness. Families are so wrapped up in their little domestic life that they have not time to spend on visiting; their social life is with people like themselves. Couples mix with other couples, finding it difficult to fit single people in. The middle class custom of balancing the sexes at dinner parties is only a formalised version of the endemic exclusion of the single, divorced and widowed. The estrangement of the sexes, outside of specifically sexual relationships, persists at all ages and increases isolation even among the elderly. The cosy image of the family makes all other settings where people can mix and live together seem like second best. Nurseries, children's homes, student residences, nursing homes, old people's homes, all in their different ways conjure pictures of bleakness, deprivation, acceptable perhaps for day care or for part of the year or a brief stage in life, but very much a *pis aller* to be resorted to only if normal family life cannot be provided.

Source: M. Barrett and M. McIntosh, *The Anti-Social Family*, p. 77, Verso Editions: London 1982

1 Evaluate the suggestion that old age is a social construction. *(5 marks)*

2 To what extent can it be argued that the aged in Britain are marginalised from society? *(10 marks)*

The important skill in longer-length evaluation questions is to consider the adequacy of various sociological explanations and to offer a judgement on the contrasting concepts and research on offer. Certain words will show the examiners that you are making judgements; they will look to see that you are doing this by noting your use of expressions such as 'in contrast', 'however', 'this research can be criticised for ...'. Unless you are using such language you are not evaluating and you will not gain the marks on offer.

Mark schemes and the examiner who reads your work

Mark schemes remain fairly general in their advice to the markers and rely on their integrity and sociological understanding. This means there is some room for individual assessments over exact marking within bands of marks. However, to gain a place in the top mark bands, certain issues and debates within the sociology of the family must be addressed in a clear and very precise manner. In question 2 you will not gain any marks unless you address the specific issue of the marginalisation of old people from society which is clearly indicated in the question. Descriptive work which lists findings. The random floating of ideas on the topic will be penalised heavily.

For the above questions you will need to do the following to gain the marks in the top band:

- Write your answers in clear grammatical language.
- Refer to a variety of studies, including those writers mentioned in the extracts. In this case you may even suggest that the study of the impact of old age is typical of the marginalisation of the old as it seems genuinely under-researched currently.
- Refer to theoretical perspectives, including the issue of the way that we only value those who are seen as productive in our society, which is raised by writers in both the Marxist and the functionalist traditions.

- Have a clear and logical conclusion which makes a judgement and refers in some way to the actual question set. You will either agree that the old are marginalised, disagree or put both sides of the case.
- Show an awareness of debates within certain sociological perspectives, because there is no absolute consensus of views even among those who work within one given sociological tradition. Your best example of this within this topic is almost certainly the range of views that fall within the category of 'the New Right and family values'. You could illustrate this by mentioning the issue of caring: the old of grandchildren and the middle aged of their parents.
- Possibly you will compare the situation in Britain with that of another culture, for instance you could mention the treatment of the old in immigrant communities.

Practice data-response questions

To practise the following full questions, you are advised to look at the extracts very carefully. Mark significant ideas or expressions of ideology so that you will notice them again when you are attempting a detailed analysis.

Look at the questions which follow. Circle the expressions such as 'evaluate' or 'assess' which tell you what you have to do in the question. Underline the important words in the questions. By following these directions you will go some way to avoid misreading the questions.

Question 3.1

Item W

Following the custom, my great-grandfather was married young, at fourteen, to a woman six years his senior. It was considered one of the duties of a wife to help bring up her husband.

The story of his wife, my great-grandmother, was typical of millions of Chinese women of her time. She came from a family of tanners called Wu. Because her family was not an intellectual one and did not hold any official post, and because she was a girl, she was not given a name at all. Being the second daughter, she was simply called 'Number Two Girl' (*Er-ya-tou*). Her father died when she was an infant, and she was brought up by an uncle. One day, when she was six years old, the uncle was dining with a friend whose wife was pregnant. Over dinner the two men agreed that if the baby was a boy he would be married to the six-year-old niece. The two young people never met before their wedding. In fact, falling in love was considered almost shameful, a family disgrace ... With luck, one could fall in love after getting married.

Source: J. Chang, *Wild Swans*, p. 29, Flamingo: London 1991

Item X

Women like my mother did marry for life. Most never discussed their pain, their disappointments or even their joys. I still wonder how many knew sexual pleasure. And yet many were glowingly happy, adored by their men (who were always described in solid terms such as 'dependable'). The art, we were constantly told as girls was to find ways of keeping the husband content and if anything was going wrong, never to talk about it. But you knew when a woman was unhappy. She was usually the one who prayed most fervently and longingly in the mosque, eyes tightly shut, the beads on her rosary rattling past her fingers at frightening speed. Sometimes there would be whispers of a suicide, always without a note, discreet to the end.

Source: Y. Alibhai-Brown, 'A Man for all Reasons', *Guardian Women's Page*.

Item Y

You see, society doesn't recognise that you can unknowingly marry a violent man. Your marriage can be declared null and void if you find out that your spouse had a contagious venereal disease at the time of the marriage. You are not protected by the law if you find out, as Margaret did, that your spouse has a criminal record. It was much too late before Margaret found out about her husband. Her collar bone had already been broken twice and she was pregnant.

Source: E. Pizzey, *Scream Quietly or the Neighbours Will Hear*, p. 38, Penguin: Harmondworth 1974

1 **Name one ground on which a marriage can be considered never to have taken place under British law in the 1970s?** *(1 mark)*

2 **With reference to Items W and X, suggest one function that an arranged marriage system may serve for cultures such as pre-Revolutionary China and westernised Muslims who both practise this method of marriage-partner selection.** *(4 marks)*

3 **What contribution have cross-cultural studies made to our sociological understandings of the modern British family?** *(8 marks)*

4 **To what extent is the family a patriarchal institution?** *(12 marks)*

Condidate's answer

1 'contagious venereal disease at the time of marriage'.

Commentary

This is a simple answer requiring no more than a careful reading of Item Y where the grounds are identified. There are other grounds for which a marriage can be considered null and void, so if the relevant piece of passage did not immediately leap to mind, take a gamble and offer 'insanity'.

Answer

2 Few cultures place the same stress on romantic love as Western societies and yet Murdoch suggested that a form of pair couple bonding can be found in every society. However, despite recent criticisms of the functionalist view of marriage which his work supports, the extracts do offer hints of the importance of marriage in societies where marriage partners are selected for each other by older people. Item W shows that marriage was viewed as a business arrangement. However, the age of the wife over her husband in Chinese society offers strong support to Parson's view that one of the two most significant functions of marriage is the stabilisation of adult personality. In Item X, the role of a woman is to please her husband and to be compliant if problems arise within the marriage. The author suggests that this compliance brings satisfaction to many women and good men are described as 'dependable'. This is a strong hint that unpredictability is not part of many arranged marriages which supports the view of functionalists that marriage and family do offer some form of stability to the adult personality.

Commentary

Functionalism is not a particularly popular tradition within British sociology and it is tempting to devalue the whole perspective because certain of the assumptions about the nature of society that it offers are unsatisfactory. This question does not ask for a criticism of the functional perspective, but for an interpretation of what it offers the sociologist in terms of understanding certain family dynamics that are basically alien to much westernised thought. This answer has clearly recognised that an understanding of functionalism is being tested. The candidate is aware of the key functions and is able to recognise what is common to two widely differing cultural situations, where arranged marriage is the norm for most people. The candidate has successfully avoided the temptation to pass judgement on the practice of arranged marriage.

Answer

3 There are two varieties of cross-cultural study. Murdoch, an American, studied families from a variety of cultures which were indigenous to the areas in which they lived. More recently, the text by Marsh (1996:395) points out that there is considerable sociological interest in the impact of the one-child-per-family policy of China. The other form of cross-cultural study includes research into family patterns among first and second generation immigrant populations living in modern Britain. It is possible to argue that both forms of cross-cultural study offer us an understanding of our own family organisations.

Work by pioneering anthropologists, such as Margaret Mead who investigated gender patterns among three tribes in New Guinea, began an argument into the status of women in our society and offered some of the first proofs that gender is a social and not a biological status. The government-imposed restriction of family size within China may offer an insight into the consequences of a more naturally evolving fall in family size in contemporary Britain where families are now averaging 1.8 children (*Social Trends: 94*). It raises real concerns for the status and care of the elderly in a society where there are fewer children to carry the burden of the sick and old.

Studies of West Indian families may presage changes in British society. A study published in 1984 suggested that there is a far higher ratio of single parent families among West Indians and that this is often planned as mothers are older at conception and many are cohabiting with a regular partner. This pattern belongs to a tradition created by the institution of slavery, but it also heralds a more recent pattern developing among the British where families are increasingly matrifocal due to rising divorce trends.

Studies of Asian families (Anwar 1979) in Britain have shown that while many immigrant populations retain certain cultural values such as the importance of the extended family, they also adopt cultural patterns from their host country such as a decline in birth rate over the generations. Although the families concerned have different cultural values from the general population, the fact of their presence in Britain makes them part of a newer modern multi-cultural British society.

It is obvious that cross-cultural studies are enormously useful because they offer us a mirror to our own society and enable us to study our cultural traditions from a fresh perspective. We are able to see in other societies the consequences of trends developing in our own patterns of living.

Commentary

The conclusion is not particularly original and there is only a cursory list of studies. However, a poorer answer would simply list the various cross-cultural studies and their general findings. What might be interpreted as a weakness in knowledge in fact demonstrates the candidate's skill in the selective use of supporting evidence in this answer. There is an attempt to limit the discussion to a well-signposted evaluation which is that cross-cultural studies offer us an insight into our own society. The conclusion therefore relates directly to the question which is being asked.

There is an awareness of the significance of cross-cultural studies in the development of sociology as an academic discipline. This also shows that the term 'cross-cultural' can be defined in two ways. There is an attempt to use the technical language of sociology correctly and the general tone is academic in style. There is a subtle acknowledgement that while not all families in Britain share the cultural beliefs of the majority of the population, they are, however, very much part of modern British society.

Answer

4 There are strong arguments both to support and to reject the view that the family is in essence a patriarchal institution. Items W and X describe extremely patriarchal and male-dominated family arrangements, but Alibhai-Brown also explains that there are, nevertheless, satisfactions for some women even within male-dominated society.

From a theoretical point of view, Marxists and feminists point to inequalities of power and labour within the modern nuclear family. For traditional Marxists, the dominance of the bourgeoisie over the working class is mirrored in the dominance of the male over the female in marriage. Marxist feminists such as De Beauvoir and Oakley have rejected marriage as an institution because, according to Engels, it is the way that capitalist ideologies are reproduced in society.

For more radical feminists, it is masculinity itself which is the enemy. Firestone points to the way that women experience loss of power and status on marriage. This can be supported with reference to statistical evidence which show that female earnings remain at about 70 per cent of male earnings. The family is a microcosm of society in which women are expected to do the labour and support the needs of males. In this view feminists share similarities with functionalist writers, but their assessment of the situation is that it is negative and hostile towards women. Women are disempowered and marginalised as a result of patriarchy. Functionalists take a more complacent view and suggest that this arrangement of power and domestic responsibility is beneficial to women and to society.

Legally and socially, it can be argued that men remain the beneficiaries of marriage. Pizzey, in Item Y, pointed out that women who marry violent partners may find it difficult to disentangle themselves from an abusive relationship. Should a marriage end in divorce, males are more likely to remain in a strong financial position and divorced women lose their rights to male occupational pensions. Divorced mothers may face financial hardship and become dependent on the state for support. The controversy over the activities of the Child Support Agency underlines the area to which this issue is a significant area of debate in our society.

However, the above debate should be seen in the context of a society where many women are actively choosing to have their children outside marriage. In some cases, women raise children without a conventional father figure, although this can carry some degree of social stigma if the mother is poor or uneducated. Men themselves are experiencing a changing role, and some writers have suggested that there is a 'New Man' with a caring masculinity. The extent to which this actually occurs remains an open question, but participation in domestic labour or child rearing no longer carries the imputation that a man is somehow inferior or inadequate. Old moralities are subject to question and while it is clear that some families are in fact patriarchal in structure, as women experience greater degree of social and moral emancipation it may be that gender roles and family structures will redefine themselves in the context of a new economic situation.

Commentary

There is a clear and definite 'maybe' in answer to this question! An evaluation is made of the suggestion that the family is patriarchal and it draws on both theory and a consideration of our society. The theoretical perspectives are reviewed and contrasts and comparisons are made. There are evaluations implicit in the language used to describe the perspectives. However, the answer then moves beyond the theoretical point of view and provides a short overview of the debates which are actually occurring in practice in our society. There is reference to changes in gender relations, the role of the CSA and the single mother debate. The answer has also used information from one of the extracts which illustrates that the material has been interpreted and wider conclusions drawn from information provided by the examiner. The candidate refers to the existence of the 'New Man' as a concept supporting the view that the family is no longer fully patriarchal, but then questions this immediately which shows that evaluations do not belong just in the conclusion but should occur throughout.

NB: Bear in mind that the answer we have included and commented on above is a very good one; and it would gain very high marks from an examiner. It provides a good example of how an answer that does not use a massive range of material can, if well organised, gain top marks

Question 3.2

Try the following question on your own. A detailed mark scheme is provided to help you organise your answers.

Item Z

What happens about the children in a divorce?

The law about children is now governed by the Children Act 1989, which came into force on 14th October 1991. It is now not automatic for the courts to make court orders for children in a divorce situation and the expectation is that the parents will try to come to an agreement. Even if parents ask the court to make orders the court will only do so if it seems that it is better for the children to make an order rather than no order should be made.

In practice, what this means is that you and your wife/husband are expected, if possible, to sort out for yourselves which of you your children should live with and the contact that they should have with the other parent. You may find it helpful to use a mediation service to work this out. If you do this by agreement no court order will be made.

Source: National Council for One Parent Families, *Splitting Up*, 1995

Item AA

Interestingly, whilst being married is associated with greater health and well-being, parenthood does not appear to work in the same way. In their review of 1980's research into health and the family Ross, Mirowsky and Goldsteen conclude that when children come along the psychological well-being of parents does not increase and in some instances parents – especially mothers – are actually more psychologically distressed than non-parents. In research at One plus One, we have found that the arrival of children presents a major challenge for couples. Most couples expected children to bring them closer but in a number of cases, parenthood actually made them feel further apart.

Source: F. McAllister, *Marital Breakdown and the Health of the Nation*, 2nd edition, p. 10, One Plus One Charity 1995

Item BB

For single women becoming a lone mother often meant giving up regular full time employment. For ex-married women becoming a lone mother had less of an impact on employment although, for those whose employment was affected, giving up work was more common than starting work. Women who had been regularly employed before becoming a lone mother were the most likely to be in employment when interviewed.

The women most likely to be economically active were older women, ex-married, with school age children, some educational or vocational qualifications, living in owner occupied housing and receiving some maintenance. An analysis of the factors affecting the probability found that the most important factors were predicted wage rates, not having young children, and child care availability.

Source: J. Bradshaw and J. Millar, *Lone Parent Families in the UK*, p. 96, HMSO: London 1991

1 **Which parent takes responsibility for a child during and after divorce?** *(1 mark)*

2 **What commonly held ideology of the impact of children on a marriage is challenged by Item AA?** *(4 marks)*

3 **To what extent can it be argued that lack of availability of childcare is the most significant cause of poverty among single parents?** *(10 marks)*

4 **Assess sociological explanations for the increase in divorce and marital breakdown since World War 2.** *(10 marks)*

Mark scheme

1 0 marks — Any answer specifying one parent or the other.

1 mark — Any form of words suggesting that the parents should decide the issue between them. In case of disagreement, the courts will decide.

2 0 marks — No relevant points.

1–2 marks — The answer will suggest in simple terms that children bring people together.

3–4 marks — The answer will refer to religious, moral, functionalist and/or New Right policies in a cogent argument.

3 0 marks — No relevant points.

1–3 marks — A commonsense argument possibly accepting without query the terms of the question.
Spelling and punctuation will show deficiencies.

3–6 marks — There will be an acceptable attempt to address the question and reach a valid conclusion.
Answers will show awareness that other factors that contribute to poverty, including level of benefit, poor educational standards, willingness of partner to pay maintenance, etc.
There will be logical expression of ideas

6–10 marks — There will be evidence of a balanced judgement.
Answers will refer to theoretical perspectives, show knowledge of recent government initiatives and policies.
There will be an awareness of the social basis of divorce statistics which suggest that divorce is more common among the lowest socio-economic groupings where poverty is endemic.
Spelling, punctuation and grammar will be of a high standard and the correct sociological terminology will be used with accuracy.

4 0 marks — No relevant points.

1–3 marks — A simplistic answer perhaps offering suggestions as to why divorce statistics have increased.
Poor expression of ideas.

4–6 marks — Answers will show evidence of an attempt to address the question in an analytical and evaluative way.
There will be a systematic attempt to link perspective with causes of divorce.
Issues will be raised such as changes in the gender status of women.
There will be some reference to statistical evidence.

7–10 marks — There will be a clear evaluation and conclusion which show awareness of factors which contribute to changes in divorce statistics. These factors and explanations will be linked to theoretical perspectives.
Mention will be made of the impact of feminism, changes in employment structure.
The best answers will refer to post-modernism and the collapse of old value structures and certainties.
Spelling, punctuation and grammar will be of a high standard.

Chapter 4

Education

Introduction

Education is one of the easiest topics to examine and one of the hardest topics to study within sociology because of the wealth of material available to provide stimulus materials.

Education can be seen in terms of being:

- a major source of employment and professional status for a large number of people;
- an institution that affects virtually all members of society at some point in their lives. It is of tremendous significance to families and children, affecting their future lifestyles and career opportunities;
- a political and ideological minefield with literally dozens of conflicting interest groups with significant points to make about its nature and purpose.

Education, then, is one of the key institutions of a modern, industrial society and has encouraged a massive amount of academic interest and research. Added to this is the complicating factor that most people consider themselves to be experts on education because they themselves have been at school at some point in their lives and have developed very strong views based on personal experience. There is a vast amount of anecdotal material which can be drawn on as stimulus.

Educational ideologies are best viewed in terms of whether they are in agreement or disagreement with certain key propositions related to the purpose and function of education. However, it is not as simple as in some other areas of study to identify sociological perspectives on education because sociologists have often adapted their analyses to previously existing philosophical positions (later in this chapter is a short section which may help you to sort out the 'pure' sociological research traditions). Nonetheless, it is important to begin your analysis with an understanding of where many sociologists fit in terms of pre-existing debates. The suggestions below are a rough statement of position.

It is often suggested by commentators that education systems should:

- prepare students for future life/careers/places in the workforce (**vocationalism**). This is likely to be a functionalist viewpoint and is also associated with the theories of the New Right and conservatism. Marxists might suggest that preparation for the needs of employers reinforces existing class divisions in society;
- correct some of the problems and evils of society (**compensatory views**). These positions may be espoused by functionalists and also those in the Marxist tradition. The variation will be in their views on how this should be carried through into practice in schools;
- provide a ladder of opportunity for the brightest and the best among us (**meritocratic opinions**). Functionalism may be associated with this type of view. A Marxist would probably claim that limiting opportunity to the best condemns others to the scrap heap;
- make society more equal by allowing people equality of access to the rewards that education offers (**egalitarianism**). Sociologically, people with these types of views tend to be Marxist or feminist. Marxists will concentrate on class differences, although they do also raise issues of ethnicity. Feminists will argue that education systems reinforce and consolidate gender inequalities;
- allow us to deconstruct knowledge, understand and thereby control our lives in society by studying (**libertarianism**). Marxists and neo-Marxists such as Friere and Illich tend to be attracted to these forms of argument. Interactionists, who are concerned with processes which take place within our educational institutions, will be positioned most clearly with this type of analysis.

Knowledge and understanding

What do you need to know? You are studying a significant social institution when you look at education. You should be familiar with its recent history and with how the system operates in society today. If you have time, one way of gaining some qualitative understanding of these areas of knowledge is to talk to practising teachers. Talk to people older than yourself about their experiences of the education system to see how changes impact upon society and how your education has differed from theirs.

You should also read the newspapers and journals written for teachers such as the supplements of *The Times*, *The Guardian* and *The Independent*. You are advised to learn some of the technical language and acronyms of education, such as DfEE (Department for Education and Employment), or SATS (Standard Attainment Tests) so that you will understand what is being discussed by professionals. Many texts will have a list or glossary of terms and you should seriously consider creating a vocabulary list of educational terms if you do not have one already. Teachers may also be able to help you here.

Although this text will try to highlight some of the more recent areas of debate, you should be aware that these may change quite quickly as a result of government initiatives or swings in the political climate.

Item A

A Staffordshire middle school has voted against **opting out** for the third time in less than two years. Parents with children at Christ Church middle in Stone rejected **opting out** by 255 votes to 180 in a re-run of a ballot ordered by John Patten, the previous Education Secretary, after the school voted against GMS earlier this year. A previous vote in November 1992 had had the same result.

Source: C. Dean, 'Ministries Split on Governors' Opt Out Stand', *Times Educational Supplement*, 12 August 1994

1 What does the term 'opting out' mean? ***(2 marks)***

This question asks you to explain the term 'opting out'. This is a knowledge question but the second mark requires that you understand some of the political philosophy underlying recent political legislation and school systems. The Conservative Government of the 1980s allowed schools the option of taking their funding from central government rather than local government. This was known as opting out. It was part of a policy of introducing market forces into the education system but was not especially popular in certain parts of the country.

Similar knowledge questions that could be asked of you might include explanations of some of these other terms used in education: comprehensive, selection, streaming and banding, direct grant school. Remember that knowledge, not just of the education system, but of recent research and legislation should inform all of your answers but it is not the point of most of them.

Interpretation and application

It is essential that you are well informed in order to make valid sociological judgements. In terms of your use of this text, you should now begin to think of applying the sociological skills of interpretation and application to your understanding of education.

Interpretation and application refer to the specific tasks of being able to select significant ideas or information from a text or a piece of statistical information and to provide an informed and sensible commentary on it. This requires higher level thinking skills, and a simple reprocessing of the information in another form will gain you few, if any, marks.

In order to gain high marks for demonstrating skills in interpretation and application, and evaluation, it is important to adopt good study techniques. When working through the questions in this chapter we suggest that you follow a few simple strategies.

- When answering data-response questions, read the items and the questions extremely carefully and get in the habit of marking off points of significance as you read.
- Under examination conditions, you should scribble very brief notes next to all of the

stimulus items to act as an aide-memoire to your writing – when doing this ensure that your notes really are short and simple (occasionally, teachers find more written on the question paper than on the answer paper!).

- One reading of a question or a stimulus piece is simply not enough and your notes will help to focus your answers and help you to select your evidence with care.

Item B

... the Chief Inspector of Schools was delivering no less a savage kick at progressive teaching methods. Chris Woodhead warned an audience at the Royal Society of Arts that 'child-centred' education was not defeated. The poison of the Sixties and the Seventies had not been eradicated. ... Mr Woodhead attacked the familiar bugbears: 'discovery learning', interactive instruction, problem solving, teachers as facilitators not hierarchs. Teachers persisted in the sacrilegious belief that 'education must be relevant to the immediate needs and interests of children'. Such a belief said Mr Woodhead, is a 'real impediment to the development of a better education system'. Facts were more important than personal skills.

Source: S. Jenkins, 'Rimbaud Without a Cause', *The Times*, 28 January 1995

1 Who was the Chief Inspector of Schools in 1995? *(1 mark)*

2 What view of the purpose of education does Mr Woodhead reject? *(3 marks)*

3 What are the typical features of 'child-centred' teaching methods? *(4 marks)*

When considering an answer to question 2, the first significant point to make is that the writer of the above passage is a journalist and not a sociologist. Sociologists should, in theory, attempt an objective analysis but journalists are under no such obligation. The writer is therefore critical of the views that he is describing and, for effect, overstates his case. Nevertheless, the words that are in quotation marks do belong to Mr Woodhead. Your answer should point out that there is a debate as to the best way to teach children. While many professionals prefer what is known as a 'child-centred approach' which should allow children to take some control over the learning process, the Chief Inspector of Schools feels that teaching should be teacher-led with the teacher and the National Curriculum in control of the pace and the content of learning.

Attempt the questions which follow Item C. They are a test of knowledge, interpretation and analysis. As a clue to help you, they reflect issues of New Right thinking as they apply to introducing market forces into schools.

Item C

Last year schools were asked to submit attendance figures for publication with the national league tables of examination results. Not all schools complied and the school by school comparison of truancy rates has been widely criticised by head-teachers and other educationalists as unreliable and misleading. For instance schools which submit scrupulously accurate returns may appear to have higher truancy rates than those which let some unauthorised absences go unrecorded. The present method of recording absence makes no distinction between children with a single unexplained absence and those who truant habitually. Also, some educationalists believe that the publication of league tables of truancy may encourage headteachers to try to exclude truants to improve their school's ratings.

Source: Bangaw (CSV Media), 'Out of School Advice Leaflet', HTV Wales, Culverhouse Cross: Caradiff 1994

1 Why have national league tables of school performance been a matter of some controversy in recent years? *(4 marks)*

2 What suggestions are made in the passage that league tables of school performance may be subject to manipulation by schools themselves. *(2 marks)*

3 Suggest social and political reasons why schools would feel a need to manipulate their public image in recent years. *(4 marks)*

One way of organising your ideas in order to prepare for interpretation and analysis is to create a frame or pattern for your revision which concentrates on linking perspective, concepts and research interests. Something like the table below (Figure 4.1) is advised and this can be adapted to suit other topics within sociology. When revising, fit some of your notes into simple frames of knowledge so that you can identify perspective, writers and main concerns of the debate. It may also prove a help when preparing notes for essay and assignment work.

A simple and unfinished sample in relation to the question of working class underachievement is shown in Figure 4.1.

In your own writing and thinking it is important to remember not to pigeon-hole research findings and writers too rigidly. Remember that much research draws on more than one perspective, so Paul Willis, for example, can be described as Marxist in his analysis but interpretative in his research methods.

Sociological perspectives in education

When you are reading work that is clearly sociological in intent you should be able to recognise the perspective that informs the author of the work. This can be recognised by the concerns of the author of the piece.

- **Functionalists** will tend to write about education with reference to how successful it is in educational terms and of the functions that it fulfils for society.
- A **Marxist** will be concerned with issues of power, social class, curriculum and knowledge control. Marxists can also be identified by a tendency to talk of systems.
- A **feminist** will look at socialisation and gender roles. A lot of early feminist sociology research of the mid 1970s took place in schools and it is fruitful study for A-level coursework.
- An **interactionist** will probably concentrate on processes which take place within schools, such as the hidden curriculum, which is all of the things that schools teach you without being aware of what they are doing.

Preparing revision frames such as the one described above should help you to appreciate the insights that the different perspectives offer a reader. Practise the skills of identifying perspectives in data-response questions by looking at the sentences in Item D, taken from a current textbook. Although intended more for undergraduates than A-level students, this offers a very helpful and up-to-date guide to current research. While you should recognise perspectives with relative ease, you can always check your answers in the text! The key phrases are underlined for you.

Figure 4.1

Perspective	Research questions	Vocabulary	Main concepts	Writers
Marxist	Why do working class fail? What is relationship between state and the education system?	hegemony domination power	The working class are socialised into failure. Education is tool of oppression.	Althusser Bowles and Gintis Willis (also Interactionalism)
Interactionist	How are working class labelled? What part do teachers play in school failure?	labels social constructions	On what basis are children streamed? How do teachers react to school failures and non-conformists?	Hargreaves Lacey Ball

Item D

(a) Although society has been created by people, individuals are seen as being born into a society which already has an identity of its own, and education as serving the function of passing on the collective consciousness, or culture, of that pre-existing society. (p. 441)

(b) In this way, the school is seen as introducing and reproducing the inequalities of social class that are perpetuated in a capitalist system, normalising them in the process so that the working class are hardly aware of them (and therefore in a state of false consciousness). (p. 444)

(c) Put simply, teachers' expectations about how well or how badly individuals will behave are likely to influence that behaviour. Pupils are likely to internalise their teachers' expectations and make them their own, eventually matching their behaviour to the predictions made. (p. 447)

Source: I. Marsh *et al.*, *Making Sense of Society*, Longman: Harlow 1996

1 Identify the perspectives which are illustrated by each extract. *(3 marks)*

2 What is the significance of the term 'collective consciousness' in extract a? *(3 marks)*

3 What is the significance of the term 'false consciousness' in extract b? *(3 marks)*

4 What is the significance of the term 'teacher expectation' in extract c? *(3 marks)*

In each of the above questions it is necessary for you to have enough awareness of the perspectives on offer to be able to understand how central the concepts underlined are to the general theory illustrated, as well as to a study and understanding of education. They require more than simple knowledge of the perspectives because you are required to develop your explanation. They are, therefore, interpretation questions.

The next item comes from a document which is more historical now than sociological. It embodied many of the truths and beliefs of its time. It is often referred to as the Newsom Report after the name of the chairman of the committee which produced it, but the actual title is 'Half Our Future'. It was influential in educational thinking in its time and ran to a second reprint some five years after its first publication as an official government report into education.

Item E

(a) A boy is usually excited by the prospect of a science course. What is it that appeals to him? He experiences a sense of wonder and a sense of power. The growth of wheat, the birth of a lamb, the movement of clouds put him in awe of nature; the locomotive and telephone he sees as man's response; the switch and throttle are his magic wands. If he cannot produce a sunset he can change the colour in his test tube. He comes readily to his teacher hoping most to learn how to control events ... (p. 142)

(b) A girl may know that when she pedals, her bicycle generator can light the lamps. She may not wish to take a generator to pieces, but by enquiry she can find out that the school or home lighting is probably produced by another generator, driven by a steam turbine ... (A discussion follows about questions which relate to science and various lessons which may be learned) ... A train of thought has been followed; experience has been used as a basis for ideas; and as a by-product and, for a moment, something about the nature of scientific enquiry may be appreciated. Like so many by-products, in relation to the less able, this one will run to waste if it is not garnered. (p. 143)

Source: Ministry of Education, 'Half Our Future': A Report of the Central Advisory Council for Education, HMSO 1963

1 What differences in gender responses to learning are identified in the item? *(3 marks)*

2 Many feminists, particularly through the 1970s, suggested that knowledge is 'gendered'. What evidence can you find in the above extracts to support their claims? *(4 marks)*

Model answer to question 2

There is much evidence to suggest that knowledge is a social construct and gendered. Although the passage is drawn from a text produced in the 1960s, even today, and despite the National Curriculum, there is much to support the view that subject choices are made on gender lines. The feminist response of the 1970s was to the views put forward by texts such as the one illustrated. Boys are described as being fascinated and stimulated by science. It is assumed that they will bring to science a sense of awe and wonder. It is also assumed that males will need to control their world. It suggests an active and positive response to external stimuli while the passage which refers to female responses suggests a more passive and receptive stance, particularly in response to her bicycle dynamo. There is an unfortunate juxtaposition of 'female' and 'less able' which would suggest that girls are somehow less well endowed with an ability to appreciate and understand scientific knowledge.

There is more than one possible response to the question above. As a general rule, select your evidence with care and do not repeat phrases from the passages given. You could perhaps state specifically what gender is in sociological terms but then you will have to consider how language is used in association with gender. Your answer to the second question using these extracts could also contain a sentence explaining that knowledge is not the same as 'fact' but is a social construct because some knowledge is considered intrinsically more valuable than other knowledge. You yourself will recognise that knowledge has been de-gendered when quiz programmes such as *University Challenge* begin to ask questions about knitting, garment construction and patchwork quilting rather than sport.

Attempt another similar question on your own. It is taken from an unpublished piece of GCSE coursework gathered by 15-year-old females who visited a primary school.

Item F

On arrival, it was obvious that girls and boys were socialised differently in the playground. Boys were playing rough games like catch and wrestling and girls were playing skipping or walking around with the teachers. This shows that aggressive play is acceptable for boys and that girls are supposed to be quiet and play cute games.

The children were definitely dressed to suit their genders. Girls wore clothes of pink, yellow, peach, etc. The boys wore blue, black, green, etc. This gives the impression girls have to be cute to be liked. This also assumes that clothes are chosen by their mothers.

When inside, the headteacher took over the questionnaire and changed the way I wanted to ask the questions. This made me feel incapable of finding out information for myself. When reading our questionnaire, he said he didn't think we would find out much because he thought there is no sexism in schools.

He asked the questions to the boys first making the girls feel inferior and unimportant. When asking the children's favourite colours, he gave them a choice of very masculine colours. This made the girls think that men were the only important species.

When one little boy said that he thought that Barbie Dolls were for boys, he was humiliated in front of the class by the headteacher. The headteacher said, 'Yes Gavin, you would!' This made the little boy embarrassed and for the rest of the questionnaire he just agreed with all the other little boys because he was afraid to have his own opinion. The headteacher gave the boy the impression that unless you like toys like cars and trains, you did not fit in.

I also noticed that there were more female teachers than male. This makes the children believe that only women can become teachers.

Source: Emma Squires, unpublished GCSE project

1 How may the working of the 'hidden curriculum' apply to gender socialisation? *(5 marks)*

2 How do schools contribute to the reinforcement of traditional gender patterns in our society? *(6 marks)*

Interpretation of statistical data-response questions

Special skills are required to answer statistical questions. Many people find themselves put off by graphs and tables so if you are not, you are at a slight advantage in this type of question. If you are worried, don't panic and try to approach the data in a logical manner. It is a good idea to have a couple of sharp pencils and a clear ruler with you in the examination room. It is easy to read the wrong line of data if you follow anything complex with a finger. Ensure that you read all of the information provided, including its source and any small detail in the legends. A legend in statistical data refers to the headings and other writing around the table or graph.

Education is a topic which lends itself to this type of questioning because so much statistical evidence is available for use. Britain spends vast amounts of money on education and employs an army of statisticians to collect and quantify trends and patterns.

This tendency was emphasised by the Thatcher administrations of the 1980s who introduced the publication of league tables to compare school performance. Local education authorities have joined the debate on the presentation of such data because they claim that raw, relatively unprocessed data can present misleading information. It is absolutely beyond argument to say that, in the UK, children from poor or deprived backgrounds will generally do significantly less well in educational terms than children from privileged and comfortable homes. Many education advisers and researchers are now applying even more sophisticated data-analysis techniques to information gained from schools to assess notions such as 'value added'. 'Value added' data takes account of pupil ability on entering a school as well as leaving so that schools with high proportions of children from socially disadvantaged backgrounds can demonstrate their achievements without being overshadowed by those whose pupils are largely from privileged backgrounds. All this adds up to a situation where we have vast amounts of data on education. It remains to be seen how much practical use this is in explaining differential and individual achievement! Your task, in the mean time, is to gain skills in interpreting and analysing some of this material.

Item G

See Figure 4.2 on page 76.

1 **What percentage of boys gained more than five GCSEs grades A–C in 1975/1976?** *(1 mark)*

2 **What percentage of boys gained more than five GCSEs grades A–C in 1994/1995?** *(1 mark)*

3 **What percentage of females gained more than one GCE A-level in 1994/1995?** *(1 mark)*

4 **What percentage of males gained more than one GCE A-level in 1994/1995?** *(1 mark)*

5 **Suggest possible reasons for the claim that boys are underachieving in public examinations.** *(4 marks)*

Questions 1 to 4 are straightforward, requiring you to read the statistical data. Question 5 requires a fuller discussion in that it is looking for you to apply your sociological knowledge to the data. It is commonly stated, and frequently believed, that boys are somehow underachieving in educational terms. If you repeat that claim you will gain no marks from this question. There is little evidence of male underachievement. Both males and females are actually improving their examination performances significantly. In 1976 for instance, approximately 25 per cent of males gained five or more GCSE passes A–C. In 1994/95, the rate for males had increased to nearly 40 per cent. The data reveal a far more interesting pattern. Males are improving their GCSE performance steadily and well. They are simply being out-paced by females who are improving their results year on year at a faster rate. At A-level, a similar pattern emerges but the performance gap by gender is much narrower. The trend, however, tends to suggest that in the future females will have an improved performance over males, given that on the basis of GCSE performance, more females than males will be qualified for A-level courses.

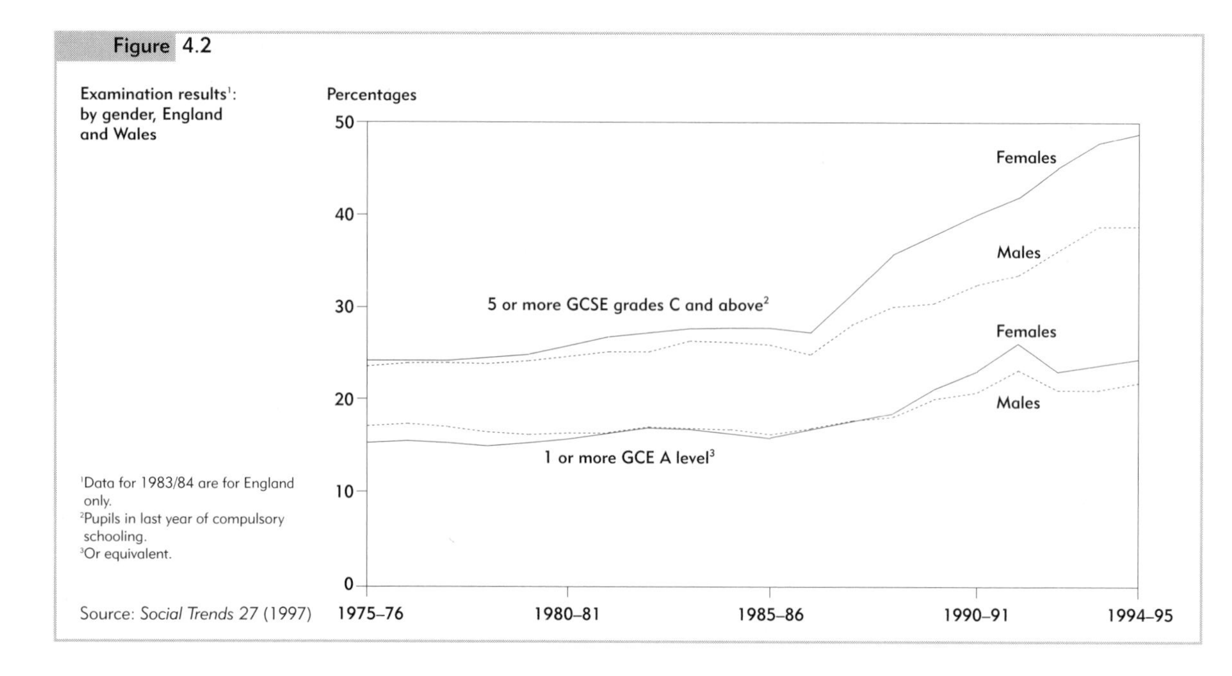

Item H

Figure 4.3

Full-time teachers: by type of school, gender and age, 1994/95

United Kingdom — Thousands

	Nursery and primary		Secondary	
	Males	Females	Males	Females
Under 25	0.8	8.9	2.1	4.5
25–29	3.0	23.2	8.1	13.8
30–34	3.5	15.4	10.2	13.1
35–39	4.2	19.4	15.4	17.0
40–44	8.0	36.8	25.3	23.4
45–49	9.1	37.8	27.0	22.0
50–54	4.6	21.3	13.9	12.6
55–59	1.8	10.8	6.1	5.5
60 and over	0.5	2.1	1.4	1.0
All ages	35.6	175.7	109.5	113.0

Source: *Social Trends* 27 (1997)

What explanations are there for teaching becoming an increasingly feminised profession? *(3 marks)*

This is an interesting question because it requires a more careful reading of the data than you may at first assume. The question does not ask about the number of women in the profession. The key word is 'increasingly' and you should have underlined it as significant if you were reading the question carefully. This word implies something about the number of entrants to the profession as well as those currently in it and the entry data are not actually available to you from the table. The table shows how many people are currently employed in teaching, their ages and gender breakdown. You are told nothing about entry or those leaving the profession. You can, of course, make logical assumptions from what you have before you, but for a top grade answer the distinction between what you are told and what you can reasonably guess should be made clear to the examiner.

Interpretation of qualitative data

Different skills are required for qualitative data-response questions. In the example below a careful reading of Item I is required because it illustrates a wider debate from a personal point of view. It is tempting to react to the immediacy of real words and therefore to ignore the real issues underlying a personal statement.

Item I

I mitch off school [local expression for 'playing truant'] when I am feeling stressed and my work is doing my head in. I also go when I haven't done my homework or if I'm doing lots of writing in my lesson or if I hate the teacher. I got caught and put on school report. The teachers phoned my Mum but my Mum didn't punish me. I just felt a bit gutted because I got caught. I also felt guilty because I promised my Mum I'd try in school and go every day.

Parents should not be punished if their children don't attend school because parents send children and it's not their fault if they don't go. If parents say to their children 'you don't have to go to school', then they should be punished.

Source: Female respondent, aged 15, from a comprehensive school

What evidence have sociologists offered to support the view that parents are responsible for their children's behaviour and school performance. *(6 marks)*

It is a popularly held view that parents are responsible for their children's behaviour. Increasingly, much public debate centres on the view that children are the responsibility of their parents. However, the popular political consensus is currently to look at schools as failing children. This respondent makes a very good case to suggest that the school takes some responsibility for her truancy. She also points out that her mother failed to punish her for non-attendance. If your answer only makes these points and is essentially just commonsense, then you will gain few marks.

The question that is being asked of you is rather more specific and the words 'What evidence ... to support ...' point to a far wider sociological debate. That debate is about the extent to which home or school is responsible for school failure. A large amount has been written over the years by various academics and researchers into education and poverty, who describe the inadequate home lives of many children, and by psychologists, such as Michael Rutter, who point the finger at school failure.

Look at the next item, the first extract of which is from A-level class notes taken during a group session discussing the relative success or failure of the comprehensive system from an individual and personal perspective.

Item J

Better students may be tempted to drop their standards in the first year. They are frightened of being called swots. We didn't think any pupils would actually drop their standards for long because of this. In any case, many pupils realise that they will gain status through being seen as intelligent. It may depend on the geographical area the school is in and people's culture.

Teachers in large schools sometimes do not realise if a pupil is being physically or emotionally mistreated whether it be at home or at school.

Comprehensives are academic enough because most have a wide range of academic subjects for both GCSE and A-level. More courses could be offered for those who are less academic.

Teachers tend to concentrate their efforts on those whom they see as bright or conformist and well-behaved.

Source: Sally James, class notes

Item K

When parents argue now for the return of selection, they usually forget that when it existed the majority of children did not go to grammar schools and the child who should have passed the 11-plus but didn't would need all his or her wits to find a way to acquire any qualifications at all, let alone enter higher education; by 15 all their educational chances were finished. What should have happened is that the comprehensive system, like American high schools, would encourage the late developer. Boys have always been held to 'mature' later than girls, which is why when more girls than boys routinely passed the 11-plus, some local authorities used to impose limits on female entry to grammar schools

Source: L. Grant, 'Under Pressure', *The Guardian*, 11 March 1996

1 **What evidence is there to support the view that comprehensive schools have brought a more egalitarian ethos into education?** *(8 marks)*

2 **What evidence is there to support the view that the comprehensive school experiment has been seen to fail more academic students?** *(6 marks)*

3 **With reference to evidence, how do you account for the continuing popularity with many parents of selective education systems?** *(8 marks)*

4 **To what extent can the perceived failures of the comprehensive system be attributed to lack of proper education funding.** *(8 marks)*

Before attempting these questions you are advised to return to the start of this chapter and remind yourself of the education debates and the perspectives that sociologists can offer to the debates. Remember that these questions are not as difficult as they look, and that you should rely on your knowledge of sociological research and your own wider reading, rather than grasping for information or research findings that you are not aware of. Take a wide ranging approach to discussion. There are ideas in the list below that you could develop and more suggestions than you could ever use in one question under examination conditions. So you will also need to practise the academic skill of selection of material and evidence.

- Quote examination trends and patterns which are to be found in this chapter.
- Discuss research on banding and streaming where it is apparent that students in low bands experience rejection and failure – you could refer to work by Stephen Ball and Auriol Stephens.
- Develop ideas about the mythology and popularity of private schooling – you could refer to work by Geoffrey Walford and Tessa Blackstone.
- Talk of government investment and the public cost of education.
- Refer to the grant-maintained system and 'city technology' college development.
- Discuss government and political commitment to ideals of equality and/or meritocracy and the work on social stratification if you have studied the topic.

Evaluation

Evaluation is perhaps the key sociological skill. This is where you are required to make a considered judgement on materials, writers and research and to assess their importance in helping you to come to a deeper understanding of social phenomena. It requires a number of things from you as a student.

You must have the confidence in yourself to criticise or support opinions with the use of evidence. One of the best ways to acquire the ability to do this is to think or talk through ideas. Your teacher may well be encouraging you to discuss ideas in lessons, but the process should not end in the classroom. Your common room or a public space such as a club can just as easily provide you with a venue for discussion work. Many people are too shy to contribute orally to lessons. However, self-consciousness is natural to most of us and few enjoy the process of public speaking initially, even those trained to it, such as teachers. The brutal reality is that you will need to overcome any reluctance to express your views out loud if you are to progress in any professional career, so it might as well be now! Shut your eyes and say what you think, with supporting evidence – some may think you wrong, some may think you loud, but few will think you stupid. You will find that the confidence you gain from articulating your views will improve the quality of your written self-expression as well.

The next set of items will ask evaluation questions. The key terms which will help you to note the difference between these and the interpretation and analysis questions which you have been studying is that evaluation questions will demand that you make a considered judgement. The active words will be 'assess', 'consider', and 'evaluate'. You are advised to re-read the introduction to the text (pages 4–5) at this point in order to clarify your own thoughts and understanding.

Item L

For this year (1997–98), with a new government, the review body has the opportunity to assert its independence and make recommendations to improve the attractiveness of teaching as a career.

This means addressing the problems of excessive and unnecessary workload, conditions of service and ensuring a competitive salary structure.

The select committee rightly points out that teachers are the key to success in raising standards and that to ensure these are able and motivated teachers means attracting enough high calibre young people to train each year.

The report quotes NUT evidence that teaching is 'blamed for the ills of the education service and the wider society' and that 'few teachers themselves would now suggest becoming a teacher to their pupils, or their own family and friends'.

Source: *The Teacher*, editorial comment, December 1997

Item M

Figure 4.4

Source: *Beano Comic Library No. 222, The Bash Street Kids in. The Cane Mutiny*

Item N

My mother was a teacher at Camden and the proudest moment of my naughtiness was when she said to me, 'I can't hold my head up in the staff room!' I thought, 'Great!' I was putting time and effort into doing badly. I was suspended twice, once for smoking dope and once for swearing at a teacher or something. I prided myself on my ability to upset teachers. At a reunion 20 years later, I went up to Miss Peak, the music teacher, and she said, 'You were the naughtiest girl I ever taught!'

Source: Arabella Weir, interviewed by Jonathan Sale in The Independent: Education, 22 January 1998

1 **Assess the extent to which one popular stereotype of teaching presented in the items varies from the reality of teaching as a profession? Use the items and your own knowledge to develop your discussion.** *(7 marks)*

2 **How reliable do you consider the views of *The Teacher* in its discussion of the failure of the teaching profession to attract high quality candidates into the profession?** *(6 marks)*

3 **To what extent do teachers contribute to the failure of some pupils to achieve?** *(10 marks)*

In each of the above questions, you will need to make a judgement. While you should be able to express a clear point of view, you will gain marks for developing and qualifying your judgements in some way. Each question has three possible conclusions.

The 'choice' of answer to question 1:

- You identify a stereotype, you think it is different from the reality and you give reasons.
- You identify a stereotype, it is very similar to reality and you give reasons.
- The stereotype contains some element of truth but there are grounds for rejection.

Possible answers to question 2 can be summarised as:

- *The Teacher* is very reliable, teaching is a dreadful occupation.
- *The Teacher* is not very reliable because teaching is a high status, highly paid and easy job.
- *The Teacher* can be said to present a reasonably accurate picture but is, nonetheless, putting forward a point of view which is, in essence, biased.

The only really acceptable answer for question 2 is the third because *The Teacher* is a union newspaper for the National Union of Teachers. It is under no obligation to be politically unbiased because it represents the views of its members who are very likely to consider teachers to be underpaid and overworked.

You should develop your account with an analysis of the problems that teachers face. There are issues of conditions of employment, hours worked and status to consider. Read the following analysis of possible lines of discussion that you could take for question 3 (and some ideas from that debate could equally be applied to question 2).

Question 3 demands a little subtlety. It will be tempting to agree that teachers do cause pupil failure and to rely on the items rather than to spread your discussion more widely. This question deserves a little more consideration than the previous two. Your possible summative conclusions are:

- teachers do cause failure;
- teachers do not cause failure;
- teachers can contribute to failure, but many pupils do succeed admirably.

Unless you refer to theory in your answer you will not be answering the question. This is hinted at in the extract from *The Independent* where an adult describes herself as a child as being as difficult as possible. The adult takes a pride in her poor (rebellious?) behaviour. A child could be a rebel against authority and therefore heroic (**Marxist perspective**), or the teacher is facing a difficult or disturbed adolescent, one of many similar children, and is dealing with problems not of her own making (**functionalist perspective**). Sub-cultures may be developing in the school (**functionalist perspective**). There may be a hidden curriculum which disadvantages some children, especially females, and causes them to reject schools and teachers (**feminist perspective**). Consider the professional status of teachers in terms of broader society and the low regard in which they are generally held in the mass media (**cultural effects**

theory). Question the role that teachers are supposed to play in correcting the ills of society (**liberal political theory**). After all, in many countries teachers do not take on a pastoral role, they exist merely to impart information and ideas (**functionalist perspective**), not to correct the faults imposed by 'bad parents' (**compensatory views**). Most of all, you must refer to labelling theory and the self-fulfilling prophecy (**interactionist theory**).

Ethnicity and inequality: a case study in analysing data

The next item comes from a newspaper. The importance of keeping yourself well briefed by reading newspapers cannot be understated. All textbooks are almost immediately out of date because by the time a piece of research makes it into a textbook as a classic piece of work, it has already had some years in which to become outdated. Newspapers are an acceptable source of more recent reports and research. However, lack of detail about how the research was conducted and what was studied forces the reader to practise evaluation of the journalist's report.

Item O

Indian and Pakistani children continue to do better than their English, Scots and Welsh classmates according to statistics on the exam performance of London teenagers.

Desmond Nuttall, of the London School of Economics, and Professor Harvey Goldstein, of the Institute of Education, have found that many white pupils still perform badly in comparison with other ethnic groups after the switch from O levels and CSEs to GCSEs.

Their figures will fuel the debate over whether class and parental expectations, and their help with homework and coursework, have as much to do with exam performances as ethnic origin.

They will also provide further ammunition for those who claim that long established British working class families pay less attention to their children's schooling than more recent immigrants.

The experts' analysis of results achieved by teenagers in 1988 reveals that Asian children still top the 'league table' converting exam grades of groups into point scores.

Only Irish and Caribbean pupils did worse than those with deep roots in Britain after allowances for various factors had been made, and their results were not significantly lower, according to the researchers.

Source: J. Meikle, 'Asian Pupils Doing Better than English Classmates', *The Guardian*, 16 February 1991

1 **To what extent can it be claimed that the British education system is racist in practice?** *(8 marks)*

2 **Evaluate the contribution of research into ethnicity and educational achievement into our understanding of the impact of home factors on school attainment.** *(12 marks)*

The same piece of writing has been used as a stimulus to two very contrasting areas of debate. This can be used to illustrate how a practised sociologist can perhaps use the same piece of evidence to support a variety of arguments.

Avoid the temptation of considering all ethnic groups to be similarly and conspicuously different from long-term British populations. The Irish may be considered as a separate ethnic group but they have also been part of mainstream British culture for a very long time. Name alone is no indication of ethnicity either, especially in the case of the Irish. Many Jewish men chose to change their very European-sounding names during the Second World War while serving in the armed forces as they were nervous of identifying themselves as Jewish if captured. Although many British people may be ignorant of the variety of cultures that are generally classed as 'Asian' or, more insultingly, 'Pakistani', those of Asian origin will not be so unaware and there will be very significant language, religious, status, educational, class and cultural variations among those of 'Asian' origin.

Question 1 is simpler than question 2, but it contains difficulties of its own, as you would expect for eight marks. Given that you have to make a decision on exactly how racist you consider the education system to be, there is little room to argue that it is racist in intent. This is against the law and would not be tolerated within our society; and most schools now have multi-ethnic, anti-racist policies in place. If you are still attending a school, you could ask to see this policy. It is probable that most colleges will have a policy as well.

Given this state of affairs, you will need to consider the extent to which racism is either covert (hidden) or unintentional within the education system. It will be tempting for you to make a commonsense answer but you will need to refer to a range of research and sources of data, such as the Swann Report, as part of your knowledge base before attempting this type of question. You should comment on the hidden curriculum and the fact that 'important' knowledge tends to be white male knowledge. There is also the significance of school attainment as an act of resistance among many Afro-Caribbean girls as suggested by the work by Fuller (1980) and, more recently, Heidi Safia Mirza (1992), which has suggested that black girls may form a counter school culture which values success. Institutions themselves may be racist in practice by not offering facilities for the practice of non-Christian worship, or by enforcing school uniform rules which infringe the religious dress codes of some ethnic groups. Outside most cities, there is a shortage of teachers from ethnic minorities and they are seriously under-represented among the older age groups of teachers.

Understanding trends in sociological debate

Question 2, Item O, requires quite a significant degree of preparation. One tip, which may help you to revise or organise your knowledge in preparation for such a question, is made fairly easy with the help of a computer. Create a table or a database with three columns. In column one you should type the name of the researcher or the research group. In column two, make a note of the date of research, and in column three, write a one-sentence summary of the research findings. Go through a number of texts and fill in your table with at least 10 pieces of relevant research. Ask the computer to sort the work by date of creation – or do it long-hand yourself if necessary! Work in texts is usually quoted in terms of a structure of argument, however, once your table is sorted you will find that you will get a very clear picture of how the debate on your chosen topic has developed over the decades. This process may also help you to organise and write your context section of the coursework paper. Part of a sample table created using a variety of textbooks is shown below.

Figure 4.5

Labour force survey	1988	West Indians and South Asians are over-represented in further education
Cohn *victim study*	1988	Bullying can be racially motivated
Blauner	1989	Many black people reject 'black pride' movements and are more concerned with integration
Gillborn *qualitative*	1990	Teachers try hard to treat all children equally. However, they perceive children differently and therefore treat them differently. Alfro-Caribbeans experience conflictual relationships with teachers.
Macdonald *et al.*	1990	Racism is covert and difficult to uncover

Having organised your notes, you now have to address the question. You must be precise in your answer because the question is quite complex.

You would be unwise to answer a question as complex as the one below without careful organisation.

Evaluate the contribution of <u>research into ethnicity and educational achievement</u> into our <u>understanding of the impact of home factors</u> on school attainment. *(12 marks)*

You must link ethnicity and home factors in school attainment. This requires quite a carefully constructed conclusion. You must judge whether research into ethnicity has made a significant contribution to the 'home–school' debate, or whether, in fact, the research is perhaps interesting but of no value when considering which has most importance to a child's attainment, home or school. First, you will need to show that you understand something of the nature of the home–school debate. You will then need to look at how the data you have learned about can be applied to the particular debate.

Practice data-response questions

Both of the practice questions on education focus on inequality. This is an area which has attracted a great deal of sociological interest and research. The most critical area of educational discussion in the past was the socio-economically class-based nature of school attainment. Since the 1970s the focus of public debate has shifted away from class differences in educational achievement and greater emphasis has been placed on the contribution of individual schools. It is clear that the children of the wealthy and privileged will be likely to gain more qualifications than the children of the poor. They will have expensive support and equipment in the home, they may attend selective schools or privately owned schools and they expect to succeed. The children of the poor are unlikely to benefit from the education system to the same extent as the children of the wealthy. Question 4.1 is based on sociological work on the relationship between the home and the school, while question 4.2 includes material on the private sector of education.

Question 4.1

Item P

Among children generally, the single factor most strongly associated with high attainment is social class. This is not surprising since, apart from any other advantage middle class children may have, the education system itself contains a 'bias' towards them in that the language used, the behaviour expected and the teachers themselves reflect middle class standards. Ability and attainment tests of various kinds also reflect the principle that a middle class way of thinking or doing things is right and should be adopted.

Source: Wedge and Prosser, *Born to Fail*, p. 54, Arrow Books: London 1973

Item Q

The area is socially disadvantaged with high unemployment and 43% of children are eligible for free school meals, which is high for the borough and over two and a half times the national average. About 20% of the pupils are of minority ethnic origin, 12% coming from homes where the first language is not English. ... The ability range is comprehensive, but with less than 18% in the highest of the three ability bands, less than 12% in Year 11. ... In 1993 only 50% of pupils remained in full time education after leaving Year 11 ... In 48% of lessons seen achievement was satisfactory or better, with 9% good.

Source: Ofsted Report on Abbey Wood School, Greenwich, 1994

Item R

The teachers say that the children from unsatisfactory homes are poor workers or lazy and that the manual working class children from these homes have poor powers of concentration in school.

Source: J. W. B. Douglas, *The Home and the School*, p. 66, Panther: London 1969

Item S

The proportion of children (those under fifteen years of age) living in households with income 50 per cent below the national average – one way of defining poverty – has risen over recent years. In 1979, 10 per cent of children were living in such households. By 1991, this proportion had grown to 31 per cent.

Source: Anthony Giddens, *Sociology*, 3rd edition, p. 271, Polity, Oxford, 1997

1 What is the approximate national average of children eligible for free school meals? *(1 mark)*

2 To what extent do schools embody middle class values and alienate the deprived? *(5 marks)*

3 What sociological links can you identify between the education of the child and subsequent adult poverty? *(9 marks)*

4 Sociologically evaluate the notion that material deprivation can result in poor school attainment among children. *(10 marks)*

In question 1 a fairly rough calculation will tell you that the approximate average number of children using free school meals is somewhere around the 15 to 20 per cent mark. If you are no good at sums, forget the question as the mark is not worth the agony. The examiners will not be too specific in their requirements either.

Question 2 might suggest a lot of detail in the particular wording but the marks allocated do not justify a lot of writing.

Candidate's answer

2 The view that schools embody middle class values is widely held and tends to be Marxian in origin. Writers such as Bordieu and Althusser point to the way that schools are the tools of the ruling classes and therefore it is natural that those of a working class background will be disadvantaged or alienated. Jackson and Marsden in the 1970s also showed a pattern of working class disadvantage in grammar schools. Bernstein has pointed out that schools embody middle class linguistic codes and the training of teachers will encourage them to value middle class conformist attitudes. However, education has long been a route to social advancement in Britain and, with the expansion of higher education in Britain in the 1960s, children of the working classes were able to make the move to higher status occupations via success in education. Figures in *Social Trends 27* show that most children generally like school. Schools may embody many middle class values, but they do not necessarily alienate the working classes.

Commentary

The candidate has referred to social theory and located the debate correctly. Evidence is relatively wide ranging and drawn from a variety of sources. There is clear knowledge of research, though the reference to Jackson and Marsden's study was vague. Perhaps mention of cultural factors might have improved this work; reference to the work of Oakley and Willis might be indicated. There is a nice, succinct conclusion which refers directly to the wording of the question.

Answer

3 There are obvious sociological links between the education of the child and subsequent adult poverty. These links are not absolute in that children who have achieved high levels of education may, in fact, not become economically successful. Graduate unemployment is a reality for many students. However, as a general principle, low levels of educational achievement will reduce the earning capacity of an individual.

This was noted by Oscar Lewis and many American functionalists who talked of a sub-culture of poverty and identified cycles of poverty in which children from poor homes adopted values and norms that would inevitably lead to low status occupations. These ideas were taken so seriously in the USA and in Britain in the 1960s that compensatory education schemes were set into place to 'correct' the values that resulted in poor economic status.

Many Marxist writers have suggested that the education system acts to create a sense of failure and poor employment. This means that there will be an acquiescent workforce to act as a reservoir of cheap labour. Gramsci appears to suggest that the intellectual classes are created by education to serve as masters for the elite and that they are rewarded for their labour in creating a society in which many are deprived.

The Ofsted Report cited in the question points out that children from the poorest economic backgrounds have a poor take up of further education. This means that they are unlikely to become high earners in a society which places value on certification. Even though graduate unemployment and under-employment are very real problems, unemployment rates are twice as high for the unskilled as the skilled (Social Trends).

Willis suggested that the behaviour of 'the lads' he studied and their rejection of the values of the school prepared boys for survival in the type of work traditionally taken by working class males. While he can be criticised for failing to recognise the authoritarian and fascist potential of the culture of the lads and for ignoring the more conformist children, he pointed to a link between education and work that is particularly pertinent now that we have become a post-industrial society.

Our society has become one where the skills of the traditional working class male are no longer required. Machines will do the work of a labour force. This has effectively de-skilled many men, particularly in areas of traditional industry, and lack of educational skills mean that these people are now unemployable and dependent on welfare payments.

There are therefore many links between education success or lack of it and a future of poverty and these are structural to our society.

Commentary

This is a wide ranging and sensible discussion. There is reference to and understanding of theory and the student is obviously very able. A critical view has been taken of the work of Willis although the criticisms are not necessarily relevant to the discussion point of the question and add nothing to the movement of the argument. There is use of the technical language of sociology and the student is clearly capable of writing fluent English. The work should be graded as an A, but not a good A. This candidate is clearly capable of structuring an answer because the introduction and the conclusion refer to the question and the argument is clearly signposted from the first sentence.

Answer

4 There is a great deal of evidence to suggest that material deprivation can result in poor school attainment among children, but that it is not the only cause of failure. Material deprivation is the lack of the goods that one requires to survive comfortably in our society.

In the last twenty years, there has been a marked difference between the wealth of the richest and the poverty of the poorest. This could be attributed to the policies of individualism followed by the New Right who controlled the Conservative Government under Margaret Thatcher. However, the poverty of the 1930s was very extreme in Britain and yet many would claim that educational standards have dropped since that time. This cannot be proved in any objective tests, but it would seem that levels of literacy may have fallen.

During the 1960s and early 1970s, many sociologists worked in the area of considering the effect of poverty on attainment. Douglas, Frank Field and others contributed to the argument. They pointed out that poor housing and poor health go together. Poor health and absenteeism also create poor education.

Commonsense also suggests that children with access to technical equipment such as computers will have a better start than those who do not when it comes to coursework and projects at GCSE. However, the items show that teachers may also be biased against those from poor backgrounds and so teacher labelling and not poverty causes the child to fail. Interactionalists point out that there is a culture of poverty which creates bad values in children, so it is not the poverty but the culture which creates failure.

Poor schools are often located in areas of poverty. There is a geographical connection between 'failing schools' and inner city areas or sink council estates. Not all schools in poor areas are bad, but children have less of a chance in schools like that than if they go to better schools.

All in all, although there is a link between poverty and school failure, other factors may be taken into account.

Commentary

This is basically a commonsense answer because there is little reference to research or theory. However, the candidate is good at writing, has clearly understood the question and has made a good attempt to discuss the issues raised. This probably justifies a B/A rather than a clear A. Terms such as material deprivation are well defined.

Question 4.2

Look carefully at the mark scheme on page 87 and then attempt to answer this question on your own.

Item T

The claim is that students from more privileged backgrounds are educationally advantaged by the time they start school and are favored (sic) even more strongly by the middle class bias of schools as they progress through the grade levels. In any case, students from more privileged family backgrounds do perform better academically.

Source: M. G. Fullan, *The New Meaning of Educational Change*, p. 14, Cassell: London 1991

Item U

Conservative thinkers argue that schools select pupils on the basis of their talents and thus ensure that the best and brightest students will get the most senior and responsible positions in society. Most sociologists are unhappy with this cheerful view: they feel that schools do operate in unfair ways and tend to disadvantage and even discriminate against certain kinds of student.

Source: Measor and Sikes, *Introduction to Education: Gender and Schools*, p. 2, Cassell: London 1992

Item V

Figure 4.6

Public school educated holders of some elite jobs in Britain in the 1980s

Category	% who attended public schools
Pupils at school in UK	7 (all independent schools)
Labour MPs	14
Conservative MPs	70
Conservative Cabinet	90
50 most senior officers in army	80
Directors of leading firms	66
Directors of banks	70
Directors of insurance companies	92
Senior civil servants	50
High court judges	83
Ambassadors	69
Church of England bishops	59

Source: K. Browne, *An Introduction to Sociology*, p.298, Polity: Oxford 1992

Item W

Whichever terms are used, one of the most important facts to note is that the distinction between State and private schools is now less clear than it was even a few years ago. An increased number of private schools receive substantial funding from the State through arrangements such as the Assisted Places Scheme and the Aided Pupils Scheme, while many parents with children in maintained schools are increasingly expected to contribute to their children's education. The introduction of city technology colleges, which are independent schools funded jointly by industry, commerce and the State, and grant maintained schools, which are State-maintained schools outside the LEA system, adds to the confusion. Such a blurring of the boundaries and the development of a range of schools can be regarded as an important part of the government's privatization strategy for schooling.

Source: G. Walford, *Private Schooling: Tradition, Change and Diversity*, p. 2, Paul Chapman: London 1991

1 **Suggest two ways in which the state may have subsidised inequality in educational provision in Britain.** *(4 marks)*

2 Can it be argued that the existence of independent education compromises the quality of education provision for those educated solely in the state sector? *(6 marks)*

3 Assess the extent to which alterations to education legislation over the last 30 years have made a difference to the class structure and life chances of the majority of people in Britain. *(6 marks)*

4 Sociologically evaluate the claim that one of the purposes of education is to provide equality of opportunity for students. *(9 marks)*

Mark scheme

1 0 marks — No relevant points.

1–2 marks — One mark each for a word/phrase specifying either the Assisted Places Scheme, the Aided Pupil's Scheme, grant-maintained schools or city technology colleges.

3–4 marks — A development of the one-word answers which specifies the form of the subsidy – e.g. money paid as fees for the more able students, additional funding for specific roles.

2 0 marks — No relevant points.

1–3 marks — A simplistic answer which concentrates on a consideration of inequality issues or independent schools. Judgements may be made that independent schools provide a 'better' education.

4–6 marks — A detailed, answer which highlights the interplay between the state and independent sectors and raises a number of relevant issues – that might include the role of an elite, quality provision and facilities, geographical inequalities, parental support. There will be a clear and supported judgement that answers the question asked. The best answers might refer to current Labour Party policy.

3 0 marks — No relevant points.

1–2 marks — A commonsense answer which accepts the terms of the question. Either class structure or educational legislation is focused on, with little attempt to relate the two separate elements of the question.

3–6 marks — An attempt will be made to relate education legislation, class structure and life chances. There will be evidence of analysis and evaluation leading to a clearly stated conclusion. The best answers will comment on the nature of the changes in, or beliefs about, the class structure of Britain.

4 0 marks — No relevant points.

1–2 marks — The terms of the question will be accepted uncritically and there will be little or no reference to theoretical perspectives. The answer will be commonsense and descriptive.

3–6 marks — There will be some, albeit limited, reference to relevant theories and writers. Better answers will probably pursue a Marxist analysis and offer limited evaluation. There will be a clear and logical expression of ideas.

7–9 marks — Answers will probably centre on a comparison of the functionalist and Marxist views of education, with some analysis of the strengths and weaknesses of each point of view and a clear conclusion drawn. There may be an acknowledgement of the political implications of the discussion with reference to the introduction of student loan schemes or similar legislation. There may be an attempt to clarify the distinction between 'equality of opportunity' and 'equality of outcome'. A range of studies and research will be used to support the discussion.

Chapter 5

Work, Organisations and Leisure

Introduction

One of the features common to the seemingly divergent themes and perspectives within sociology is the notion that it is the economy which is of fundamental importance. **Parsons**, writing from a functionalist perspective, sees the economic system as the prime mover in the evolution of societies from simple to more complex forms of organisation. Similarly, for **Marx**, the capitalist economy, through its system of class relations, is nothing less than the determinant of all aspects of human social behaviour. A different view is taken by **Weber** who argues that the ideas of individuals can alter the nature of work and its organisation, thus transforming society. This approach is taken up by **phenomenologists** who tend to concentrate upon the subjective experience of work and its effect upon the individual and their families.

The rapid transition of society from a labour-intensive to a technocratic system with capital-intensive, machine-based and controlled production is especially topical at present. The growth of an increasingly market-oriented economy has brought with it a different managerial approach both to industrial relations and to organisational structure within industry and society. The change in the organisational structure within industry has reflected, and induced, corresponding changes in the wider society. Non-work and leisure pursuits have assumed greater significance, not only for the large numbers for whom loss of employment has been a shattering blow, but also to those for whom it has meant increased job opportunities within an expanding service and leisure sector of the economy.

It is clear, then, that work, organisations and leisure have a primary significance in the lives of people and are, in consequence, of great importance within sociology. In this chapter you will be given help in developing and using the skills necessary to answer successfully the questions on this vast, complex yet interesting topic. Examiners will seek to test your ability in three skill domains:

1. **Knowledge and understanding** – This examines what you know about specific topics in sociology (in this case work, organisations and leisure) and how well you understand what you have studied.
2. **Interpretation and application** – Here your ability to express data in your own words or to explain them and use them to show your understanding of some other aspect of sociology is tested.
3. **Evaluation** – This is where your capacity to measure the usefulness of given information against other evidence, empirical research or theoretical concept is assessed. Having assessed each, are you able to make an informed judgement of the relative merit of each, and produce your own conclusion? It is this skill that examiners look for in the more substantial data-response questions; that is those parts of the question which attract the highest marks.

Alongside all of the above, examiners also seek to discover the extent to which you are able to express your answers in a clear, logical and concise manner. In order to satisfy all the above demands adequately certain techniques will produce the required results more effectively than others.

Knowledge and understanding

Your ability to show that you have a broad and deep knowledge will hinge upon your capacity to see the topic from a variety of different perspectives. Work, organisations and leisure is a topic which is riven by many diverging political views, each reflecting a specific sociological perspective.

It is unlikely that you will be asked only for knowledge and understanding but these aspects are of such importance that it is well worthwhile practising and assessing the extent of your knowledge. You could attempt to answer questions such as:

- Summarise the views of Durkheim on the division of labour in society.

- What do you understand by the term 'alienation'?
- Give an outline of the interactionist approach to work and leisure.
- Summarise Weber's views on bureaucracy.

Answering any questions effectively requires a sound basis of knowledge and understanding. In the phrasing of the question and/or in the items presented there will be clues on how best to respond. Specific commands may be given to you, which should be the trigger to use your knowledge and to show how well you understand it. Examples of 'action words' associated with the skill area of knowledge and understanding are provided in Chapter 1 (page 5). These words will indicate that knowledge and understanding are required in your answer.

In addition, there are a number of things you **must** do in order to satisfy examination requirements adequately.

- You must show that you have relevant sociological knowledge of the many theories, perspectives and empirical studies which relate to work, organisations and leisure.
- You must have appropriate knowledge of the aspects of British society which form the basis of the question. This means you have to have information on such matters as patterns of employment, leisure pursuits.
- You must use appropriate sociological terms and concepts in a way which shows that you clearly understand them.

While not completely exhaustive, the following indicates the major **issues** and **debates** which you should include in your answers. You must be able to mention a number of **relevant studies** and place them accurately within their various perspectives. A brief summary of the essential items to be deposited in your '**knowledge bank**' is given below. It is intended only as a guide and cannot replace your textbooks, class notes and the use of good sociological magazines such as *Sociology Review*. You could, however, use the summary as a guide to your revision programme.

Work

- The definition of work and leisure. An outline of different working patterns such as the informal economy and the 'black economy'. The importance of work in providing status to an individual.
- Changes in the structure of employment. The decline of primary and secondary industries and the growth of tertiary (service) and quaternary (new technologies) industries. The increase in short-term contracts and part-time work, together with an increase in middle class home-working with computers and advance technologies. Fordism and post-Fordism.
- The changing situation of women in the workforce and how their situation differs from that of men. The explanations for this change in status, such as lack of qualification, sexual discrimination and the 'glass ceiling'.
- The experience of work, the debate about technology and alienation and the de-skilling debate. Industrial conflicts with an explanation of this and examples of recent events. Different explanations for the fall in the number of strikes.
- Issues of unemployment, with reasons for its increase across all sectors and its effect on individuals and their families. Regional variations. Unemployment statistics and the problems associated with them. Issues surrounding 'workfare'. The links between occupation, social class and unemployment.

Leisure

The problems of defining this concept. Parker and criticism of his work. The leisured classes, the leisure-rich and the leisure-poor. Changes in the nature of leisure.

Organisations

Weber and bureaucracy; management studies and the Weberian legacy; Taylorism; Mayo and the human relations school; Marxist and conflict views;

Braverman and the degradation of work in the twentieth century; postmodernism; Foucault; Garland and Burrell.

Interpretation

Being able to interpret requires that you have clearly understood the question and that you have been able to identify correctly any specific perspective which is taken in the items. For example, is the item written from a functionalist, Marxist, interactionist, feminist or other perspective? It is also important to be able to interpret data given in numerical form. This will require careful attention to the dimensions of the numerical data. Are they referring to percentages, to rates? Are they expressed in thousands, or in millions? Have you noted the source and the date of the material, because this can frequently give indications of the specific perspective taken. For example, statistics from the Adam Smith Institute may well represent support for a right-wing, possibly functionalist stance.

One of the nice things about interpretation questions is that they only use the information given. This helps in the search for relevant material from your knowledge store when you address the question. In general, too, these questions only carry low(ish) marks, say, within the 2 to 4 mark band, and so you must not spend too much time on them. A good rule of thumb is to take the number of marks awarded and multiply by two – this gives you a fair idea of the time you should spend on answering this part of the question. Obviously, you need to answer the question but only do enough, do not waste valuable time writing a mini-essay when two words would gain the same (or more!)marks. Also **do not** rewrite the question. This is unnecessary, it wastes time and examiners are unimpressed by your ability to copy text!

Interpreting quantitative data

Most statistics are straightforward, but they create havoc for many students because they are unfamiliar with them. First, **do not panic**! Remember that you will be more likely to make a mistake if you try to rush everything so read any tables slowly, using a ruler or other straight edge to read across a line of figures. Look for the main **trends**, such as increase in unemployment, and look for any significant **differences**, as between ethnic groups, for example. You will find that the data are presented to you in the form of charts, graphs, text or columns of figures.

Item A

Trends in male and female employment 1971–88

Figure 5.1

	Males (thousands)	Females (thousands)	Females % of total	% Females full-time	% Females part-time
1971	13,424	8,224	38.0	25.3	12.6
1976	13,097	8,951	40.4	24.3	16.3
1981	12,878	9,108	42.6	24.7	17.8
1986	11,643	9,462	44.3	25.2	19.6
1988	11,978	10,096	45.7	26.2	19.5

Source: *Department of Employment Gazette* HMSO, 1989

1 By how many did male employment exceed that of female in 1986? *(1 mark)*

2 What trends in male and female employment arise from Item A? *(2 marks)*

Answer

1 2,281,000.

2 The number of men has decreased and the number of women has increased significantly. There has been a 7.7 per cent increase in the number of women in employment during the period. The great majority of this increased female employment has occurred within the part-time sector.

Commentary

1 All you have to do here is to subtract the female from the male employment figures in the chart. Although straightforward, the wrong columns or rows may be chosen, or the figure may be calculated wrongly or expressed as 2281 only. This misses the dimensions of the figures quoted which are in thousands. Simple errors can throw away marks which are, in effect, a gift!

2 This type of question requires that you include **two** trends to gain the two marks on offer. What you have to do is to compare the colums of data and look for obvious movements. Is there any clear direction to the way the figures rise or fall? The trends are fairly clear once a calm analysis is carried out.

Interpreting qualitative data

Generally in these questions you are asked to give the meaning of a specific element within the given text. Alternatively, you may be invited to state what perspective is represented by a particular item or series of items. This is if the items are all of the same perspective, but more usually they will be contradictory and you may be asked to explain what debate they form part of in sociology.

Once again the number of marks available should be your guide as to the time you spend on each question. This is also a guide to the amount of knowledge element you are expected to provide. The higher the marks the more you are expected to put in. Low marks, say, one or two, can usually be answered by the use of the data on their own. Anything higher and you will be expected to add some further knowledge from your studies. Remember, always gauge the amount you write in accordance with the marks on offer.

Item B

Undoubtedly the labour market is more flexible. Non-standard types of work such as part-time and contract jobs and self-employment have boomed in the past decade. One British worker in four is now a part-timer. Add in temporary staff and the self-employed and two workers in five are outside permanent, full-time employment. Firms such as the Burton Group in tailoring, British Home Stores and British Airways are rushing to convert full-time workers into part-timers.

As many as two-thirds of Sears, the Saxone-to-Selfridges group, are now part-timers. These firms say part-time work enables them to boost staff at busy periods, improving customer service.

In the long run more flexibility in the labour market should mean more jobs ... if firms are now hiring two part-timers rather than one full-timer it ... may explain why unemployment has started to fall earlier than expected.

Source: The *Economist*, 22 May 1993

1 What is meant by the term 'non-standard types of work' in Item B? *(1 mark)*

2 Explain, with examples what 'flexibility in the labour market' is shown in Item B. *(4 marks)*

Answer

1 Part-time and contract jobs and self-employment.

2 The term means that the workforce is not now socialised into expecting that there will be a career track for them within the same enterprise. There is much more acceptance of part-time and seasonal work. 'One British worker in four is now a part-timer.' In addition, the growth of the 'enterprise culture' has meant that a significant number of people are involved in setting up their own small business.

Commentary

1 As there is only one mark available it is clear that the answer to this part of the question should be brief. You may recall that we suggested that a good guide would be to take the number of marks awarded and multiply by two. This should indicate the approximate time to spend on this part of the question. In this case, only two minutes should be spent on your answer.

Careful reading of the item will usually indicate what the required answer is. In this case it is very easy – the 'non-standard types of work' are listed immediately after the phrase. Sometimes the answers are rather more difficult to spot, but not very often! In any case if you keep calm and read the item carefully you will have little difficulty in finding the correct answer.

2 The four marks available here indicate that you should spend a little longer (approximately eight minutes) and that you are expected to give more information, this time in your own words. You are asked to interpret the phrase 'flexibility in the labour market'. This will require you to pause and consider that you are trying to explain this to someone who has no knowledge or understanding of sociology. Make your answer as clear and as concise as possible. It is also important not to try to impress by using long words which you may *think* you understand but which may, in fact, have a quite separate and distinct meaning. Keep it simple and clear!

Interpreting pictures

Occasionally one of the items presented to you will be in the form of a photograph, drawing, engraving or cartoon representing some aspect of either work or leisure. There are not very many points which can usefully be demanded of you and if this format is used at all you may be asked to describe the perspective indicated, or to determine which debate or concept the image claims to represent.

Item C

Figure 5.3

What perspective is illustrated in Item C? *(1 mark)*

Answer

Marxist.

Commentary

This is a question which requires you to decide which of the major perspectives is represented in the picture. In this case the representation is rather overt and lacking in subtlety. There is a clear political statement which is implied through the harsh cynicism of the stereotypical 'bloated capitalist' exhorting his workers to greater sacrifice and effort. Clearly the portrayal of capitalism as a voracious monster could only come from Marx and Engels and might well have been ideal for inclusion in the original version of the 'Communist Manifesto'. One word will therefore suffice to explain the perspective of the image presented.

Application

This is a special skill which requires you to be able to apply your knowledge and understanding to illustrate or explain a particular sociological idea. For instance, you could use current events, which may not yet have appeared in any textbook or sociological study, and relate them to points raised in the items.

The question will give you plenty of information indicating what the examiner is looking for. For example, if the question asks, 'To what extent does empirical evidence support Marx's concept of alienation?', you should immediately think of **Blauner**, **Braverman** or **Beynon** in support of the argument, perhaps pointing out, in contrast, that **Weber** takes issue with the view that organisations are necessarily alienating since they improve job security and therefore provide a focus of stability for the employee. This will gain you good marks, but you could equally well use information adapted from the items, or you could use evidence from recent events (such as the 'corporate' approach of Japanese companies) to explain the nature of alienation and the arguments surrounding it.

It will help if you keep a 'cuttings file' of relevant information from newspapers and periodicals. Try to get into the habit of scanning the daily papers for information which relates to the topics you are studying. If you try to interpret the articles as you cut them out you will find that you begin to adopt the habit of interpreting what you read and applying your knowledge, thus honing your application skills.

Questions in this skill domain tend to be variable in the marks awarded. Again it is useful to apply the rule of thumb mentioned earlier, and multiply the marks available by two to give you a rough idea of the time you should spend on this piece. Occasionally you will find a question carrying relatively high marks, say, 6 to 8. This will require you to interpret the items concisely, and clearly and to provide a detailed outline of the competing sociological theories together with relevant examples.

As previously, data may be given in three forms: quantitative, qualitative and pictorial. The same words, asking you to do certain things, will indicate how you should address the skill of application to the particular question. You may be asked, for example, to 'identify' or 'describe'; then again you may be asked to perform a more complex task such as, 'Provide examples from your studies which support Marx's theory of alienation', or 'Using material from the items and elsewhere explain ...'.

Applying quantitative data

The skill of applying statistics when answering questions on work, organisations and leisure is in the interpretation being used as a platform on which you can show your knowledge and understanding.

Using material from Item D and other sources, identify the patterns of unemployment and describe how sociologists may explain the reasons for them. *(6 marks)*

Item D

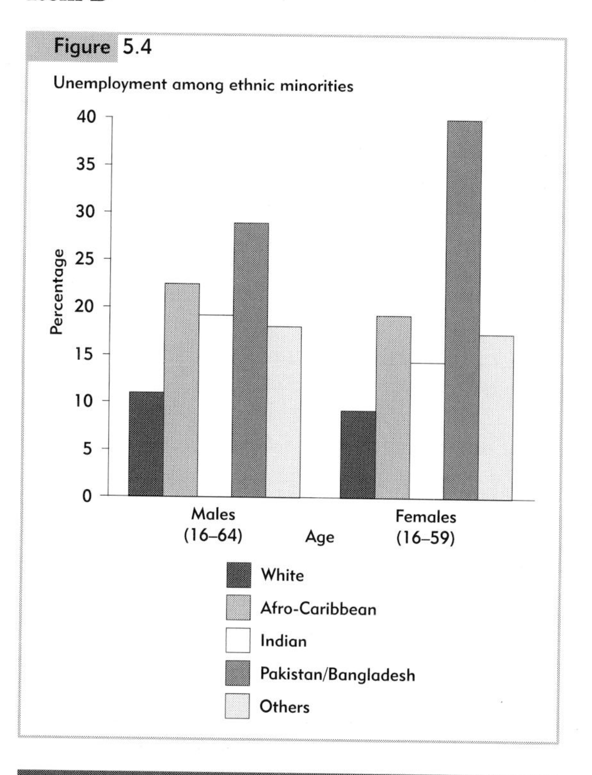

Answer

The patterns of unemployment in Item D show that both white males and white females of working age had the same level of unemployment (10 per cent). Among ethnic groups referred to as 'Others', for example African and Chinese, there were also unemployment similarities between the sexes (15 per cent). However, both Indian and Afro-Caribbean males had higher unemployment rates than their female counterparts. The most marked difference was between Pakistani/Bangladeshi males at about 25 per cent and females at nearly 40 per cent, the highest unemployment level in Item B.

Sociological explanations of the above patterns vary. A major issue has been the extent to which ethnic minority groups occupy a different labour market in the United Kingdom. Rex and Tomlinson argued that there were two separate labour markets and they therefore posited a 'dual labour market theory'. Asians and Afro-Caribbeans are found mainly in jobs in the secondary labour market, consisting of low status, poorly paid jobs with little job security and therefore at higher risk of unemployment. Rex and Tomlinson also found differences in female employment, for example, in the West Midlands. Whereas white women usually held secretarial or shop-working positions, women from ethnic minority groups worked mainly in factories rather than in service industries.

Castles and Kosack, in their study of immigrant workers in France, Germany, Switzerland and the United Kingdom, found that these workers faced similar problems in the labour market as identified by Rex and Tomlinson. Most were manual workers in unskilled or semi-skilled jobs and they experienced high rates of unemployment. According to Castles and Kosack, writing from a Marxist perspective, such high rates of unemployment are based upon the needs of capitalist society for a 'reserve army of labour'. It is necessary to have a labour surplus to keep wages cost down because the greater the labour supply, the weaker will be the bargaining power of workers. As capitalistic economies go through periods of boom and slump, a reserve army of labour is required to be hired and fired in relation to the situation pertaining in the capitalist economy at any specific time.

Commentary

This question is typical of those requiring a much higher level of input. You will notice that, in addition to correctly applying data to certain patterns of unemployment, as requested, wider knowledge must be applied in order to explain adequately the full range of the theoretical position taken. You will only gain a few marks for interpreting the information in the item. The main element for which marks are awarded is the application phase. The key word 'explain' is your 'trigger' to put a lot of detail into your answer. If the question had asked you merely to 'describe' or 'outline' reasons you would not be required to spend so much time.

Applying qualitative data

It is very common to find that examiners look for your knowledge of, and abilities in explaining, theoretical perspectives in the qualitative element. You must, therefore, be well informed and be selective. In other words, *make your answers concise, clear and relevant.* Many students, through panic, reach for their suitcase marked 'Theory and Methods' and proceed to unload its contents in a jumbled heap on their examination paper. This is something you must not do!

Item E

The working class of today, far from being a homogeneous group of equally unskilled and impoverished people, is in fact differentiated by numerous distinctions. Within the labour force we have to distinguish at least three skill groups: a growing stratum of highly skilled relatively stable workers, a stratum of semi-skilled workers and a dwindling stratum of totally unskilled labourers who are often newcomers to industry (such as immigrants). These three groups differ not only in their level of skill, but also in other attributes and determinants of social status. As with the capitalist class, it has become doubtful whether speaking of the working class still makes much sense.

Source: R. Dahrendorf, *Class and Class Conflict in Industrial Society*, Routledge & Kegan Paul: London 1959

Explain why sociologists might expect the working class of today to be a homogeneous group of equally unskilled and impoverished people? ***(6–8 marks)***

Candidate's answer

Karl Marx predicted that as proletarianisation developed the working class would become increasingly similar in outlook and organisation. This process of homogenisation would result in the working class becoming more or less equally impoverished and de-powered.

Braverman, in 'Labour and Monopoly Capitalism' (1974), in support of Marx, has led to technological innovation whereby workers are replaced by machines. The result is a decline in the need for skilled workers and, increasingly, for unskilled workers across the whole spectrum of industrial production. What has resulted is a de-skilled society, with workers increasingly becoming the appendages to a machine. These unskilled workers are more likely to be impoverished because, due to technological improvements they are more prone to unemployment. Even when in employment they often lack the pay increments, fringe benefits, opportunities for promotion, job security and other benefits accorded to their full-time colleagues. Unskilled workers are more likely to be at risk for short-time, lay-off and redundancy. They are, in short, members of a homogeneous group with little or no career track in employment and insecure, low-paid employment.

Commentary

This is a rather short answer to be given a full eight marks. The first paragraph lacks accuracy as Marx did not use the concept of proletarianisation. This came much later with the work of Braverman. Marx did predict the impoverishment and de-powering of the proletarian class but much more detail could have been given about Marx's vision of the process by which this would come about. The structural process of capitalism contains the seeds of this inequity and should be explained clearly.

Modern Marxists use the concept of de-skilling and proletarianisation in connection with the analysis of work situations in advanced capitalism; especially in connection with factory and production line labour. They point out that what results is increasingly alienated labour. The second paragraph could therefore have linked the notion of the homogenisation of the working class with the concept of alienation.

You may want the opportunity to practise using your application skills on a simulated answer. What follows is a question and answer which, by careful reading, you will be able to analyse in terms of application skills. Underline those parts of the answer which you consider to be examples of interpretation. Remember that there are a number of indications based on the following list of possible phrases, such as:

- the use of relevant examples from everyday life – topical events;
- the application of empirical studies and theoretical analyses to the question;
- the linking with other topics, where relevant, to show your knowledge and understanding.

Explain why ethnic minorities are over-represented in unskilled jobs largely because they are recent immigrants. *(8 marks)*

Candidate's answer

From the information given in the item, ethnic minorities do seem to be predominant in unskilled jobs. This bears out information given in a report from the Race Relations Commission in 1994, which showed that a comparison of white employees with black and Asian employees showed a large discrepancy. Over 40 per cent of whites were employed in non-manual jobs, as compared with only about 8 per cent for the black and Asian groups. As Rex and Tomlinson pointed out in 'Colonial Immigrants in a British Society', there is apparently a dual labour market. The primary market is in stable, permanent jobs with a reasonable wage level and a career enhancement pathway The secondary market is in unstable, low-paid jobs with poor working conditions and no career track. In general, it is into the secondary market that blacks and Asians are recruited. Rex and Tomlinson also noted that the gender effect led to the same situation. Over 27 per cent of white females were employed as clerical workers, while black and Asian women tended to work in factories.

Such patterns of employment appear to mirror the needs of the British economy for workers to fill the low-paid jobs which have been left behind by the white workers. The relatively unskilled immigrant workers are content to work in any establishment which will present them with the opportunity to earn their living. When they are fixed in one of these unskilled manual jobs, the immigrants begin to experience discrimination in many other areas of their lives.

Pilkington, in his work entitled 'Race Relations in Britain' has tried to show that black workers are employed without any real chance to move out and better themselves. He points out that ethnic minority members have become trapped into these poor jobs with little or no prospects. There is, Pilkington asserts, significant evidence from a 1974 survey which showed that 32 per cent of West Indians, 58 per cent of Pakistanis and 36 per cent of Indians were in skilled or semi-skilled jobs. This gives support to the notion that the immigrants are trapped in ghettos made up of large extended families.

He goes on to argue that the concept of an underclass and the support it receives from many committed Marxist and Trotskyite sources does not have much support from empirical studies. He does accept that there has been a decline in the proportion of ethnic minorities at the very lowest levels of the job market. Empirical evidence shows that there have been spectacular falls in the numbers of black people and Asians clustered at the bottom of the employment hierarchy. It is clear, Pilkington claims, that while these groups are relatively disadvantaged in the economic scramble for jobs, they by no means constitute anything remotely like an underclass.

Commentary

This is a capable answer which provides a critical analysis using evidence from a range of relevant studies. The first paragraph links information from the item with knowledge which is directly supportive of the data derived from the item. The mark awarded for this answer would be seven. The highest mark could have been gained for an explanation of the concept of the 'underclass', and some evidence of knowledge of the debate which surrounds the use of this term.

Evaluation

This is arguably the most difficult and therefore potentially the most rewarding of all the skill domains tested in the examination. It is the element which gains the highest marks and where the student can make the difference between a mediocre pass and an outstanding grade A. The essence of evaluation is the ability to assess how effective respective explanations, perspectives or empirical studies – be they functionalist, Marxist, interactionist – are in explaining specific data given in the question.

You are, in effect, a member of a jury trying to judge which piece of evidence or explanation most adequately explains the facts presented to you. Of course, when you are writing your answer you are expected to reach a final verdict based upon all the evidence you have at your disposal. What the examiners are looking for is that you reach a balanced and coherent decision, having examined and given credence to the items and other evidence from your own knowledge base.

What is required is that you weigh up the strengths and the weaknesses respectively of the items presented. Then you make up your mind as to which you consider offers the most adequate explanation. Above all, you must justify the conclusion you have reached. This is no easy task given that the knowledge base is so vast, so you will have to be both well read and selective in your response.

The amount of information and the time allocated will, as always, be in proportion to the marks awarded. Questions in this skill domain carry high marks and, consequently, will require lots of information from a range of perspectives. You may, if you wish, begin your answer with these high score questions. This will ensure that the time you have spent is the most profitable. You may think, however, that if you allocate your time strictly according to the two-minute rule of thumb (where one mark is approximately equal to two minutes) it does not matter what order you answer the questions in as you will have managed your time successfully and have ample time for answering and checking your work.

As in all previous skill domains, certain action words and phrases should alert you to what the examiners are expecting of you (see Chapter 1, page 5 for examples of these).

Evaluating quantitative data

It is uncommon for an evaluative question to be asked about purely numerical data in the items. However, be prepared for anything!

It is very important to remember that in this, the most searching of the skill domains, you may be asked to identify a concept or perspective as part of an interpretation and application exercise. Using the interpretation you have made as the 'base line', you may then be required to evaluate what you have identified, as in the following example.

Item F

Figure 5.5

	Percentage of the working week lost through sickness	Days lost through strikes and other stoppages
1981	2.7	1350
1986	2.7	1050
1988	3.0	800
1990	3.0	750
1991	3.3	650
1994	3.4	600

How far do you agree that the data given in Item F support the concept of alienation? *(10 marks)*

Answer

The figures show that a high proportion of time is lost through both strikes and sickness. An interesting trend emerges on close examination. The number of stoppages due to strikes and industrial action **decreases** while, at the same time, the percentage of the working week lost through sickness **increases**. This trend has to be seen in the context of a report from the Office of Health Economics which maintained that, in their view, '... the most significant factor associated with sickness absence is job satisfaction'.

Marxist analysts would claim that the figures quoted support the concept of alienation. This is the feeling of estrangement from the work process which is experienced by workers within a capitalist enterprise. Instead of feeling a sense of value, dignity and worth in the pursuit of labour, workers in capitalist enterprises share a sense of worthlessness, futility and misery as they engage in the process of work. It is only the dubious pleasure of the pay-packet – **extrinsic reward** – which provides the motivation for each worker. This accent on the extrinsic reward has the effect of reducing workers to the level of being simply adjuncts to a machine, mere components in the production cycle. Each individual worker thus experiences a loss of both power and control over the work situation. This is because, as Marx points out, they are a 'wage-slave' tied to an employer by the powerful bonds of capitalism and consumerism. It is scarcely surprising, therefore, that they seek whatever opportunity they can find in order to escape from the drudgery of the workplace.

During times when worker solidarity was at a high level, industrial stresses, which built up due to the forces of alienation experienced by each worker, frequently found expression and some release through strikes and other forms of corporate industrial action. In recent times the power and extent of the trade union movement has been significantly reduced on two fronts. First, the number of active members of unions has reduced dramatically due to increased unemployment and changes in worker attitude. Second, increasingly restrictive legislation has considerably reduced the capacity of the union movement to act in support of members. The net result is that the previous 'safety valve' for worker stress and dissatisfaction is now no longer as readily available. Workers feel an increased force of compulsion to submit to the powerful forces of alienation and to endure them for longer periods. The stress levels increase cumulatively and this, perhaps, is an indication of why in the long term the result is absence due to sickness.

Blauner ('Alienation and Freedom'), used a Marxist definition of alienation as a basis but refined it into a **Weberian** view involving both a subjective and an objective element. Specifically he maintained that workers were more likely to experience alienating forces when they were involved in repetitive, routine and highly differentiated work. This is typically to be found on a production line where the workers are involved as makers or assemblers of components with which they had no identity or, occasionally, knowledge. **Braverman** ('Labour and Monopoly Capitalism'), following a specifically Marxist stance, has shown how workers have become successively de-skilled as technology has developed. He noted that as workers increasingly perceive themselves as little more than a commodity, they become more militant. The inability to find an outlet for this militancy results in increased stress felt subjectively by each worker. Attempts to make the experience of work more acceptable and enjoyable results in workers being forced to accept more subtle, yet equally frustrating and restrictive, management control. Because of the increased level of part-time work – especially involving women – the ability to act corporately is even further reduced and there is greater exploitation as work is de-skilled.

Critics of this view, such as Penn ('Skilled Manual Workers in the Labour Process'), point out that many industries have consistently used part-time labour and there has been little, if any, dissatisfaction expressed. Others, for example **Piore** ('Perspectives on Labour Market Flexibility') point out that skill levels are actually increasing as the level of technology in the workplace increases.

Writing from a **Weberian** stance, **Woodward** ('Industrial Organisation and Control'), remarks that the attitudes of workers towards their work experience have to be seen in the context of the technical organisation of production. In contrast, writers from a **functionalist**, or **New Right** perspective have pointed out that many workers are satisfied with their work. **Thierry** and **Iwema** ('Work and Organisational Psychology') found that as many as 85 per cent of workers expressed satisfaction with their experience of work. Should workers feel they are unwell then, as **Parsons's** analysis of the 'sick role' attempts to show, there are adequate institutional safeguards and responses to enable them legitimately to find treatment and to be restored to functional health.

Allen ('The Sociology of Industrial Relations') follows a Marxist line and argues that alienation is an inevitable feature of work under capitalism. Dissatisfaction with work is thus a consistent theme and, irrespective of the ways in which the organisation of work is modified, the workers will always be nothing more than 'wage slaves', with all the corresponding stresses and strains which must find an outlet either through group action (strikes) or, if this is not available, through personal illness, either physical, mental or both.

Wedderburn and Crompton ('Workers' Attitudes and Technology') follow a classically Weberian view supporting Woodward in claiming that changing technology will induce different attitudes and response to the work situation. There have been many suggestions proposed to try and introduce effective ways of reducing worker alienation and stress levels. High among these is the transition from assembly-line work to a group-oriented system – as, for example, in Volvo.

It seems from the statistics that whatever methods are experimented with, the fact remains that, under capitalism, workers will continue to experience alienating forces which detach them from the meaning and fulfilment of labour. The lack of availability of expressing discontent and stress in a public, group manner through strikes or other action will, inevitably, result in higher levels of absence due to sickness.

Commentary

This question, as you should have noted from the number of marks on offer, *involves* you in all the skill domains. You should approach it by first **interpreting** the question and looking for clues in the way the question is phrased. Let us examine the question more closely. You are asked 'How far do you agree ...'. This means that the examiner wants you to put your point of view after having carefully examined and weighed up other, contrary and supporting views. In short, this is **evaluation**. You must therefore put as much information for and against, as you work through your answer. Do not leave your evaluation until the very end of your answer.

The evaluation in the above answer involves critical views on alienation, which is a Marxist concept. This should be your starting point – it is the bench mark against which you should measure all other perspectives from your knowledge store. Obviously you must come to your own conclusion or, if you cannot definitely arrive at a conclusion, you should point out that the evidence presented is inconclusive and perhaps suggest avenues for further research.

Now, read the answer again and mark the points at which you think evaluation has been carried out. The first few sentences have been done for you as a guide.

Evaluating qualitative data

The following question still requires you to evaluate in great detail and you also have to interpret the question. You will need to follow the stages you went through with the earlier question.

Item G

We are not yet at the stage where the civil servants could be accepted as the real rulers of the country. But the tendency in that direction at the present day arises from the increasing difficulty and complexity not only of government but of all organised life and activity. Those who would try to avoid it by reducing the activities of government would, from the point of view of the democrat, not be solving the problem but abandoning any attempt at its solution. For they would be handing over the decisions in many matters which affect us all to even less responsible people, for instance to the managerial class which increasingly exercises the real power in matters of business and finance. Everywhere the 'iron law' of oligarchy holds, that the more difficult and complicated things become the more those who are on the spot all the time and devote their whole attention to the work will exercise effective control over the decisions taken.

Source: G. C. Field, *Political Theory*, p. 12, Methuen: London 1965

In any organisation oligarchy is inevitable. Critically analyse this view and explain why large organisations have problems in being democratic. *(10 marks)*

Answer

Robert Michels (*Political Parties*) thought that in any large organisation, from the state to industrial enterprises, democracy was impossible without an effective system of organisation. By democracy he means the election of people to positions of power by the will of the people as expressed through a majority in a free election. Michels also notes that, inside these large organisations, there is a paradox. This is the fact that organisations are inevitably arranged in a hierarchical manner and therefore any real democracy becomes lost as decision making has been distilled to be conferred upon a small group. Representative democracy is, by definition, control by a small representative group. 'Who says organisation, says oligarchy,' wrote Michels, and this was to form the basis of his famous 'Iron law of oligarchy'. Michels believes that all bureaucracies are the 'sworn enemy of individual liberty'.

Selznick (*TVA and the Grass Roots*), writing from a functionalist perspective, stated that his study of an American Government institution set up in 1933 to tackle the problem of poverty had developed into an oligarchy. He pointed out that when the survival of the organisation was threatened the original ideals were ignored – including the notion of democracy. He concluded that the scheme was run largely to serve the interests of the leadership rather than the public as originally envisaged.

An opposing view, claiming that bureaucratic organisations may be democratic, has been expressed by **Lipset *et al.*** (*Union Democracy*). They carried out a study of a printing union in America and found that democracy was effectively carried out. There were regular free elections for all officials, together with a powerful 'separation of powers', resulting in checks and balances throughout the organisation. In addition the officials did not have special 'perks' which might induce them to hold on to their position using any means at their disposal. They did note, however, that the organisation they studied was not representative of other organisations they had studied. They agreed that, generally, large organisations were not conducive to democratic principles.

One of the main reasons given for the introduction of representational democracy is that it is efficient, given the large numbers being dealt with in any population. This was, of course, the position held by **Weber** in his construction of the ideal type bureaucracy. He pointed out that they are most efficient because they provide a rigid framework within which those involved have to operate. The rules governing the rights and the duties of each individual are prescribed and limited with very precise detail. Not every theorist is in agreement with this view however.

Gouldner (*Patterns of Industrial Bureaucracy*) made a study of a gypsum plant in America. He found that there was a distinct separation of bureaucratic influence between the gypsum mine and the factory attached to it. The miners were far more autonomous than the factory and they were often able to make their own decisions concerning work procedures. Inside the gypsum plant there was a clear hierarchy and, on the surface, a strong bureaucratic system seemed to operate. The main problem was at the interface where the management of the plant tried to increase bureaucratic control within the mine area. This was successfully resisted by the miners because of their powerful unionisation and solidarity of purpose.

Burns and Stalker (*The Management of Innovation*) have tried to enhance Weber's ideal type of bureaucracy by dividing it into two types. First, a **mechanistic** type where there is a clear hierarchy of power and a stable organisation. All personnel are given clearly defined roles and chains of command. Second, an **organic** type where there is no clear hierarchy of power and an unstable market. There are no clearly defined roles and decision making is an 'ad hoc', corporate event.

Blau (*The Dynamics of Bureaucracy*) has shown that the introduction of bureaucratic systems is not always a guarantee of efficiency. He noted in his study that many practices of an informal nature were 'short cuts' introduced by the staff against regulated practice. The end result was a more efficient and smoother processing than would have been possible under the prescribed system.

It appears, from the evidence provided in the item and from empirical studies mentioned, that oligarchies are perhaps an inevitable part of large-scale organisations. If this is the case then democracy is increasingly difficult to equate with large organisations.

Commentary

There are two separate instructions in the question which indicate clearly what is expected of you. You have to **critically analyse** and **explain**. You should, by now, be at the stage when instructions like this set your mind looking for arguments **for** and arguments **against**. You have to be sure, however, that you are arguing for and against the correct issue or sociological concept. This is where your interpretative and application skills will be of the utmost importance.

Having correctly identified what it is that the examiner is seeking you are still not ready to begin writing. Remember, a few minutes' planning can save you hours of regret later. Imagine you are a barrister preparing an argument for a jury. You have, of course, to be convinced of your client's situation. (You can ascertain this from the way in which the question is phrased – **interpretation** and **application**.) A rough list of theoretical arguments and empirical studies supporting them can be placed in two columns – one in support of your position, the other against. Try to include as many perspectives as possible – but only if they are relevant! Don't try to introduce, say, an interactionist view simply because you feel compelled to do so. It may be that the point at issue is one which is not addressed by the interactionists and you will look silly if you try to invent an explanation from this perspective.

Finally, you should produce a conclusion which either supports or refutes the stance taken by your 'client'. In other words you have to change roles and be a member of the jury. Don't be afraid to have an opinion. Examiners like you to show you have independence of thought but, remember, you must make a balanced, rational decision. Avoid writing a political tract which is a one-sided outburst in support of your own ideological stance.

The question on Item I gives you an opportunity to try out your skills of evaluation.

Item H

Leisure activities are principally the domain of the large capitalist enterprises and are part of the system of false consciousness which seeks to divert the attention of the working class away from the exploitation they experience. The state and capitalist industrialists combine in this assault upon the consciousness of the working class. This assault is made through control of their leisure activities in the provision of licensed premises for the sale of alcohol and gambling (in which the state, through the National Lottery, has become even more financially involved). As John Lennon remarks in his song 'Working Class Hero', all the above conspire to keep the working class quiet 'with sex and TV'. The commercialisation and control of leisure is simply a way of ensuring a docile and compliant working class. Their working week is aimed towards the 'weekend' and their 'holidays' – all of which are provided for by the large leisure and tourism industry and from which they make enormous profits.

Using information from the item and elsewhere discuss the validity of the arguments expressed in Item H.

Practice data-response questions

The two questions below are complete data-response questions which cover all aspects of the skill domains we have discussed. The first question (5.1) includes student answers to each of the five parts and a brief commentary on these answers. The comments suggest what sort of mark would be awarded for each of the answers. In looking at the student answers you should try to get inside the head of the examiners. For example, you might consider how well the student has **interpreted** the question and the data in the items, how well their knowledge has been **applied** and the extent of any **evaluation** offered. Question 5.2 gives you an opportunity to answer a full data-response question in the area of work, organisations and leisure and then to mark your own answers following the mark scheme provided – a mark scheme similar to those used by the examiners when they mark your paper.

Question 5.1

Item I

Figure 5.6

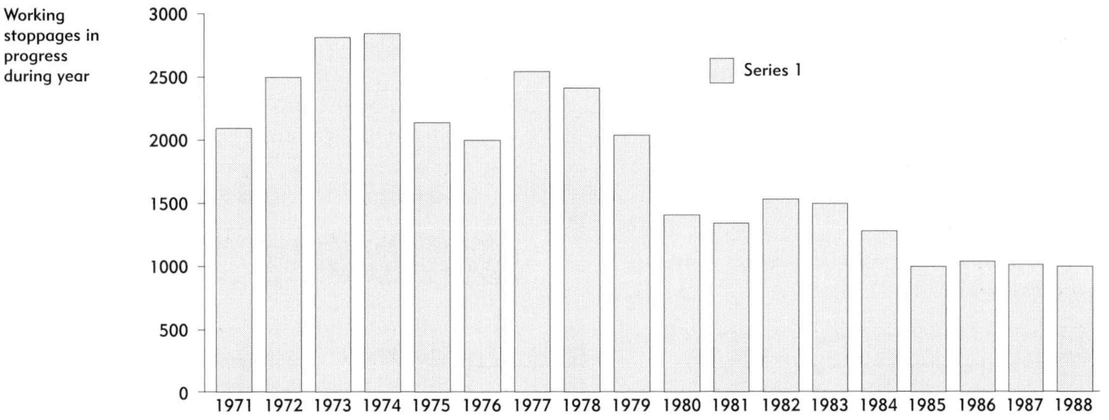

Working stoppages in progress during year

3000
2500
2000
1500
1000
500
0
Series 1
1971 1972 1973 1974 1975 1976 1977 1978 1979 1980 1981 1982 1983 1984 1985 1986 1987 1988

Source: *Social Trends* 27 (1997)

Item J

Scientific management and control over production

Taylor first published his views in the early part of the twentieth century in the USA, and Braverman has analysed the consequences of the principles upon which scientific management was based.

1 Taylor's first principle was that management should gather together all the traditional knowledge of working people in a particular industry and reduce this knowledge to 'rules, laws and formulae'. To Braverman this greatly diminished the power of the workers and their control over production because managers took from them the knowledge necessary to make production possible.

2 Taylor's second principle was that 'brain work' should be taken away from the factory floor and carried out in a planning department. Braverman calls this the 'separation of conception from execution' and he argues that it makes the detailed control of the labour process by the management easier.

3 The third principle was that management should plan out and give written instructions to every worker specifying exactly what they should do.

To Braverman, when all three steps were followed the management achieved control over the workforce.

Source: M. Haralambos, and M. Holborn, *Sociology, Themes and Perspectives*, 1995, p. 209, Harper Collins: London 1995

Item K
Marx and alienation

What, then, constitutes the alienation of labour? First, the fact that labour is *external* to the worker, i.e. it does not belong to his essential being; that, in his work, therefore, he does not affirm himself but denies himself, does not feel content but unhappy, does not develop freely but mortifies his body and ruins his mind. The worker therefore only feels himself outside his work, and in his work feels outside himself. He is at home when he is not working, and when he is working he is not at home. His labour is therefore not voluntary, but coerced, it is *forced labour*. It is therefore not the satisfaction of a need; it is merely a *means* to satisfy needs external to it. Its alien character emerges clearly in the fact that as soon as no physical or other compulsion exists, labour is shunned like the plague. External labour, labour in which man alienates his self, is a labour of self-sacrifice, of mortification. Lastly, the external character of labour for the worker appears in the fact that it is not his own, but someone else's, that it does not belong to him, that in it he belongs, not to himself, but to another. Just as in religion the spontaneous activity of the human imagination, of the human brain and the human heart, operates independently of the individual – that is, operates on him as an alien, divine or diabolical activity – so is the worker's activity not his spontaneous activity. It belongs to another; it is the loss of his self.

Source: K. Marx, *Economic and Philosophical Manuscripts of 1844*, p. 110–111, Lawrence & Wishart: London 1970

1 **In Item I, how many work stoppages were in progress in 1977?** *(1 mark)*

2 **Identify, and briefly explain, two reasons for the decline in the number of works stoppages in progress between 1977 and 1988.** *(4 marks)*

3 **Explain in your own words what Braverman means by the 'separation of conception from execution' in Item J.** *(3 marks)*

4 **Using material from Item J and other sources, assess the degree to which the main aim of industrial labour research is increased control of the workforce.** *(8 marks)*

5 **Using information from Item K and other sources, compare the ways in which sociologists have looked at alienation in the workplace.** *(9 marks)*

Candidate's answer

1 2,550

Commentary

This is correct within the parameters of the accuracy of the chart in Item I.

Answer

2 Unemployment began to fall because of the recession and workers were more concerned about keeping their jobs than fighting the management over pay and conditions. The Thatcher Government introduced strong laws to stop strikes and the power of the Trade Unions. This made strikes much more difficult to do.

Commentary

A good answer that demonstrates the skills of interpretation and application. It is concise and to the point. The grammar could have been better, but the essentials are there and this would merit the full four marks.

Answer

3 This means that the ideas which make new products or technological breakthroughs are separated from the workforce. They become the responsibility of an educated elite which is separate from the workers. This is in line with what Braverman calls the 'deskilling' of work.

Commentary

This answer accurately explains the meaning of the required phrase. In addition there is further explanation which shows that the student has understood the context within which this was used. A good answer, again meriting full (three) marks.

Answer

4 Taylor introduced scientific management in order to make sure that the workers' efficiency would be improved as industry became larger and more production was needed. He suggested that workers should be working as part of a factory 'machine' system and that they should be kept apart from each other as far as possible to avoid distractions. Not only this but the workers were not expected to think or to try and make any corrections to the work process. The design of the system was to be given to management. His work provided the foundation of the factory system and what Braverman has called the 'deskilling' of work.

Other thinkers have looked at ways of increasing output from workers. Among these Elton Mayo introduced his Human Relations School theory. He showed that the workers could not be treated as if they were nothing more than a part of a machine and that they needed to feel part of a human workgroup in order to be happy and content with their work. If they are treated like Taylor wanted then the alienation will arrive and they will not be as happy or as productive in their work.

When all is said and done it seems that the main aim of the studies carried out has been to maximise production and to make sure that the workers are controlled effectively.

Commentary

This is a well-argued answer but is too short to achieve high marks. Its shows that the student has a knowledge of Taylor's 'Scientific Management' and that there has been some evaluative reading. This is shown by the reference to Elton Mayo and the 'human relations' approach. The mark awarded could have been improved by showing how Taylor reflects the bureaucratic theory of Max Weber, and by extending a Marxist critique which is implicit in Braverman's work and which could have been linked with modern developments in industrial relations; that is an effective linking of Braverman with the widespread de-skilling of industrial production shown in many contemporary studies. Enough to gain perhaps five out of the eight marks available.

Answer

Marx thought that alienation was the separation of the worker from any meaning in work. What is produced is made because the worker works for money only. This is extrinsic satisfaction and occurs under capitalism where workers are made greedy and are treated as little more than 'things' to be bought and sold by the capitalists. Work does not have any meaning except as a means of getting money. The worker is not in control of anything and has to obey the managers and the owners of the factory where they work.

Marx said that the only way in which alienation could be removed from work was to get rid of the capitalist system which was the basis of all the problems in society, making people greedy and lose their basic humanity. The Marxists concentrate their studies on factory, production line working and see this as the main area of alienation in industry. The main criticism is that the division of labour into smaller and smaller parts creates a boring, monotonous and repetitive system where the worker has no control or say in production.

Weber, who can be said to be a sort of updated Marx, has pointed out that bureaucracy is an efficient system of production which can give benefits to both the workers and industry. It was Taylor who devised the Scientific Management approach which increased the division of the work process into smaller sections and increased the separation of the worker from the work process.

Blauner has tried to show that it is not only capitalism which causes alienation. He says that it is caused as a by-product of increased technology in industry. Blauner noted four kinds of technology in history. Craft, machine-minding, production line, and process production. These are in an increasingly alienated order. Alienation, for Blauner, has four elements: powerlessness, isolation, meaninglessness and estrangement. In the more modern system, process production, Blauner thinks that alienation is beginning to be reduced.

Braverman has shown that the deskilling of society and the concentration of workers in the same area is a calculated plot to ensure that they will be powerless and easier to control. The division of labour with deskilling makes each worker cheap and easy to replace. This can also be used to explain why workers do not go on strike so often because they realise that they are easy to replace and so they concentrate on keeping the job instead of arguing about pay and conditions.

Commentary

This is a reasonable account which includes some good analyses of studies which are relevant to the question. There is an attempt to place each theorist in context and the student would be given credit for this. Under the time available (calculated using the 'marks x 2' approach) the student has produced a quite sophisticated answer, but it is fairly short in length and restricted in evaluative content – although there is some evaluation of the Marxist position, little is offered on the work of Blauner or Braverman. Further studies, perhaps including Goldthorpe and Lockwood's famous 'Affluent Worker' study (which shows how the source of workers' instrumentalism is to be found away from the workplace, in the new 'privatised' family structure) and more recent work on increasing flexibility in the workplace (maybe debates on post-Fordism), could have been considered. This would have greatly enhanced the marks awarded; as it is this answer might be awarded five marks.

Question 5.2

Item L

Figure 5.7

Number of strikes and percentage of workforce registered unemployed 1978–87

	Number of strikes	Registered unemployed (%)
1978	2498	5.7
1979	2125	5.3
1980	1348	6.8
1981	1344	10.4
1982	1538	12.1
1983	1364	12.9
1984	1221	13.1
1985	903	13.5
1986	1074	11.7
1987	1016	10.7

Source: Adapted from R. Hyman, 'What's Happening to the Unions?', *Social Studies Review*, March 1989

Item M

Not all industrial disputes end in strikes. Sometimes it is possible to settle conflict peacefully through existing negotiating machinery. Should this not work there are various options open to employees. These can include work to rule, overtime bans, token strikes, strikes by key personnel and all out stoppages. To some extent these different forms of industrial action can be seen as alternatives and which one workers choose will depend upon local circumstances and workers' definition of the situation.

In addition to the above types of organised conflict there are also various forms of unorganised conflict. Before collective action can take place there needs to be a shared sense of grievance, a degree of solidarity, and a belief amongst the workers that by taking collective action they have the means to do something about their problem. If one or more of these conditions is not present it is likely that workers who experience deprivation at work will resort to unorganised conflict.

Source: J. K. Lane, *A Practical Guide to 'A' Level Sociology*, p. 46, Nelson: London 1985

Item N

The functionalist view of strikes is not of inevitability. Their belief in a society based on consensus extends to employers and employees, who ultimately share the same goals, but play different roles in the production of goods and services. Strikes are seen as a problem caused by the break-down in communication between employers and workers, which can be solved, providing adequate bargaining machinery is set up to settle disputes. More recent initiatives aimed at eliminating conflict and extending industrial democracy include the encouragement of workers' participation in management via the ownership of shares in industry. For Marxists, participation still does nothing to remove the fundamental inequalities within the system, which can only be removed by workers' control of the industry. The limited attempts at cooperative industries in Britain (e.g. Triumph Motorcycles at Meriden) have failed due to lack of development capital. It has also been argued that the culture of the British working class is against industrial democracy, as workers are socialised either to conform or conflict, not to participate.

Source: adapted from Catherine Court, *Basic Concepts in Sociology*

1 What trend is apparent in the figures shown in Item L? *(1 mark)*

2 What was the percentage difference between the number of registered unemployed in 1978 and in 1985? *(1 mark)*

3 (a) Item M differentiates between organised and unorganised industrial conflict. Suggest two forms of unorganised conflict. *(2 marks)*

(b) Using information from Item M and elsewhere give reasons why strike action tends to be concentrated in certain industries. *(4 marks)*

4 Evaluate the two sociological analyses of industrial democracy outlined in Item N. *(8 marks)*

5 Critically analyse the various sociological explanations for strikes. You should use information from the items and other sources you may have studied. *(9 marks)*

Mark scheme

1 Fewer strikes as unemployment rises (or similarly phrased explanation) – 1 mark.

2 13.5 – 5.2 = 7.8% – 1 mark.

3 (a) Any two from: persistent lateness, absenteeism, sabotage, limiting production, labour turnover high, reduced goodwill – 1 mark for each suggestion (up to the maximum 2).

(b)

0 marks	No relevant points made.
1–2 marks	A limited interpretation. There is a recognition of the greater strike activity in some industries (probably citing one or two traditional heavy industries as examples).
3–4 marks	Answers in this band will provide a range of reasons why industries with large workforces pursuing similar tasks and gaining similar rewards are more prone to strike action. For 4 marks a clear awareness of the relationship between industrial organisation and workers' attitudes and behaviour should be demonstrated.

4

0 marks	No relevant points made.
1–2 marks	Answers in this band will merely restate the information given in the item.
3–4 marks	Here, in addition to material from the item, answers will give some other sources, although evaluation will not be explicit.
5–8 marks	In this band, evaluation will be explicit, using material from a range of sources, illustrating both Marxist and functionalist arguments. Comments on the dangers of an over-rigid division between the perspectives is legitimate and should be rewarded.

5 0 marks No relevant points made.

1–2 marks Answers here tend to concentrate on one perspective and exclude other views. Evaluation is therefore severely limited.

3–5 marks This band will have a restricted number of explanations and, while evaluation is present, it will not be comprehensive.

6–9 marks A wide range of explanations, supported by further evidence. The evaluation will be *clear* and *explicit*.

Chapter 6

Social Stratification and Differentiation

Introduction

Knowledge and understanding

How to use your knowledge and understanding of stratification

Interpretation

Defining the area of stratification to be interpreted
Interpreting numerical data
Interpreting written data
Interpreting pictorial data

Application

Choosing how to apply your knowledge of stratification
Applying numerical data
Applying written data
Applying diagrammatic data

Evaluation

How to show evaluation in stratification questions
Evaluating written data

Practice data response questions

Introduction

Social stratification and differentiation are central to the understanding of the contemporary social (and political economic) world. Stratification systems are socially constructed forms of inequality which become manifest through concepts such as class, caste, gender, 'race', ethnicity, age, regionalism and disability. Social stratification can be defined as a hierarchical ranking system based on unequal amounts of power, wealth and prestige. Differentiation refers to the unequal treatment of individuals, groups, communities or even societies because of their assumed differences.

The concept of stratification will have been evident within all the substantive areas you have studied – for example, differential educational achievement, poverty, discrimination in employment – as well as being a topic in its own right. In this chapter you will be guided through the systematic development of skills, resulting in the successful application of the skill domains to questions specifically relating to social stratification and differentiation.

Knowledge and understanding

How to use your knowledge and understanding of stratification

The skill of knowledge and understanding in stratification terms refers to your ability to make reference to, and use effectively, sociological concepts such as embourgeoisement, theories (for example the New Right perspective) and studies (for example Anne Oakley's work). You should have learned a lot about social stratification and differentiation during your course, thereby equipping yourself with a thorough knowledge and understanding of the subject area. However, it is worth remembering that if you attempt to enter the examination with only a 'commonsense' understanding of stratification, you will fail that section.

A sociological answer requires some sociological knowledge. It may seem difficult to relate your sociological knowledge to the question at first, especially considering all the 'jargon' used within the issue of stratification. For example, words and phrases such as 'egalitarian', 'vertical segregation', 'a class in itself', 'gerontocracy', 'bourgeoisie', 'value consensus' and 'fatalism' can all seem quite confusing at first. However, persistent and determined revision throughout the course will provide you with a knowledge and understanding of this jargon. This is very important because such jargon is an essential tool for the sociologist as it provides precise meanings which will enable you to answer questions more effectively. For instance, you will be able to answer questions in sentences rather than paragraphs (which will save time), while still displaying your sociological understanding of the terminology.

The skill of knowledge also means knowing about the empirical basis of sociology, about the research that contributes to sociological understanding. In other words, it is not enough to list all of the names, concepts, theories or studies you can remember on the question area, you must know the basic ideas of different perspectives and the standard criticisms and be able to apply these as relevant to the question in hand.

This said, you still cannot pass Sociology A-level just through knowledge alone. You must also understand what the knowledge you possess *means*. Therefore be careful not to use the knowledge skill alone to answer all the questions. Try to find a balance in your answers that displays your knowledge and understanding of stratification, but which also demonstrates the other skill domains required by the question. For example, you can gain application marks for illustrating your answer with examples from newspapers, but the articles must be seen to support your sociological knowledge and understanding. Only when you understand

stratification issues can you interpret the questions and apply your knowledge in a relevant and evaluative way. Therefore, to demonstrate your knowledge and understanding skill when answering stratification questions you must:

- show familiarity with, and an understanding of, stratification concepts, approaches, theories, studies and evidence;
- show familiarity with, and an understanding of, the theoretical and practical considerations influencing sociological enquiry into stratification issues.

Answering the questions

Knowledge and understanding of stratification will help you to answer all the stimulus-response questions in that section, even if you are only required to demonstrate the skill of interpretation. They will make it easier for you to interpret what you are required to put in your answers, i.e. which knowledge is relevant and useful in answering the question. The 'action' words in a question provide information on how to answer it (look back to Chapter 1, page 5 where we list some of the typical 'action' words used when knowledge and understanding are directly required for answering a question).

Remember, however, that it is very important to use your knowledge and understanding of stratification when answering *all* the questions. For example, a one-mark interpretation question may not display your knowledge of that area, but your knowledge and understanding will help you to interpret the data supplied in the item accurately.

A pure knowledge and understanding question is unlikely to occur in the examination, but to help you practise this skill the following questions call only for knowledge and understanding:

1 Summarise the main features of liberal feminism. *(3 marks)*

2 What do you understand by the term 'polarisation'? *(3 marks)*

3 Outline the Weberian view of social stratification. *(6 marks)*

Interpretation

Defining the area of stratification to be interpreted

The skill of interpretation necessitates an accurate interpretation of the questions, but it also requires you to select from, and suggest the meaning of, a variety of data such as extracts from books, graphs, charts, tables, photographs or even cartoons. Data on stratification can often seem confusing because they cover such a wide area of social life. Sometimes it can take time just deciding which area of stratification the question is referring to; for example, is it class or 'race' or what? The best approach is to remember that all the clues are provided in the data and careful reading will inform you of the knowledge area in stratification that you are required to remember and use. For example, a chart headed 'Gross weekly earnings by occupation grouping (£)' is telling you which information to use from what you have learned. The key words are *earnings* and *occupation*, which should steer you towards identifying *wealth* and *class* as the relevant sections.

Interpretation questions require you to use *only* the information provided in the data (and will usually direct you to the appropriate item as well), therefore the area of stratification should be fairly clear. If you cannot decide which area is being asked about, you may be making the question more complicated than it actually is. It is amazing how often students make comments, such as 'I didn't think it was referring to gender/ethnicity/class, because it was *too obvious*.'

If you are finding it difficult to interpret the area, relax and approach the question and data again with a more open mind and straightforward approach. You know it is about stratification, so it can only be one of a limited choice of options, i.e. class, caste, social mobility, 'race', ethnicity, gender, wealth, etc.

Once you have defined the area of questioning, you must remember to keep an eye on the clock. These questions are worth only one or two marks and should take only about two to four minutes to write. Consequently, your answers should not provide too much detail, even if you do have a vast amount of knowledge about stratification issues, concepts and theories. Do not be tempted to write down more than is necessary. Interpretation questions do not need answering in full sentences – one or two-word/figure answers are fine. For example, a question may ask you to examine a table and decide something like 'What percentage of a certain group were in part-time employment in 1997?' Do not bother to rewrite the question in your answer; simply note down the percentage. The same rule applies if you are asked to identify a specific group, social concept or situation.

Answering the questions

Interpreting the question itself will be based on your knowledge and understanding of stratification and also your familiarity with the 'action' words which provide information on how to answer the question (each section of this chapter deals with interpreting the different skills and content required by the question). Examples of the sorts of 'action' words which call for the interpretation of data were provided in Chapter 1 (page 5). It is important to identify the 'action' word quickly to ensure that your answer is utilising the correct skill.

Interpretation questions ask you to select/interpret information from three forms of data:

1 numerical, for example, statistics on ethnic minority employment in the UK;

2 written, for example, an extract from Charles Murray's *Underclass: The Crisis Deepens* (1994);

3 pictorial (occasionally), for example, a photograph of a female in gender stereotypical employment.

This can get confusing, especially with stratification questions, because of the huge amount of statistical and written data available. Again, the best approach is a calm one. You have already defined the area of stratification that the data are about, you know how to answer the question by identification of the 'action' word, you have decided on the amount of detail necessary, therefore all you have to do now is decipher the numbers, text or picture.

Interpreting numerical data

Interpretation questions on stratification displayed in numerical form tend to be quite predictable, asking about:

- similarities or differences between or within groups, for example, men and women, black people and white people, rich and poor, old and young, etc., or between times such as the 1950s and 1990s;
- patterns portrayed by the data, for example, a trend in ownership wealth, average income, etc.;
- statistics or figures displayed in the data, for example, the percentage of children in poverty or the total of people in RGS group IIIM.

These questions require you to transfer diagrams into text or figures, as the following example shows.

Item A

Figure 6.1

Average gross weekly earnings (£)
April 1995 Great Britain

	Men	Women	All
Full-time	375	270	336
Full-time manual	291	188	272
Full-time non-manual	443	288	372
Part-time	126	102	105

Source: *New Earnings Survey*, CSO, 1995

What is the difference in average gross weekly earnings between men and women in full-time, non-manual employment? ***(1 mark)***

Answer

£155

Commentary

This question is simply asking you to subtract the earnings of women in full-time, non-manual employment from those of men in the same category. First, therefore, you need to identify the correct row and columns:

Item A

Figure 6.2

Average gross weekly earnings (£)
April 1995 Great Britain

	Men	Women	All
Full-time	375	270	336
Full-time manual	291	188	272
Full-time non-manual	443	288	372
Part-time	126	102	105

Source: *New Earnings Survey*, CSO, 1995

Second, subtract £288 from £443 to find the difference. The difference – £155 – is the only answer you are required to write. One word can gain one mark for this type of question.

What trends in average weekly earnings are indicated in Item A? *(2 marks)*

Answer

In Great Britain women earned less than men in the same category of employment (horizontal segregation) in 1995. Manual employees earned less than non-manual employees. Full-time employees earned more than part-time employees.

Commentary

This question is slightly trickier and requires you to interpret the data fully. It also asks you to identify **trends** and is worth two marks, therefore you must include **two** trends. Do not lose a mark by missing the clues in the question. There are actually three obvious trends in the earning figures, but any two will do nicely. The easiest way to identify the trends is to compare figures. Which are the highest? Do they have anything in common? Are they in the same column? If so, what does this show? Which are the lowest? Are they in the same column? Does this mean that column has something in common? If it does, then this is the trend. For example,

Item A

Figure 6.3

Average gross weekly earnings (£)
April 1995 Great Britain

	Men	Women	All
Full-time	375	270	336
Full-time manual	291	188	272
Full-time non-manual	443	288	372
Part-time	126	102	105

Source: *New Earnings Survey*, CSO, 1995

The shaded column shows that highest figures are all for men, while the boxed figures are the lowest and are all for women. Consequently, we can conclude that women's average gross weekly earnings are less than men's.

Item A

Figure 6.4

Average gross weekly earnings (£)
April 1995 Great Britain

	Men	Women	All
Full-time	375	270	336
Full-time manual	291	188	272
Full-time non-manual	443	288	372
Part-time	126	102	105

Source: *New Earnings Survey*, CSO, 1995

The same routine can be practised to find another trend in the data. The boxed figures show full-time, manual earnings, while the shaded area shows full-time, non-manual earnings. The 'all' figures show an amazing difference in the earnings between the two types of employment. Manual workers earned £100 gross a week less than non-manual workers in 1995. Therefore another trend shown is that manual workers earned less than non-manual workers.

Interpreting written data

Social stratification questions which ask you to interpret a piece of text from one of the 'items' provided usually require you to identify:

- the meaning of a sociological term or sentence, for example, data may implicitly or explicitly (not-so-obviously or obviously) provide information on the meaning of a term or sentence, such as class consciousness;
- implicit or explicit theories and/or concepts, for example, data describing the positive functions of income inequality can be interpreted as being written from a functionalist theoretical perspective;
- implicit or explicit sociological issues or debates, for example, the above example could be interpreted as being part of the 'role of stratification' debate.

The more implicit the information is in the data, the more likely it is that you will be required to use some knowledge as well. If this is the case, the answers will be worth more marks than if you were using only interpretation skills. Therefore the amount of marks given for the answer will inform you about whether to use your classroom knowledge or not. If it is worth one or two marks, the meaning can be interpreted/identified from the data provided as the question below demonstrates.

Item B

... there is not a single known society which is egalitarian in all respects. Functionalists see this as empirical support for their view that inequality is necessary for social equilibrium and they discuss the views of those radicals who have worked for the creation of an equal society as utopian ideology.

Source: J. K. Lane, *A Practical Guide to 'A' Level Sociology*, p. 75, Nelson: London 1985

What is meant by 'egalitarian' in Item B, line 2? *(1 mark)*

This question requires you to read the data referred to and interpret the meaning of 'egalitarian' from it. It is worth only one mark, which provides you with a massive clue about the information – it is going to be quite explicit. It may appear at first that you need knowledge to answer this question. However, careful reading will reveal the answer. Weaker students may misinterpret the data and use line 3 for the answer, but you can find the correct answer in line 6.

Explain briefly what is meant by 'egalitarian' in Item B, line 2? *(2 marks)*

This question appears very similar to question 1, but you will notice that it is worth two marks. Consequently, more detail is required for this answer than the first. You should interpret and draw information from Item A as before, but expand it with one piece of information from your own knowledge too. For example, you could support your definition by making a very brief reference to Marx's theory of communism, or by providing an example of an egalitarian society/community. However, do remember that this question is worth only two marks, so do not spend too much time mentally fishing in your vast pool of stratification knowledge to answer it (about four minutes will do).

Interpreting pictorial data

Very occasionally you may be asked to interpret sociological information provided in a pictorial form, such as a photograph or a cartoon. Although rare, this still requires you to demonstrate the same level of interpretation skills as numerical or written data would. Most of the time the picture will be accompanied by a caption or captions which will provide you with further information to help your interpretation. Social stratification questions requiring you to interpret a picture might ask you to identify a:

- **sociological perspective**, for example, a cartoon depicting former Conservative Prime Minister John Major taking a benefits cheque from the hand of an obviously poor person as they walk out of a post office could be interpreted as the New Right perspective;
- **sociological concept**, for example, a photograph of an elderly person reading the employment section of a newspaper could be interpreted as the concept of gerontocracy;
- **sociological debate or issue**, for example, an illustration showing a Sikh being rejected for a job on a building site because of his turban could be interpreted as part of the debate about ethnicity and employment.

You may be required to use a little more knowledge to answer these interpretation questions (the information given is usually more implicit than that contained in numerical or written data), but remember that the pictures and captions provide huge clues about the answer, as the following example shows.

Item C

See Figure 6.5.

Figure 6.5

Source: J. Fleming, 'Call Me Old Fashioned', Leeds Postcards

Which sociological perspective is illustrated in Item C? *(1 mark)*

This question asks you to look at the cartoon and read the captions. It is obviously a gender issue – the woman appears to be a secretary who is fed up with her boss's attitude – so, based on this interpretation, which perspective examines issues of patriarchy? It is as straightforward as that, and remember, one word can gain one mark, there is no need to write a great deal for this type of answer.

Interpretation skills of social stratification and differentiation issues can be practised in many different contexts, not just within the confines of the classroom. Any situation which provides you with the three forms of data can be used to practise this skill domain. For example, you may be sitting on a bus when you discover an old copy of *The Big Issue* which contains an article on homelessness. You decide to read the article and find it contains some statistics on homelessness over the last 10 years. Suddenly you notice from these figures that homelessness has increased over time. You have identified a trend and that is *interpretation in action.*

Activity

1 **Take any daily newspaper (preferably a broadsheet, e.g. *The Independent* – especially if you never read one) and read it.**

2 **Cut out any articles on stratification issues. These could be written, numerical and/or pictorial data. You have already performed some interpretation by identifying the relevant articles.**

3 **Now interpret the article fully by writing a summary of what it shows or argues. It may be useful to record the information in the format below.**

Newspaper/date	Article title	Summary/ interpretation
Times Educational Supplement, 24 October 1997	'The Fight Against Racism'	Black teachers have succeeded despite racial inequality in the education system (Beulah Ainley)

NB: File the articles in the stratification section of your folder. They could come in useful for obtaining application marks at a later date.

Application

Choosing how to apply your knowledge of stratification

Application requires you to use your sociological knowledge and understanding in a particular context, for example, to draw on ideas, explanations and arguments from other relevant sociological areas and link them to the question. In relation to application skills in stimulus-response questions on stratification, this means you must select material very carefully, because the only way to obtain application marks is to apply your chosen data relevantly to the question being asked. This may seem straightforward but, considering the huge amount of knowledge you have about stratification, it is sometimes difficult to decide exactly which issue/concept/theory is the most relevant.

The questions will, as always, provide you with clues about which information is being sought. For example, if you are asked, 'How far does sociological evidence support the embourgeoisement thesis?', you are alerted to the area of stratification being tested (affluent working class attaining middle class status) and should have the knowledge from specific or relevant studies to apply to the question (Goldthorpe, Lockwood, Bechoffer and Platt, etc.). The information provided in the items will also give you clues about which material is relevant or appropriate to use. The data given in the question will tend to focus on specific stratification issues which, once identified or interpreted, will provide you with an area of stratification that could be applied to an answer. You can either apply the information directly from the item or expand on the issue with your own sociological (or even personal) knowledge. As long as all information is applied relevantly to the question, i.e. it is clear how your answer is linked to the question, you will receive marks.

Remember that the material you apply to a question can be drawn from any topic area you have been taught, or from information gathered from other sources, for example, films, books, newspapers, etc., but do make sure that you use it within a stratification context relevant to the question. For example, if you are answering a question on stratification systems and choose to illuminate your answer with reference to Huxley's *Brave New World*, show how and why this book is relevant. If you can answer 'yes' to the following two questions after completing your answer, you have demonstrated your application skill correctly:

1 Are the studies/theories/concepts I have selected appropriate to this area of social stratification?

2 Have I used the studies/theories/concepts relevantly to the stratification question being asked?

Once you are sure that you have chosen the correct area of stratification to apply to the question, it is time to decide on the length of your answer. Application marks, unlike interpretation marks, are generally given in association with any combination of the other skills. For example, you may be asked to interpret and apply statistics on female employment, and this would require you to use the item provided and back it up with your own relevantly applied sociological knowledge. Consequently, it is quite difficult to advise you on the amount of information to include for an 'application question', because it will depend on the other skills required in the answer. As a general rule, however, an application question will never be worth less than two marks and the amount of marks will let you know about the depth of the answer, i.e. if the answer is worth two or three marks it will involve some interpretation and a little application. If it is worth eight or nine marks then all the skill domains will be called into full force, necessitating the detailed application of more complex sociological theories and concepts.

Applying numerical data

Applying numerical data when answering stratification questions will involve using relevant or appropriate statistics or figures. These data will usually be most effective when you are attempting to back up or reaffirm a written statement about a concept or theory. For example, if you have just applied your knowledge about the employment of ethnic minorities in the British workforce, official statistics could be used to substantiate any claims you have made.

The question below displays how numerical data can help you to apply your knowledge and thereby show your understanding of the issue.

Item D

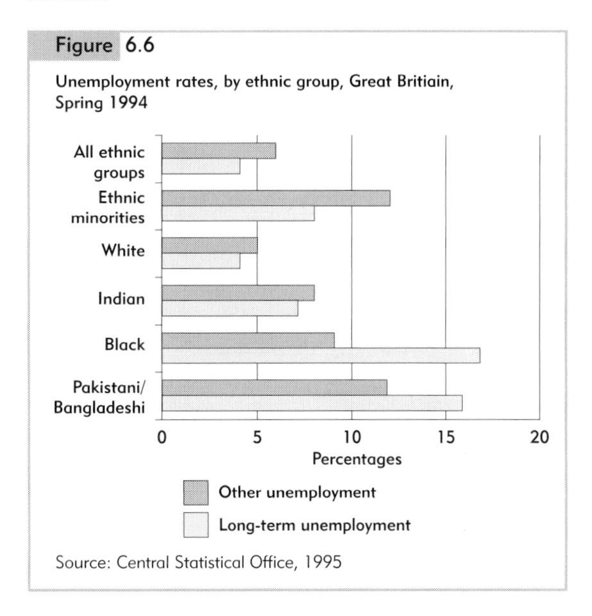

Using material from Item D and elsewhere, describe the relationship between recent levels of unemployment and ethnic minorities in Britain. *(3 marks)*

Answer

Minority ethnic group unemployment reveals disproportionate disadvantages for Pakistani/ Bangladeshi, black and Indian groups compared to that of the white population in Britain *interpretation of data in Item D*. Accurate figures on ethnic group unemployment are unknown, because the DfEE no longer provides a breakdown by ethnic group. However, Labour Force Surveys (LFS) indicate that as unemployment rises, minority ethnic group unemployment rises faster. The overall unemployment rate for minority ethnic groups, according to the LFS for 1987–89, was 14 per cent compared to 9 per cent for whites. *Application of knowledge from elsewhere*.

Commentary

The answer provided above is just one way of answering the question. As long as you interpret the question accurately, you can't go far wrong. This question requires you to use the data provided (interpretation) as a basis for applying your knowledge of the subject. The data shows that only 9 per cent of whites were unemployed at this time, compared with 28 per cent of Pakistanis and Bangladeshis, 27 per cent of black people and 14 per cent of Indians. Consequently, the relationship between unemployment and ethnic minorities in Britain shown by the numerical data provided is that they are more likely to be unemployed than the white population (see highlighted area on the chart below).

Figure 6.8

Unemployment rates, by ethnic group, Great Britiain, Spring 1994

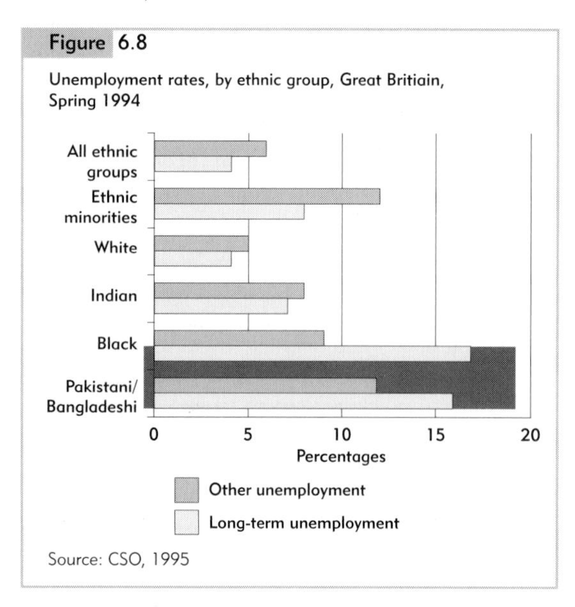

Source: CSO, 1995

Remember that you will receive one or two marks for interpreting the data correctly and one or two marks for providing further relevant information that you have learned in class (application of knowledge). You cannot attain full marks by only interpreting the data or just applying knowledge. If the question asks you to use the items and information from elsewhere, you *must* do both things.

You should be able to determine what is required by the action words used in the question, for example, 'Using material from Item D' calls for interpretation skills; 'and elsewhere' invites the application of knowledge; while 'describe' means that you are required to apply the information relevantly. It is also important to remember that a 'describe' command only requires you to outline the social phenomenon (in this case ethnic minority unemployment in Britain), not to explain why it occurs or to evaluate it in any way. Therefore, to answer the second part of the question you would simply apply your knowledge of minority group unemployment, probably with the support of statistical data, i.e. What studies do you know of on ethnic minority unemployment? What have these studies shown about unemployment levels for ethnic minorities in Britain? How can you apply this knowledge relevantly to the question? On this basis the question is only worth three marks, indicating that a long answer is not necessary. However, the answer would have been more detailed had the question read:

Using material from Item D and elsewhere, explain the relationship between recent levels of unemployment and ethnic minorities in Britain.
(6 marks)

This is because you would not only have to outline the relationship between unemployment and ethnic minorities, but also apply your knowledge in explaining why or how it happens, for example, racial discrimination, theories of ethnic minority disadvantage in employment, etc. Therefore, always identify the 'action' and 'command' phrases accurately in order to apply your knowledge relevantly.

Applying written data

Stratification theories/concepts/issues are applied, on the whole, through writing. To achieve the best application marks possible, you must convey your knowledge of stratification in a way that is relevant to the question. For example, if you are asked to explain the subjective nature of class, focus *only* on this part of class, i.e. subjective versus objective definitions of class. *Do not* fall into the trap of writing everything you know about class. The following question will focus your attention on the application of relevant written knowledge.

Item E

The future orientation of the middle-class person presumes, among other things, a surplus of resources to be invested in the future and a belief that the future will be sufficiently stable both to justify his investment (money in the bank, time and effort in the job, investment of himself in marriage and family, etc.) and to permit the consumption of his investment at a time, place and manner of his own choosing and to his great satisfaction. But the streetcorner man lives in a sea of want. He does not, as a rule, have a surplus of resources, either economic or psychological. Gratification of hunger and desire from simple creature comforts cannot be long deferred. Neither can support for one's flagging self-esteem. Living on the edge of both economic and psychological subsistence, the streetcorner man is obliged to expend all his resources on maintaining himself from moment to moment.

Source: E. Liebow, *Tally's Corner*, p. 68, Little, Brown and Co: London 1967

What explanations have sociologists offered for the differences between rich and poor, as shown in Item E? *(6 marks)*

The answer to this question requires you to interpret the extract provided in Item E and identify the differences that exist between a middle class lifestyle and that of the poor streetcorner men. Realising the massive inequalities that exist between rich and poor, you will then apply your own relevant sociological knowledge of the explanations sociologists have given for these inequalities, for example, individualistic theories, cultural theories and structural theories.

It is worth remembering that this question is worth six marks and should therefore be completed in some detail (two to three paragraphs). However, do not become tempted to evaluate the explanations. If this was required the question would have read:

Assess the explanations sociologists have offered for the differences between rich and poor, as shown in Item E? *(6 marks)*

Understanding what skill/s are required in answering stratification questions is vitally important because it ultimately determines the mark you get. The skill of application enables you to use sociological information relevantly which is crucial when showing your understanding of written data.

Applying diagrammatic data

Diagrams may be useful when trying to apply your knowledge and understanding to a stratification issue which lacks clarity. For example, an explanation of Ralph Miliband's concept of economic deprivation (lack of money) and political deprivation (lack of power) creating a vicious circle for those at the bottom of the stratification system may benefit from the support of a diagram to make your application clearer.

Figure 6.8

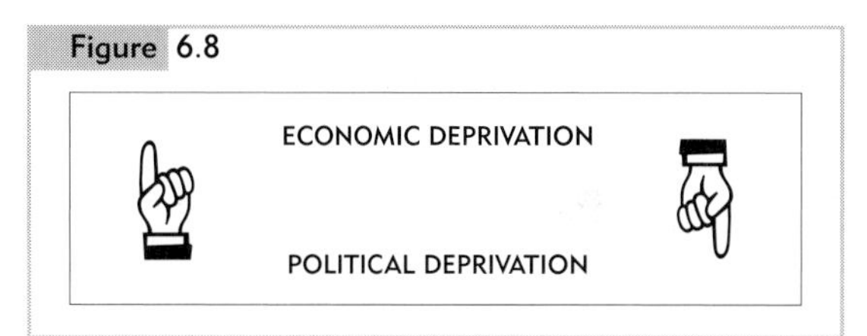

Using a diagram to clarify your relevant application of knowledge and understanding to a question will support your answer. For example, the following question requires a written response, but you could also apply your understanding with the aid of a diagram or two:

Identify and outline two different types of social stratification systems. *(4 marks)*

Answer

Two different types of social stratification systems are class and caste (see diagram).

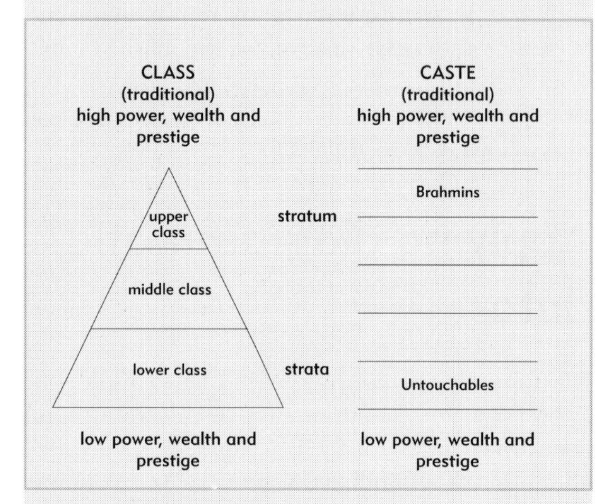

Both systems are hierarchical, based on unequal amounts of power, wealth and prestige. However, class is an open society where status is achieved and movement occurs between stratum, while caste is a closed society where status is ascribed, thereby not allowing any social mobility.

Commentary

Note how the diagrams support and clarify what is written in the answer. The question is worth four marks and should therefore take you about eight to ten minutes. It requires the application of knowledge and understanding, but does not call for too much detail. Half of the marks are gained simply by identifying two different types of stratification systems. However you must show that you understand *how* they are different. Using the diagrams immediately shows the examiner (in a very obvious way) that you have identified and understand the basic differences between the two systems.

Identifying when the skill of application has been used in a piece of work will help you to apply your knowledge of stratification in the examination. Read the following question and answer, and underline each phrase or sentence which demonstrates the skill of application, based on one or more of the following criteria:

- relevant use of knowledge in answering the question;
- applies a study, theory or concept relevantly;
- draws from other relevant areas of the syllabus;
- uses examples from appropriate political, social, economic and cultural events;
- contemporary events are used to support sociological points.

Explain why sociologists argue that 'race' is a socially constructed classification. ***(6 marks)***

Answer

There is no scientific evidence, according to Donald and Rattansi (1992), to support the idea that 'race', as a biologically differentiating category, exists. Society appears to construct labels which identify people according to a presumed 'race', when really it only exists within a social context. There are obvious physical differences between 'races' , such as colour of skin, and it is on the basis of these differences that racial stereotypes are based. Racial prejudice (an avertive or hostile attitude towards someone because of their presumed 'race') and racial discrimination (the behavioural manifestation of racial prejudice) are a common feature of our society, e.g. the Steven Lawrence 'race' murder, and show that even if 'race' is a social construction, people believe that racial groups exist and are different to one another.

Some sociologists, such as Herrnstein and Murray (1994) and Kohn (1995), have tried to sustain the ideas of Morton by arguing that 'race' is biologically determined and therefore not a social construct. However, over the past 50 years scientists and social scientists have investigated racial classifications and realised that all human beings come from a single origin. Consequently, even differences in skin colour are merely a reaction to environment and overlap constantly (who of us are truly 'white' or completely 'black'?). 'Race' as a classification is commonly accepted by sociologists to be a social construct based on socially created myths to differentiate between people who appear to be physically different.

Evaluation

How to show evaluation in stratification questions

Sociology is constantly either questioning society's commonsense assumptions or standing back and assessing the relative merits of different pieces of evidence. These processes are known as evaluation. Evaluation in stratification stimulus-response questions requires you to look at the strengths and weaknesses of an argument/concept/theory or study and make an overall judgement on which argument etc. offers the most convincing case. In other words, evaluation displays a balanced opinion based on all appropriate sociological and non-sociological evidence.

Evaluation could be seen as the most important skill you will utilise in the examination because it is given the highest amount of marks. It is a very difficult skill to acquire, as it consists of more than unsubstantiated personal opinion. It is not even enough to 'sit on the fence' and merely summarise all the different viewpoints associated with that area of stratification. The easiest way to master evaluation is to pretend you are a judge overseeing a court case. You hear competing claims about the case and have to weigh up all the evidence presented to you in a fair and objective way to reach your verdict. In order to justify your decision, you will consider which claim seems the most convincing and why. Once you are able to show an awareness and understanding of the main arguments on each side, you will have the basis of good evaluation.

Two elements should be observed as having equal importance when evaluating stratification questions.

1 **Critical analysis** – identify arguments and points *against* the concept/theory/study under discussion, for example, when assessing the social construction of gender roles you must present the biological arguments too.

2 **Balanced judgement/reasoned conclusion** – discuss both strengths *and* weaknesses of the concept/theory/study being examined and decide on which is the most/least convincing and why. Your conclusion *must* be clearly justified, for example, when assessing the functionalist concept of 'role allocation' you must present the positive contributions it has made to the debate on stratification, and also its weaknesses and whether the idea of value consensus and an open society lacks support from other sociological theories and contemporary societal references.

The second element of evaluation requires you to present the strengths and weaknesses of stratification issues which is not always straightforward. Social stratification and differentiation cover a vast amount of sociological information, therefore knowing all the 'pros' and 'cons' of different ideas, studies and theories, requires clear and compre-hensive learning. Once you have acquired 'the knowledge', you can examine the strengths and weaknesses of any stratification issue by answering the questions shown in Figure 6.9.

Test your understanding about the strengths and weaknesses of the following stratification concepts by completing the checklist in Figure 6.9:

- functionalist theory of stratification;
- New Right theory of social stratification;
- occupational grouping as an objective measure of class;
- the Essex Social Mobility Study;
- the underclass thesis;
- government measurements of wealth in Britain.

Remember that if you come down clearly on one side of the argument, you must justify this decision based on the strengths, weaknesses and alternatives you have presented. If you decide, however, to compromise in your evaluation, stating that the argument has equal strengths and weaknesses, make sure that you show very clearly why your judgement is balanced between the two sides (otherwise it will look as though you cannot make up your mind!). Finally, it is worth considering that there are no absolutely right or wrong evaluations – even sociologists disagree about the answers to social questions. Therefore, as long as you show awareness and

Figure 6.9

Strengths and weaknesses checklist stratification

Concept/theory/study ....

Questions	Yes/no	If yes, how?
STRENGTHS Does it clarify key concepts in sociology?		
Does it extend any sociological discussions/debates?		
Does it provide an alternative argument?		
Does it add to the understanding of the area?		
Is it supported by empirical evidence?		
Is it useful to future sociologists?		
WEAKNESSES Does it fail to address relevant issues?		
Do alternative arguments offer valid critiques?		
Does it lack empirical evidence to support its case?		
Does it overlook any important issues?		
Is it bias?		
Is it outdated?		

understanding of the main advantages and disadvantages of an argument, you have the basis for good evaluation.

Questions which require you to evaluate stratification issues will carry high marks (6–10 AEB; 8–16 IBS) and therefore necessitate a long and detailed answer. You will be required to use the information provided in the data and any other relevant sociological knowledge and understanding to evaluate the question. For example, you may be asked to examine whether class exists in modern Britain, which means that you must provide the arguments for and against this view and arrive at a balanced judgement on whether class does or does not exist.

It is worth remembering that evaluation questions will also call for you to use all the other skill domains, hence the high marks and depth of answer required. This also means that you have to be quite careful about the amount of time you spend on planning and writing your answer. You should have paced yourself throughout the stimulus-response question on stratification and therefore have a good idea about the amount of time you have available for each individual question.

Unfortunately, evaluation questions tend to be placed at the end of each section, but then always require the most time and consideration. Consequently, many students end up rushing the answer they should be spending most time on. To avoid this, attempt to work to the one mark = two minutes rule, saving **at least** 15 to 20 minutes for the evaluation question. If by some remote chance you do run out of time at the end of the section, don't panic! Use whatever time you have left to construct a detailed plan of your answer (with as thorough a conclusion as possible) and write this down instead. You should achieve more marks for this than you would for a hurried introduction alone, because you will have displayed all of the skills being examined.

Answering the questions

As ever, fast and accurate identification of the 'action' words and the marks available will enable you to start planning how to evaluate the question, for example, whether to emphasise the strengths or weaknesses of a concept, depending on your balanced judge-ment of the answer to the question. It is very unlikely that you will have to evaluate numerical, pictorial or diagrammatic data in a stratification question. This is because statistics and pictures tend to be evaluated methodologically, (for example, are statistics on class valid?) which means that questions evaluating numerical data are generally placed in the theory and methods section. As a result of this you can concentrate on evaluating written data (which may be supported with numerical data and diagrammatic data as part of your application skill).

Evaluating written data

All the studies, theories and concepts you have learned as part of social stratification, and the data provided in the question, will provide you with the material to evaluate any questions. Just remember that your evaluation should emerge from a balanced consideration of the different points of view about an issue, which you have supported with sociological evidence. You will be juggling a lot of complex information, both in your head and on paper, but what seems like an impossible task at the beginning of the course will become easier with practice. The following questions will familiarise you with, and enable you to practise, the skill of evaluation in relation to stratification stimulus-response (and structured) questions.

Item F

There is consensus, then, that feminism survives as a body of thought rather than as an action-based movement. As such, it has had some influence on academic disciplines, including sociology, where in recent decades, gender has come to be recognised as a fundamental basis of inequality in the distribution of power and resources in society. There are, though, a range of feminist perspectives. This theoretical plurality has taken place partly as a consequence of challenges to notions of there being a unitary category of women, influenced by postmodernist critiques. Differences between women, on the basis of class, ethnicity and sexuality, for example, have come to be seen as equally, if not more, important than their shared gender.

Source: J. Pilcher, '"I'm not a Feminist but ...", Understanding Feminism', *Sociology Review*, 1993

Assess the contribution of different feminist perspectives to the recognition of gender 'as a fundamental basis of inequality in the distribution of power and resources in society' (Item F, lines 6–7). *(12 marks)*

Candidate's answer

British feminism began in the 19th century with the aim of achieving equal rights for women. It was evident that women were disadvantaged in society because of their sex, for example women did not have equal rights in marriage or employment. Therefore women decided to seek emancipation through the movement of feminism, a movement which has changed and developed over the last hundred years to include a range of different female focuses. Consequently British feminism can be broadly divided into five perspectives: Liberal feminism, Radical feminism, Marxist feminism, Socialist feminism and Black feminism. <u>All of these feminist perspectives have expanded our knowledge of gender inequality by concentrating on particular areas of power and wealth differentials between men and women.</u>

Liberal feminists base their ideas on the principal of individual rights and freedoms, which means that women should have equal opportunities to men. Sociologists, such as Anne Oakley (*Housewife*, *Subject Woman*), have investigated gender socialisation and conjugal roles in order to show that differences between the sexes are socially constructed, e.g. girls learn to behave in a socially acceptable feminine way and women take on the role of mother-housewife in marriage as a consequence of that socialisation. Liberal feminists believe that there are no natural differences between the behaviour of the sexes, only nurtured ones. As a result of this they argue that removing discrimination through legal means would bring equality for women, because people would realise the socially constructed differences for the myth that they are.

The other feminist perspectives have challenged this liberal attitude by arguing that it ignores the power of patriarchy (sex discrimination laws being relatively ineffective, e.g. Sex Discrimination Act 1976) and the associated problems of class and 'race' inequality. Liberal feminism initiated discussion about the power and resource differentials experienced by men and women, which Marxist feminists used to develop their class based feminist analysis. Marxist feminists, such as Barrett, argue that women's lack of power (ownership of the means of production) results from capitalism, which needs the unpaid domestic labour of women to survive. Therefore the solution to gender inequality is the abolition of capitalism and the freeing of women to undertake paid employment on an equal basis to men.

Although this last theory enables us to see how capitalism can benefit from women, e.g. they supply free domestic labour which supports and nurtures generations of healthy and happy workers (Benston), it fails to acknowledge the benefits women give to men. Radical feminism concentrates on this issue, stating that women are subordinate in society because of patriarchy. Radical feminists, such as Firestone, believe that men sustain the inferiority of women in society and only by freeing themselves of men can women be free. Power is lost by women through the control men have over them, especially considering women suffer the burden of childbirth. Firestone argues that women are dependent on men when they are pregnant and when their children are young, therefore women can only be released from patriarchy when they are freed from the process of childbirth.

Radical feminism has been criticised for ignoring the differences in patriarchy over time and place, and the effect of class and 'race' on women. Socialist feminism addresses the issue of gender, class and patriarchy by combining Marxist and Radical feminism in a 'dual systems theory'. It is argued that both capitalism and men benefit from women's inequality in society. For example, Ansley argues that women act as a 'safety valve' for their husbands' work induced frustrations. In other words, men feel better about being oppressed at work (and so remain a committed proletariat) after taking out their anger on their wives (who unwittingly support capitalism by protecting the workplace from their husbands' 'revolutionary ire'). Consequently women become the slaves of the slaves. Women have limited access to resources and power, because they serve the interests of men and the state, the solution therefore is to get rid of capitalism and patriarchy.

It seems that Socialist feminists give equal weighting to class and patriarchy, but ignore 'race' and ethnicity. Black feminism believes that any feminist theory should examine racism, because it fundamentally changes the experience of some women. Sociologists, such as Yuval-Davis and Brah, have argued that racism must be challenged alongside patriarchy and class if women from all sections of society are to achieve equality.

The different feminist perspectives have emphasised different factors as the cause of female subordination, but all accept gender as the fundamental basis of sex role inequality. It is evident that women lack power and resources (consider the relatively low number of female MPs and the differentials in the average wage of nearly £100 per week in favour of men) and the perspectives outlined above have all contributed to our understanding of gender inequality by drawing our attention to social situations that may cause or perpetuate discrimination, e.g. socialisation, class, patriarchy and 'race'.

Commentary

You will be aware after reading this answer that it is a very good one. Do not be put off by this, instead use it as a model on which to base the structure of your future answers. This question is worth 12 marks and therefore requires detail (as you can see by the length of the answer) and thorough use of all the skill domains. Your first task is to **interpret** the question and spot the 'action' words. The question asks you to **assess** (action word), i.e. **evaluate**, what **different** (more than one) feminist perspectives have written about gender inequality (female subordination), specifically in relation to power and resources. You are therefore required to show **knowledge and understanding** of the main feminist perspectives (and associated studies), **apply** them relevantly to the title and **examine their strengths and weaknesses**, to reach a balanced judgement on their contribution to the sociological understanding of female subordination.

The evaluation in the answer above is evident in the critical analysis of the perspectives, contribution to the understanding of women's lack of power, i.e. the way in which the perspectives have been outlined and their strengths and weaknesses assessed.

You will notice that this evaluation takes place throughout the essay, not only in the conclusion. This is an important point worth remembering, because many students lose marks as a consequence of leaving any evaluation until the conclusion, thereby missing or forgetting to include valuable criticisms or observations about theories/concepts/studies which could have been effectively discussed in the main body of the essay. Also, by raising evaluative points in the main body of the answer you stand a good chance of picking up interpretation/application marks for keeping your answer relevant to the question.

Now read the answer again, but this time underline or highlight the sentences or sections which would achieve evaluation marks in the examination. To start you off the first evaluative statement has been underlined. If you have difficulty recognising what information is evaluative, use this as a guide.

NB: It is possible to pass this question without including all of the different feminist perspectives (you could argue that the above answer has failed to examine Walby's 'theorising patriarchy'), but only if you assess more than one perspective thoroughly to show critical analysis.

The next question calls for a great deal of evaluation based on providing evidence for and against a concept. The process in answering the question will be similar to that outlined above, but will require you to apply more knowledge from outside the social stratification topic area, in this case from 'poverty, wealth and welfare'.

Item G

Inequality in Britain has rapidly increased since the late 1970s, and only far-reaching economic and social reforms can avert the damaging consequences of the widening gulf between rich and poor, according to a study by the Joseph Rowntree Foundation published this week.

The study is the final report of the foundation's year-long inquiry into income and wealth. Its analysis details how the steadily increasing equality that characterised Britain during the post-war period sharply reversed from the late 1970s onwards ... The report also shows that as the rich have got richer during that time, the poor have undeniably become poorer.

Source: *New Statesman and Society*, 10 February 1995, p. 7.

Evaluate the evidence for and against the view that 'only far-reaching economic and social reforms can avert the damaging consequences of the widening gulf between rich and poor' (Item G, lines 2–5). ***(9 marks)***

The 'action' word in this question is a gift, as it actually tells you that evaluation is required ('**Evaluate** the evidence for and against ...'). Therefore you know right from the beginning that you will have to critically examine the arguments both for and against the concept that structural and political changes are necessary to stop the rich becoming richer and the poor poorer. You can apply and evaluate information from Item G, but the main body of knowledge for your analysis will come from elsewhere. The question is worth nine marks, which means that a detailed answer is required.

The best approach to take with this question is to make a basic plan before you start. Jot down all the studies/theories which support the view in one column and all those that disagree with it in another. You may find that some theories only agree with half of the title, for example, Marxists believe that only economic reforms (revolution to communism) are necessary to get rid of poverty (Capitalism), but that social reforms merely prolong the problem by removing the proletariats' revolutionary tendencies. Put these theories/studies in a separate column because this shows the examiner that you are really analysing the question and understand the 'pros' and 'cons' of each theory. Remember to include not only structural and system blaming theories, but also the individualistic and cultural theories which offer an alternative solution to income inequality. Only by providing all the evidence can you reach a balanced judgement about the value of the theories/studies you intend to use.

When you write your answer remember that your conclusion should answer the title based on the evidence you have provided, i.e. evaluate the validity of all the theories/studies in relation to your contemporary understanding of income inequality. The structure of this answer could take many forms, therefore the conclusion you reach could be very different to someone else's. This does not mean that you are wrong, just that your examination of the evidence has taken an alternative direction. For example, you may conclude from a functionalist perspective (structural) that there is a gap between rich and poor, but that it does not have 'damaging consequences' because it sustains the equilibrium of society (capitalism). Someone else may argue from a conflict perspective (structural) and agree that the title is correct in that the welfare state needs to be more generous and taxation systems have to be made more progressive. It all depends on your critical analysis of the evidence.

Taking into account all the advice above, have a go at answering the question. As the old saying goes, practice makes perfect and you really cannot get enough practice in evaluation. With this in mind, the following question has been left without an answer or a commentary. It is hoped that your ability to answer evaluation questions on stratification has been developed enough in this section to 'go it alone'.

Item H

Seemingly, the absolute necessity of children as real presences throughout history, as opposed to the temporary and fragile character of other phenomena such as capitalism, HIV and the European Community – however serious their impact on human beings – has rendered childhood completely mundane; we simply take it for granted. Unlike the poor, in reality it is children who are always with us. As an event childhood is not even different enough to specify a mode of experience that is peculiar to certain groups of people; it is what everyone does or has done at a stage in their lives. Beyond this childhood is a transitory phenomenon, we 'grow out of it', it is routinely disregarded on our way to achieving our proper destiny; adult rational life.

Source: C. Jenks, *Childhood*, p.60, Routledge: London 1996

Using information from Item H and elsewhere, assess the argument that childhood is a social construction. *(9 marks)*

Practice data-response questions

Question 6.1

A model answer is provided for each of the four parts of this question. These model answers are preceded by a brief commentary on the skills that the answers are expected to demonstrate.

Item I

Figure 6.10

Percentage of employees in managerial and professional occupational groups, by ethnic origin and sex

(Labour Force Survey 1987–89)	Men	Women
White	35%	27%
West Indian/Guyanese	17%	31%
Pakistani/Bangladeshi	27%	23%
Indian	41%	not available
All ethnic groups	34%	29%
All other origins	43%	30%

Source: Department of Employment, 1991

Item J

John Rex has provided the major Weberian analysis of 'race', linking racial disadvantage to class position and market situation. His analysis was formed in South Africa where the situation did not conform to a classical Marxist model. He noticed that 'real' privileges existed for whites, rather than the Marxist notion of 'false class consciousness' making them appear so to disadvantaged blacks. Rex realised that Weber used the concept of capitalism in both a 'wide' sense (i.e. that it allowed market opportunity to develop peacefully or in the spirit of adventure as in imperialism), and in a 'narrow' sense (i.e. just in imperialism). The relatively unfree labour of black workers could only be understood, argued Rex, in terms of a Weberian approach, which allowed for classes being generated by differential control of, or access to, property.

Source: M. Kirby *et al.*, *Sociology in Perspective*, p. 216, Heinemann: Oxford 1997

Item K

Above all, the concept of social class, which in British sociology has traditionally been the most important concept for understanding social divisions and social inequality, has come under sustained scrutiny. An increasing number of sociologists feel that the concept is no longer useful (see the debate in Lee and Turner, 1996), although a prominent group of powerful and vociferous sociologists continue to insist of its value (see notably Goldthorpe and Marshall, 1992). The controversy over class is partly related to the wider social and political context in which we live. The decline of the manufacturing industry, the rise of female employment, the growing visibility of ethnic and racial groups, the rise of consumer cultures and the growing importance of leisure all appear to suggest that traditional class divisions are of declining importance.

Source: M. Savage, 'Class and Stratification' in M. Haralambos (ed.) *Developments in Sociology*, vol. 13, p. 2, Causeway Press: Ormskirk 1997

1 **Re-write in your own words what is meant by '"real" privileges existed for whites, rather than the Marxist notion of "false class consciousness" making them appear so to disadvantaged blacks' (Item J, lines 5–8).** *(2 marks)*

2 **Identify and explain the trends shown in Item I on ethnic minority employment in the professions in Britain.** *(6 marks)*

3 **Examine the ways in which 'The decline of the manufacturing industry, the rise of female employment, the growing visibility of ethnic and racial groups, the rise of consumer cultures and the growing importance of leisure' (Item K, lines 12–16) could affect the usefulness of a concept of class in contemporary Britain?** *(9 marks)*

4 **Assess the contribution of Marxist and Weberian perspectives to the understanding of ethnic minorities' generally disadvantaged position within the stratification system in Britain.** *(8 marks)*

1 This is quite a difficult question for two marks, involving interpretation, knowledge and understanding. You are required to put the extract from Item J into your own words, which requires an understanding of the term 'false class consciousness'. However, one mark could easily be extracted from the data provided.

Answer

White South Africans received definite benefits in society which only they could achieve. Black people would never have had the chance of achieving these benefits, even if they had realised that they were in an exploited and oppressed position.

2 This question calls for interpretation, application, knowledge and understanding. The 'action' words and mark reveal that it does not necessitate evaluation. It is best to begin by outlining the trends shown in Item I, followed by an explanation of why these trends occur based on the application of knowledge from elsewhere.

Answer

The Labour Force Survey (LFS) data (1987–89) reveals that Indian men are much more likely to be employed in the professions than any other ethnic minority group (or whites) in Britain. Ethnic minority women generally (like white women) are not as prevalent in the professions as men, although West Indian/Guyanese women have almost doubled the employment rate of their male counterparts. As a whole, however, minority ethnic groups (men and women) are less likely to be in the professional/ managerial occupation groups than white people.

Skellington (1992) argues that the relatively high proportion of Indian men in the professions can be explained in part by self-employment. Limited job opportunities in Britain and a culture which values hard work to support the family resulted in many Indian men turning to self-employment (a professional occupation) to survive. Female ethnic minority representation in the professions can partly be explained by female discrimination in society as a whole (Barron and

Norris's Weberian 'dual labour market' theory suggests that women are more likely than men to enter lower occupations), however the success of West Indian women challenges this theory. It seems that young black women are becoming increasingly upwardly mobile, entering white collar employment with advanced qualifications. This could be a result of more equality in education, the absence of cultural restrictions to career choices for West Indian/ Guyanese women (these ethnic groups having quite a strong matriarchal history) and the fact that these ethnic groups have been resident longest in the UK.

Racial prejudice and discrimination remain evident in Britain (Social Attitudes Survey, 1984 and Runnymede Trust NOP, 1991), with two thirds of black people believing that they have been discriminated against in employment. This could explain the lower figure of ethnic minority employment in the professions, because a racist society would attempt to retain the highest rewards (which professional occupations tend to offer) for themselves.

3 The answer required by this question has to be detailed (it is worth nine marks), using all the skill domains to satisfy the 'action' words ('Examine the ways in which'). The question itself appears complicated because of the quotation used, but it is actually quite straightforward. You should start by interpreting the question, i.e. put the extract from Item K into your own words. This reveals that occupational changes, increased ethnic presence, growing capitalist culture and privatisation have all affected our sociological understanding of the concept of class. It suggests that class is not the main determinant of social status in contemporary Britain; it may not even be part of our understanding of social positions.

Once you have deciphered the question, you are expected to critically analyse the argument that class has lost its usefulness as a concept. It is useful to start by showing how class could help to explain social positions/differentiation in contemporary Britain (use studies/theories as evidence of your knowledge and understanding) and then provide the opposite arguments (remembering to apply them relevantly to the question). By doing this you are displaying clear evaluation skills, i.e. you are examining the strengths and weaknesses of the argument. Once you have completed this, you will be able to arrive at a balanced judgement on whether the factors in the question do affect the usefulness of the concept of class or not. The answer below is an ideal model and can be useful for planning answers when revising.

Answer

Class has been the classic sociological explanation of differential social positions in Britain. Marxist and Weberian perspectives believe that class (economic relations) is central to our understanding of stratification in society. More contemporary perspectives, such as feminism and post-modernism, however, have challenged the relevance of class in explaining societal differentiations, arguing that changes in the stratification system, e.g. increased female employment and a greater emphasis on privatisation, contribute more to a valid understanding of modern British social relations.

Marx defined class as a group of people who share the same relationship to the means of production. Weber defined class as a group of people who share a similar position in the market economy and therefore receive similar rewards. Generally class can be defined as a group of people who share a similar identity, have a similar lifestyle and therefore similar life chances. Examination of these definitions reveals that members of a class should have a great deal in common, they have to be similar in order to create solidarity, or, to use a less Marxist term, unity within the stratum. Therefore it becomes quite evident why sociologists have challenged the concept of class as the main determinant of social relations in contemporary Britain. Changes have occurred in the way in which society is organised and operates, resulting in other factors influencing people's understanding of their position in society. Marshall et al. may argue that class is still relevant to the British population, but they associate their status with gender, 'race'/ ethnicity, affluence and leisure activities, just as much as with occupation (the objective measure of class).

Classes therefore appear to contain very differentiated groups of people. It may be asked what similarity exists between an unemployed white male welder and a black female factory worker. Both are supposedly working class, according to occupational classifications, yet their life experiences, lifestyles and even life chances would be completely different. The decline of the manufacturing industries has resulted in whole communities losing their class status. Traditional working class people in areas based on industry, such as Sheffield, have started to identify with either their unemployed status as an 'underclass', or strata lower than the working class (as depicted in the film *The Full Monty*, 1997), or with the new middle class service industry they have been forced to enter. This has resulted in divisions within the 'so called' working class between those who can afford to indulge in the growing consumer culture and those who cannot even afford to live. Add to this the complex nature of 'race' and gender relations, which will affect a large number of this 'class', and you have a group of people who only share a similar past life as workers for industries such as steel.

Rising female employment is another change in the occupational structure that has altered perceptions of identity. Women are entering the workforce in ever increasing numbers; according to the Labour Force Survey, 1993, 44.43% of those in employment were women. However, women are overwhelmingly employed in part-time, low-paid employment. Beechy has argued that they constitute a reserve army of labour, available in times of need, but expendable when cut backs occur. This had resulted in radical feminists, such as Firestone, claiming that gender is the main influence on social position, with 'class status' actually being determined by sex. Consequently, female employment changes traditional perceptions of class. Women cannot be placed alongside men in terms of class/occupation. It seems, as radical feminists argue, that women are a distinct group in their own right. As Eichler argues, 'social stratification on bases other than sex are real, but so is sex stratification'.

It is worth noting that despite their disadvantaged position in the labour market, women still have more independence through access to employment. In some cases this can free married women from the traditional association with their husbands' class, allowing them to claim their social position from their role as worker, women, wife, etc. This situation can be applied to ethnic minority groups in Britain. 'Racial' groups have become more visible in all areas of the occupational structure. Indian men now constitute, according to Labour Force Survey statistics 1987–89, the highest proportion of workers in the professional/managerial occupational group. Increased access to the labour market for some ethnic minorities and high unemployment for others, e.g. Pakistani/Bangladeshi, has meant that assuming a general ethnic minority class position through occupation cannot be. In fact, it has been argued that ethnic groups are constituted from such varied and complex cultures, occupational groups etc. (Modood) that to assign them to a class identity makes no sense at all. It is more valid to examine the social positions of ethnic groups based on a range of criteria, including the effect of their presumed 'race'. As Weber argued, status groups (to which ethnic membership can be seen to conform) can cut across class to influence the amount of power possessed by that group and so affect their position in the stratification system.

Capitalist ideology, especially in the form of media pressure to consume everything from fad foods, such as 'pop tarts', to new exercise equipment for the home, has changed popular culture. It is claimed that we live in a post-modern society and that we have access to a 'mix 'n' match' culture, in which everything is relative and true meaning cannot be established. Consequently, it could be argued that society's members are searching for something 'solid' or real when participating in mass consumerism and extended leisure activities. Therefore class does not hold the key to modern social identity, as Cohen argued, individuals identify with what they can afford to buy, what they can afford to do, what sex they are, what 'race', what 'ethnicity', etc., etc.

The concept of class is useful as a tool for examining social stratification, because it provides a well researched starting point for identifying similarities in social groups. Its weakness lies, however, in its application to contemporary society, where social changes have caused many differentiations to become evident between its members. These differences can also form the basis of an individual's or group's social position and therefore need to be taken into account when attempting to form a valid account of stratification in modern Britain.

4 This question requires you once again to use all of the skill domains in order to achieve the full eight marks. You must start by **interpreting** the question, which involves critically assessing or evaluating the Marxist and Weberian approaches to racial inequality in Britain. It is quite a straightforward question, in that you are expected to explain (**apply** your **knowledge and understanding**, from the items and elsewhere, relevantly), and then show the strengths and weaknesses of (**evaluate**) each theory. Do not forget to include relevant contemporary studies, articles or issues if they support your argument. Your final **evaluation** will be based upon how much you think each has contributed towards a valid understanding of the race relations situation in contemporary society. Again, this is a model answer and should encourage you to revise stratification fully in order to reproduce this standard in the examinations.

Answer

Labour Force Surveys show that although there has been a reduction in most types of inequality between minority ethnic groups and whites, there still appears to be a considerable difference in the life chances experienced by ethnic minorities. Minority ethnic groups in Britain continue to experience disadvantage, compared to whites, in many areas, such as overall employment (Labour Force Surveys, Item I), education (Swann Report), private housing ownership and crime (*Social Trends*). It should be noted, however, that there is a great deal of variation in the pattern of inequality for each ethnic group. For example, people of African-Caribbean origin are much more likely to be the victim of all types of crime (*Social Trends*, 1994).

Both Marxist and Weberian perspectives on racial inequality approach the problem from a structural perspective. They both argue that racialism is linked to the economic structure of society, i.e. competition for scarce resources. This seems quite an appropriate and valid starting place, because Britain is a capitalist economy based on a free market and competition. Consequently, as Dahrendorf argues, everybody is searching for their place in the sun, or in other words, every worker and owner want to have the best lifestyle that can be achieved. However, in the quest for success some individuals or groups have to fail and these are likely to be the ones who lack power, wealth and prestige in society. Unfortunately, ethnic minorities in Britain have a history of disadvantage and despite the introduction of anti-discriminatory legislation, such as the Race Relations Act 1976, a legacy of racialism still affects their life chances today. Racial discrimination therefore affects the ability of ethnic minorities, according to Marx and Weber, to become owners of the means of production, a source of power. Weberian analysis parts from Marxist at this point to explain that issues of status and party, as well as class, can affect the market situation of minority ethnic groups in Britain.

Marxists argue that 'race' is a particular type of labour/capital relation which serves the interests of capitalism. Cox argued that it provides another differentiating point to divide the subject class and thereby prevent a communist revolution. The ruling class also perpetuates racial prejudice within society to justify the exploitation of that group. Therefore racialism is an ideological construction which was established to support class oppression. Cox has been criticised, however, for not taking into account that racialism can exist outside of capitalism. Neo-Marxists have taken this criticism on board, arguing that capitalism does not determine all social phenomena.

Another Marxist sociologist, Miles, argued that racial groups are stereotyped as different in Britain and this results in them being discriminated against. The manifestation of this discrimination is maintenance of black workers in the ranks of the proletariat. However, even in this class they experience worse conditions than their white counterparts, being treated as an expendable reserve army of labour, as Castles and Kosack found in their study of migrant workers. 'Race' is seen to be ideologically, rather than biologically, based, but with real consequences for those who are discriminated against because of it. Miles concludes that racism can only be understood in terms of capitalist class relations, because as an ideology it promotes false class consciousness by hiding true economic relations.

Marxism therefore assumes that racism is the result of capitalism, supported by hegemony to sustain false class consciousness and divisions within the subject class. Ethnic minorities are seen as having poor life chances, because they constitute a reserve army of labour based on negative images developed to perpetuate their disadvantage. It is a useful approach because it examines the exploitation of labour in a capitalist society and how racist policies are supported by the state (which seems quite pertinent considering recent legislation such as The Nationality Act 1981 and The Asylums Act 1996 which restrict immigration to Britain, suggesting that ethnic minority presence is a problem). However, Marxism does tend to over-emphasise the role of class, thereby marginalising the concept of 'race' and ethnicity. It is also assumed that all ethnic groups form part of the subject class, but as Item I shows, many ethnic minorities have 'escaped' proletarian occupations, entering middle class professional occupations. Weberian sociologists have argued that Marxist approaches have ignored the concept of power, which is very important in explaining the differential inequality experienced by minority ethnic groups.

Weberian sociologist Rex, and Marxist sociologist Miles, agree that ideology forms the basis of racism and that it reflects structural realities, such as colonial belief in the biological inferiority of black people. However, despite basic similarities between the two approaches, many differences are apparent. Weber argued that power distribution results in stratification. Parkin applied this to the study of race relations and concluded that ethnic minorities were negative status groups who lacked power. Rex developed the Weberian analysis of 'race' inequality further, 'linking racial disadvantage to class position and market situation', as shown in Item J. He argued that ethnic minorities form an 'underclass' (a class below the working class), because they are disadvantaged in housing, education and employment. Black workers were seen to be limited to the 'secondary labour market', experiencing poor pay, poor prospects and poor conditions. They have a very low market situation and lack power to enter the 'primary labour market' to improve their life chances.

The Weberian analysis of racial inequality moves beyond the economic determinism of Marxism. It acknowledges that racism is created by society through daily interactions and historical context. It realises the influence of power (or lack of it) on individual and group life chances. Marxists, however, would challenge the emphasis on status, rather than class, and racism's refusal to identify class as the main cause of discrimination. In conclusion, both theories develop our understanding of ethnic minorities' disadvantaged position in the stratification system, allowing us to realise that the ideological nature of 'race' has very real consequences for those involved.

Question 6.2

A detailed mark scheme is provided after the questions. Think about the skills that are being examined by each part of the question before attempting your answers.

Item L

According to the prevailing sociological perspective, our masculinity or femininity is not biologically determined. Although our biological or genetic inheritance gives each of us the sex organs of a male or female, how our 'maleness' or 'femaleness' is expressed depends on what we learn. Our masculinity or femininity, that is, what we are like as sexual beings – our orientations and how we behave as a male or a female – does not depend on our biology but on social learning. It can be said that while our gender is part of our biological inheritance, our sexuality (or masculinity or femininity) is part of our social inheritance.

Source: J. M. Henslin, 'On Becoming Male: Reflections of a Sociologist on Childhood and Early Socialisation', in *Down to Earth Sociology*, pp. 122–3, New York Free Press 1993

Item N

Marx defines class with reference to ownership of the means of production. As Geoffrey Kay explains in his clear presentation of Marx's theory of the working class, the proletariat is defined by its complete dependence on the wage. Yet for Marx the typical wage-labourer is male. In his discussion of the introduction of machinery, Marx refers to 'women and children' as 'that mighty substitute for labour and labourers'. He states that the 'value of labour power was determined not only by the labour-time necessary to maintain the individual adult labourer, but also by that necessary to maintain his family'. Marx goes on to argue that capital's expansion into the employment of women and children had the consequences of usurping the labour necessary in the home, of depreciating the value of labour power and raising the degree of exploitation. It is currently a matter of dispute as to whether Marx is correct in this argument.

Source: M. Barrett, *Women's Oppression Today*, p. 125, Verso: London 1980

1 What is meant by 'capital's expansion into the employment of women and children had the consequence(s) of usurping the labour necessary in the home' in Item N, lines 15–17? *(2 marks)*

2 Illustrate, with reference to Item N, the Marxist feminist contribution to the sociological understanding of female employment in Britain. *(6 marks)*

3 Critically examine the view that the division of domestic labour by sex in Britain has become more equal over the last 40 years. *(8 marks)*

4 Assess the arguments for and against the view that 'our sexuality (or masculinity or femininity) is part of our social inheritance' (Item L, lines 12–13). *(9 marks)*

Mark scheme

1	0 marks	No relevant interpretation.
	2 marks	Any relevant form of words which encompasses the notion that women's and children's domestic labour is seen as supporting capitalism.
2	0 marks	No relevant points.
	1–2 marks	For the clear identification of what Marxist feminism believes causes female subordination, for example, capitalism requires the unpaid labour of women to survive.
	3–6 marks	For applying the Marxist feminist perspective to female employment, including the use of relevant studies.
3	0 marks	No relevant points.
	1–2 marks	A commonsense understanding of the domestic labour debate is likely to be given, with evidence not being very well applied. As a consequence evaluation is likely to be asserted rather than argued. Spelling, punctuation and grammar may show serious deficiencies and frequent errors.

3–5 marks Answers show awareness of the debate surrounding divisions in domestic labour by sex, and are able to apply appropriate material and evidence towards it. However, in terms of evaluation, there may be some imbalance, with answers tending to take the inequality of women in the home as a constant since 1957.

Fair to good logical expression of ideas and competent use of a range of conceptual terms.

There may be minor errors of punctuation and grammar, however, they will not affect the clarity of the answer.

6–8 marks Answers are likely to be more balanced, displaying a good coverage of the arguments for and against growing female equality in the home. Reference to the effect of occupational changes in male employment/unemployment on the allocation of domestic labour by sex, where applied, should be rewarded. Evidence will be applied directly towards the question set.

Very good expression of ideas and the precise use of a broad range of conceptual terms.

Spelling, punctuation and grammar will be of a very good to excellent standard. Commonly and less commonly used sociological terms will almost always be spelt correctly.

5 0 marks No relevant points.

1–3 marks A commonsense understanding of the social construction of gender is likely to be given, with evidence not being very well applied. Any studies cited are likely to be described, rather than applied. Long descriptions of the differences between men and women are likely. As a consequence evaluation is likely to be asserted rather than argued.

Spelling, punctuation and grammar may show serious deficiencies and frequent errors.

4–6 marks Answers show awareness of the debate surrounding the nature/nurture debate and are able to apply appropriate material and evidence towards it. There will be an attempt to examine the strengths and weaknesses of each side of the argument. However, in terms of evaluation, there may be some imbalance, with answers tending to provide more evidence for the argument than against it.

Fair to good logical expression of ideas and competent use of a range of conceptual terms.

Spelling, punctuation and grammar will be of a reasonable standard.

7–9 marks Answers provide a balanced debate concerning the allocation of gender roles. The evidence used will provide good coverage of the arguments for and against nature versus nurture as the determinant of gender behaviour. Evidence will be applied directly towards the question set and a clear justification will emerge for an evaluative conclusion, which will emerge directly from the debate.

Very good to excellent expression of ideas and the precise use of a broad range of conceptual terms.

Spelling, punctuation and grammar will be of a very good to excellent standard.

Chapter 7

Culture and Identity

Introduction

This chapter covers some of the fundamental philosophical and sociological questions which have concerned generations of writers. For example, what is a person and how is society possible? In other words, what are the bonds that link people in terms of shared values, attitudes and beliefs – what is the nature of culture?

Culture is created by people. In everyday life we commonly assume culture to be 'high' culture such as great art, literature and classical music. Alternatively, we speak of 'popular' culture such as Oasis, *Coronation Street* or tabloid newspapers. For sociologists, however, 'culture' has a much wider meaning and includes all human creations: the clothes we wear, the houses we live in, and the food we eat are all products of our common culture.

All sociologists are concerned with the relationship between the individual human being and the culture that they live in. People may produce culture but, at the same time, the culture of a society will help to shape the personality of the individual. People have to learn how to become a member of society, and this learning process is called the process of **'socialisation'**. This is an ongoing process of development which starts at birth and continues throughout our lives.

Most textbooks which look at issues of culture and identity tend to concentrate on the effects of race, gender, social class and ideology, particularly as passed on via the mass media. In this chapter we relate culture and identity to the very nature of 'the self' and look at how the self is affected by such factors as race and gender. In summary, we see the person as an agent – a unique individual with an identity of their own.

Knowledge and understanding

Questions about issues of culture and identity can be drawn from any area of social life and you can gain a significant number of marks by using knowledge points from other areas of the syllabus. For example, if you are reading about 'class cultures' in the stratification chapter of your textbook, ask yourself if these class cultures could play a role in the formation of a person's identity.

Culture and identity knowledge questions usually ask you to identify a piece of text or perhaps a particular theory.

The following data-response question will give you a clear idea of what is expected in order to gain one knowledge and understanding mark in the examination. To gain this mark you must demonstrate your ability to read and understand the passage by picking out the key word and giving a very brief outline of the process the key word describes.

Item A

When Itard found and took Victor, the 'Wild Boy of Aveyron', into his family, he provided the basis for a continuing debate about the social and the natural. Victor could not feel pain and could not talk. Possible explanations for this included the idea that he was physically damaged as a result of living in the wild or that he had perhaps not been socialized to experience pain and to talk. Itard eventually trained Victor to talk and to feel pain, but his speech always remained underdeveloped. Now, most sociologists and psychologists would argue that socialization plays an important part of language learning and that there is an ideal time when children learn to speak. If children do not hear speech during that time, they may have great difficulty in learning to speak.

Source: N. Jorgensen *et al.*, *Sociology: An Interactive Approach*, p. 37, Collins Educational: London 1997

What is the name of the sociological concept used to describe the process of how children learn the culture of society? *(1 mark)*

In order to get the one mark you would need to make reference to the process of socialisation.

Interpretation and application

If the question is about interpreting a theory, you may be asked to explain the sociological perspective that an item contains. For example, is the item written from an interactionist perspective or some other viewpoint? The information provided in the items will give you some information on the meanings asked for. However, the meaning of the concept or theory may not be explicit. In other words, you will have to give your interpretation of what the item means by drawing upon both your own knowledge of sociology and your skill in interpreting the text.

You may be asked to describe a sociological debate. In the example given below, from Joanne Finkelstein, you are asked to comment on the relationship between agency and structure. The following questions focus on the power of an individual. Do people have power irrespective of the circumstances in which they find themselves? All sociological theories make assumptions about the 'human agent' or the self. Some theories suggest that people are pushed about by forces outside of their control; other theories suggest that people are not pushed about by outside forces. The information you obtain from this exercise can be used to form evaluative points and interpretation points in relation to a range of sociological theories.

Item B

Clearly, physical appearances are understood to do more than differentiate the sexes; they act as social passports and credentials, often speaking out more eloquently than the individual might desire ... In the following example from Primo Levi, appearances are used as a credential of one's humanity. In his document of the Nazi concentration camps, *If This Be A Man* (1987), Levi described an episode where an inmate of Auschwitz, L, understood even in the torturous circumstances of the camps, that there was power to be gained through deliberately fashioning one's appearance. L went to extreme lengths to cultivate his appearance, so, in the barbaric conditions of the concentration camp where everyone was soiled and fouled, his hands and face were always perfectly clean, and his striped prison suit was also 'clean and new': 'L knew that the step was short from being judged powerful to effectively becoming so ... a respectable appearance is the best guarantee of being respected ... He needed no more than his spruce suit and his emaciated and shaven face in the midst of the flock of his sordid and slovenly colleagues' to stand out and thereby receive benefits from his captors.

Source: J. Finkelstein, p. 136, *The Fashioned Self*, Polity: Oxford 1995

1. **What do you understand by the comment in the item 'appearances ... act as social passports and credentials'?** *(2 marks)*
2. **According to the information in the item, does L have power?** *(2 marks)*
3. **According to the information in the item what, if any, is the origin of his power?** *(2 marks)*

What are examiners looking for in answer to these questions? Your answers should give the examiner an insight into your understanding of the nature of power. Power is not simply something which governments, classes or large companies have, but a capacity which we all have and which we can all draw upon, even in circumstances in which we look to be totally powerless. The suggestion in this passage is that power is the ability of the person to make another person do something that the first person wants them to do. The questions give you an opportunity to explore your own opinions and beliefs about the nature of an individual's power.

Answer

1 By the phrase 'appearances ... act as social passports and credentials', the item suggests that people treat individuals differently according to the way that a person looks. In the case of L, because he looked like a human being, the guards treated him like a human being.

2 There are two possible responses, both of which are valid.

Response A: Although L manipulates his appearance in an effort to secure advantages, the item makes it clear that L is a prisoner in a concentration camp and, as such, may lose his life at any moment. On balance, therefore, L has little power over his own future.

Response B: As the item clearly shows, by maintaining his own appearance L is able to influence a degree of control over his captors. This shows that even in the most oppressive of situations an individual can still exercise control over her or himself which can be used to exercise power over others. On balance, L has a degree of power over his own future.

Commentary

These two responses are contradictory but equally valid answers. They are very different interpretations of the item, but each makes a short but convincing response to the question by drawing upon the item and making sense of the information given.

3 If you believe that L has a degree of power, then you must state this and follow it with a short explanation for the basis of your opinion. For example:

In my view the item clearly shows that L has a degree of power. L manipulates his appearance in an effort to mould the captors' perception of him as a person. This manipulation of his appearance is the source of L's power.

However, if your view is that L is relatively powerless, then again you must state your view and follow it with a short justification. Consider the following example:

In my view the item clearly shows that L has no power over most areas of his life. L manipulates his appearance in an effort to mould the captors' perception of him as a person. The item may suggest that this manipulation of his appearance is the source of L's power. However, the captors could at any time take L's life or subject him to any indignity, and L would be powerless to resist.

Commentary

As above, these two responses are contradictory, but equally valid, responses and would gain marks.

In essence, you have to be confident when answering interpretation questions. State what you think the item is about and why you think what you do.

The aim of the extracts of text in this exercise is that you will further develop your understanding of what it means to be a human agent or a self. In the previous exercises we have implied that all humans have power and that all humans learn how to live a life and what it means to be a person by going through a process of socialisation. This exercise looks specifically at what it means to be a person. A person is a physical object, but what is it that makes people different from a range of other physical objects? When answering data-response questions, interpretation and application marks can be gained by drawing upon novels and films to highlight relevant sociological points about what it means to be a person.

Read the following item and answer the questions.

Item C

... androids equipped with the new Nexus-6 brain unit had the sort of rough, pragmatic, no-nonsense standpoint evolved beyond a major – but inferior – segment of mankind. For better or worse. The servant had in some cases become more adroit than its master. But new scales of achievement; for example the Voigt-Kampff Empathy Test had emerged ... Empathy evidently only existed within the human community, whereas intelligence to some degree could be found through out every phylum and order including the arachnida. For one thing, the empathic faculty probably required an unimpaired group instinct; a solitary organism, such as a spider, would have no use for it; in fact it would tend to abort a spider's ability to survive. It would make him conscious of the desire to live on the part of his prey. Hence all predators, even highly developed mammals such as cats, would starve ... the empathic gift blurred the boundaries between hunter and victim, between the successful and the defeated.

Source: P. Dick, *'Do Androids Dream of Electric Sheep?', Blade Runner*, Grafton Books: London 1986

1 According to Phillip Dick's text, what differentiates a human from an android? *(1 mark)*

2 Outline two attributes that we attribute to ourselves as humans that we would not attribute to androids? *(2 marks)*

Question 1 is an interpretation question. To score one mark you must read and understand the passage and write a sentence about the 'empathy' test. If the question was worth more than one mark you would be expected to comment on whether you agree or disagree with the point Phillip Dick is making and why you have come to the conclusions that you have.

Question 2 is an application question. To score the two marks you have to identify any two characteristics you think humans have that androids do not have. Remember, you have to be confident. State what you think the item is about and why you think what you do.

Although the content of the following passages is rather difficult, it could certainly form an examination question. The purpose of the exercise is to enhance all three of the skills you will be assessed on. Mead is one of the founders of sociology and he made a significant contribution to our understanding of the self. Anthony Giddens is arguably one of the most influential sociologists working today and his critiques of Mead will score marks in the examination as evaluative points. However, in order to write down Giddens's critiques of Mead you must understand the passages, which is an interpretation and application skill.

Item D

Symbolic interactionism is perhaps the only leading school of thought in English speaking sociology that assigns a central place to agency and reflexivity. G. H. Mead's social philosophy hinges upon the relation of 'I' and 'we' in social interaction and the development of personality. But even in Mead's own writings, the 'I' appears as a more shadowy element than the socially determined self, which is elaborately discussed. In the works of most of Mead's followers, the social self displaces the 'I' altogether, thus foreclosing the option that Mead took out on the possibility of incorporating reflexivity into the theory of action. Where this happens, symbolic interactionism is readily assimilated within the mainstream of sociological thought, as a sort of 'sociological social psychology' concentrated upon face to face interaction.

Source: A. Giddens, *Politics, Sociology and Social Theory*, p. 236, Polity: Oxford 1995

Item E

We might suppose that the 'I' is the agent ... The constitution of the 'I' comes about only via the 'discourse of the Other' – that is, through the acquisition of language – but the 'I' has to be related to the body as the sphere of action ... the 'I' only refers to who is speaking, the 'subject' of a sentence or utterance. An agent who has mastered the use of 'I' as Mead says has also mastered the use of 'me' ... For I have to know that I am 'I' when I speak to you, but that you are an 'I' when you speak to 'me', and that I am a 'you' when you speak to me ... and so on.

Source: A. Giddens, *The Constitution of Society: Outline of the Theory of Structuration*, p. 43, Polity: Oxford 1984

In the two items from Giddens identify and briefly comment on two of the points that Giddens makes. *(4 marks)*

Candidate's answer

In the above items Anthony Giddens explains that G. H. Mead made a distinction between the 'I' and the 'Me' in his analysis of the self. However, many of Mead's followers do not explore fully Mead's analysis of the 'I'. In addition, Giddens also explains that Mead's work is one of the first examples of what became known as the 'linguistic turn' in sociology. As Item B clearly shows, Mead places language at the very centre of his analysis of self-formation. Communication between people through language is a precondition for the emergence of self. It is only when an individual can organise their thoughts in terms of language that they become a self. Language allows a person to reflect upon themselves in an objective fashion, which is essential for the formation of the 'me'. A number of recent accounts of the self fall within this 'linguistic turn' notably Jurgen Habermas, Rom Harre and Charles Taylor.

Commentary

Answers in the three to five-mark category need to identify the relevant points from the items and to draw upon sociological knowledge as part of an explicit evaluation. The answer above clearly outlines two points from the comments by Giddens: first, that Mead made a distinction between 'I' and 'me', although these terms are not explained. Second, the point is made that language use is a key element in the process of self formation, or becoming a self. However, the idea that language allows people to form relationships with others – and that these relationships with other selves is crucial for the self is not fully explained. The candidate could also draw similarities with the work of Charles Taylor, whom we review in the next section. In terms of scoring marks for interpretation the candidate could have added points about 'feral children', for example the case of Victor, the 'Wild Boy of Aveyron' (see Item A, page 135). The suggestion that children who cannot speak are not selves could have been commented on, perhaps with reference to the film *Nell* which explores these issues.

The following example gives some information on how to attempt a four-mark question. As in the last item, the content is rather difficult but worth grappling with. Christopher Lasch made a significant contribution to our understanding of the self.

Item F

The history of modern society, from one point of view, is the assertion of social control over activities once left to individuals or their families. During the first stage of the industrial revolution, capitalists took production out of the household and collectivized it, under their own supervision, in the factory. They proceeded to appropriate the workers' skills and technical knowledge, by means of 'scientific management', and to bring these skills together under managerial direction. Finally they extended their control over the worker's private life as well, as doctors, psychiatrists, teachers, child guidance experts, officers of the juvenile courts, and other specialists began to supervise child-rearing, formerly the business of the family ...

Increasingly the same forces that have impoverished work and civic life invade the private realm and its last stronghold, the family ...

Instead of serving as a refuge, it more and more closely resembled the harsh world of work. Relations within the family took on the same character as relations elsewhere ...

Source: C. Lasch, *Haven in a Heartless World*, pp. 53–4, New Havey 1977

1 According to the item, people have lost control over personal life in their families, but who is responsible for this loss? *(1 mark)*

2 Outline four ways in which Lasch's view of the family differs from any other sociological theory of the family with which you are familiar. *(4 marks)*

In order to score the one mark available in question 1 the candidate must write a sentence which is based upon, and briefly explains, the relevant passage from the item which is: 'Finally they extended their control over the worker's private life as well, as doctors, psychiatrists, teachers, child guidance experts, officers of the juvenile courts, and other specialists began to supervise child-rearing, formerly the business of the family ...'

To score all four marks available for question 2 the candidate must explain briefly what Lasch is saying about the family. This would be worth two marks, and would include observations such as:

> In Item A Christopher Lasch argues that parents are becoming de-skilled in the modern world. In other words, parents are losing their traditional parenting skills to specialists from outside of the family unit. In addition, Lasch suggests that relations within the family are becoming more formal and are taking on the same character as relations elsewhere. This means, as Item A makes clear, that: 'Instead of serving as a refuge, it more and more closely resembled the harsh world of work.'

A good contrast with Christopher Lasch is the work of Talcott Parsons. As you may recall from your reading on the family in your textbook, in sharp contrast to Lasch, Parsons suggests that the modern nuclear family is responsible for the 'socialisation of young children' and the 'stabilisation of adult personalities'. You need to explain these two points, with a short account of how they differ from the points raised by Lasch. In short, this would include explaining that, in Parsons's view, parents are not becoming de-skilled and that the relationships with the family are not becoming harsh and formal.

The next example could be an examination question and is written in that form. As above, the purpose of the exercise is to enhance all three of the skills you will be assessed upon. This exercise will give you an opportunity to explore what you need to do to gain all the marks in a six-mark question. Like Christopher Lasch, Richard Sennett has also made a significant contribution to our understanding of the self.

Read the following passages by Richard Sennett and answer the questions.

Item G

In such a society, the basic human energies of narcissism are so mobilized that they enter systematically and perversely into human relationships ... Narcissism [is] a character disorder, it is self-absorption which prevents one from understanding what belongs within the domain of the self and self-gratification and what belongs outside it. ... This absorption in self, oddly enough, prevents gratification of self needs; it makes the person at the moment of attaining an end or connecting with another person feel that 'this isn't what I wanted.' ...

The withdrawal of commitment, the continual search for definition from within of 'who I am,' produces pain ... narcissism withdraws physical love from any kind of commitment, personal or social.

The most common form in which narcissism makes itself known to the person is by a process of inversion: If only I could feel more, or if only I could really feel, then I could relate to others or have 'real' relations with them.

... [destructive gemeinschaft or the market exchange of intimacies] ... reinforces this fruitless search for an identity ...

Source: R. Sennett, *The Fall of Public Man*, pp. 8–9, Cambridge University Press: Cambridge 1977

Item H

Narcissism and the market exchange of self-revelations structure the conditions under which the expression of feeling in intimate circumstances becomes destructive.

Source: R. Sennett, *The Fall of Public Man*, p. 10, 1977

Item I

Broadly stated, when people today seek to have full and open emotional relations with each other, they succeed only in wounding each other. This is the logical consequence of the destructive gemeinschaft.

Source: R. Sennett, *The Fall of Public Man*, p. 223, 1977

1. **What do you think Richard Sennett understands by the term 'the Intimate Society'?** ***(6 marks)***
2. **Outline four similarities between the work of Lasch and the work of Sennett in relation to 'the self'.** ***(4 marks)***

3 Would you describe Richard Sennett's contribution to our understanding of the self as an 'optimistic' or 'pessimistic' contribution? Give four reasons for your answer. *(4 marks)*

Question 1 is a difficult interpretation question which requires careful thought before answering. As the items suggest, Sennett refers to 'the Intimate Society' as a society organised on the basis of two principles:

- **Narcissism**, by which Sennett means the hunt for enjoyment for the self which at the same time prevents that enjoyment from taking place.
- **Destructive gemeinschaft** or 'a market exchange of intimacies', in which individuals are encouraged to make revelations on the grounds that this activity is a moral good in itself.

To score all six marks the candidate would be expected not only to mention narcissism and destructive gemeinschaft or 'a market exchange of intimacies', but also to give a short outline of what these difficult terms mean.

The four similarities asked for in question 2 could include:

- the notion of narcissism in their work;
- the pessimistic view which underpins their work;
- when individuals attempt to develop open and emotional relations with each other, they succeed only in causing damage to each other;
- the withdrawal of physical love from any kind of commitment, either personal or social.

To get all the available marks for question 3 the candidate would have to say that, on balance, Sennett presents a rather pessimistic view of both the self and of city life. He argues that the public space in the city is viewed as 'dead' and the inhabitants of the city are isolated, inhibited from fulfilling personal relationships, transported in cars which diminish their relationship with their surroundings and isolated at work in buildings which place an individual under a high degree of constant surveillance.

The city becomes organised around two principles: narcissism, 'the search for gratification of the self', and destructive gemeinschaft, which is characterised by: repression, loss of participation and violence.

Identity

Identity is concerned with questions of who we are as individuals and who we are as a group. In other words, our identity defines which groups we belong to. The philosopher A. J. Ayer suggested that the general criteria of personal identity may be solely physical in nature. In other words, that our personal identity may be based upon our physical appearance. In contrast to this view, the philosopher Hume viewed the self as a 'bundle of perceptions', and in this sense our identity may be built upon such experiences and exist as a factual relationship between experiences. In contrast to this view, Ayer argues that only persons can have experiences and one must be a person before one can do any experiencing. Hume's argument suggests that our identity can exist as a disembodied spirit and as a memory trace. Ayer's conclusion is that: '... we would appear to have no alternative but to make people's identities depend upon the identity of their bodies ...' (A. J. Ayer, p. 192, Macmillan: London 1956).

Before you attempt the following question you might find it useful to read in your textbook about Harold Garfinkel's study of Agnes, the transsexual.

The purpose of the following exercise is to get you to think about 'passing techniques' – how Agnes, who had been born and brought up for 18 years as a man, decided that she was really a woman trapped in a man's body and attempted to 'pass' as a woman, not only dressing as a woman, but living as a 'normal' woman.

Item J

... Agnes had to furnish a urine specimen when she was examined as part of a physical examination for a job with an insurance company ... Agnes made the excuse to the physician ... that she was unable to urinate but that she would be happy to return the specimen later in the day. ... It then occurred to her that it might be possible from an examination of the urine to determine the sex of the person. ... [Agnes] told her roommate that she had a mild kidney infection and was afraid that if the infection showed up in the urine she would be turned down for the job. The room-mate did her the favour of furnishing her with the bottle of urine which Agnes submitted as her own.

Source: H. Garfinkel, p. 143, *Studies in Ethnomethodology*, Prentice Hall: New Jersey 1967

What are the implications of the technique described by Garfinkel in Item J for our understanding of how individual people manage impressions of themselves? *(6 marks)*

Candidate's answer

The techniques described by Garfinkel in the item, which were used by Agnes, are known as 'passing techniques'. These are attempts to manage impressions, in a similar fashion to the activity of the self with stigma in Goffman's analysis. Garfinkel discusses 'passing' in terms of 'management devices': '... attempts to come to terms with practical circumstances as a texture of relevances over the continuing occasions of interpersonal transactions.' (Garfinkel, 1967)

One of the techniques Agnes used was 'anticipatory following', learning from people's questions or from situations by successfully attempting to analyse questions and situations in an effort to find clues hidden within them on 'normal' ways of behaving. However, Agnes was forced to reveal the truth about her body and her upbringing to her boyfriend Bill. Agnes had been going out with Bill for some time and Bill wished to marry Agnes. Although she was in love with Bill and told him this, she had always refused to have intercourse with him. At first she said she had an infection and then explained that she had a condition which prevented her from having sexual intercourse. Bill demanded to know more about 'the condition' and eventually Agnes had to tell Bill the truth.

Commentary

This response is excellent in terms of the knowledge expressed, including as it does a quote from Garfinkel and some knowledge of Garfinkel's text. In addition there is a very good contrast between the work of Garfinkel and the work of Goffman on the management of impressions. However, it is limited on interpretation and application. What do you need to need to do in order to gain the marks available for these skills? Consider the following points.

Put yourself in the position of Bill. What would you do? Would you end the relationship or would you continue with the relationship? Outline your reasons as if you were talking to other sociology students.

In the interpretation and application skill domain you will score marks for outlining your own relevant personal experience. This question aims to make you explore you own thoughts, feelings and prejudices. Even if you have not lived your life as a person of the opposite sex to which you were born, you will still have used some 'passing techniques'. On your first day as a sociology student did you dress in a fashion in which you believed sociology students would dress? Did you carry your textbook around with you in an effort to look more like a student? Have you ever attempted to give your sociology teacher the impression that you knew what he or she was talking about when you did not have a clue? These are all examples of passing techniques, and you could make use of them in your answer.

Evaluation in culture and identity questions: contemplate, contend and convince

As sociologists we are constantly challenging the commonsense presuppositions that make up everyday life. In addition, as sociologists we are constantly looking at the merits and failings of arguments, evidence and theories. If you ask yourself which theories are the most successful, which are the most convincing, which are based solely upon personal opinion, then you already have an awareness of the skill of evaluation. This questioning is what we understand by evaluation, and if you can do this well in the examination you will be successful. Your evaluation should contain reasoned judgements which are:

- balanced;
- critical;
- contain a justification for what you think and why you think it.

A typical culture and identity A-level question, which would be worth about 10 marks, is:

Outline and evaluate any one sociological contribution to our understanding of sexual identity. *(10 marks)*

In responding, always present both the strengths and the weaknesses of any theories which are relevant to the question or which you yourself introduce into the discussion.

In order to gain all 10 marks you need first to give a brief outline of what you understand by the term 'sexual identity'. Traditionally, '**identity**' has had two key elements:

- being part of a group;
- the common categorising of outward phenomena, such as race or the clothes people wear.

'**Sexual**' can have a purely physical meaning, such as having sexual intercourse or reference to differences between the sexual organs of men and women. Alternatively, 'sexual' can be a cultural notion, related to ideas of masculinity and femininity. In other words, what it means to look and behave as a man or woman. Your answer should include some mention of all these issues.

The answer could then go on to outline the work of Harold Garfinkel on Agnes, the transsexual, together with any positive points you may want to raise about Garfinkel's study and any criticism you may have of it.

Culture

Sociologists argue that culture should be understood as 'common ways of behaving' within a community, which have a considerable role to play in the creation of our identity. Most sociologists have some theory of culture within their analyses. However, you may want to ask yourself if some cultures are better than others?

Two terms are important for your understanding of this question:

- cultural relativism – the argument that all cultures are different, but of equal validity. Cultures simply reflect the shared meaning within a given context;
- ethnocentrism – the idea that one's own culture is superior to any other.

The next example involves you in considering your own views. As suggested above, the interpretation and application skill domain rewards people for making valid sociological points by drawing upon their own personal experience. Evaluation is about making judgements on questions such as:

1. **What do you think are the essential elements of human cultures?**
2. **What do you believe are the essential elements of British or English culture?**
3. **Is your culture superior to any other culture? Outline some reasons for your answer.**

Once you have attempted these questions, compare your answers with other sociology students. If you or the other sociology students accept the cultural relativist position, ask yourself if the people who wanted to kill Salman Rushdie because in his book, *The Satanic Verses*, he made a number of offensive comments about Islam and the Prophet Mohammed, had a valid case?

Take a range of A-level Sociology textbooks and have a close look at the work of Talcott Parsons and Emile Durkheim. In particular, look at what both Parsons and Durkheim have to say about the 'conscience collective' and what Parsons has to say about common values or 'pattern variables'. Draw up a list of any similarities between what Parsons has to say and what Durkheim has to say on these issues.

The purpose of this exercise is to allow you to develop your interpretative skills in terms of identifying similarities between theories. You will then be able to use your critique of Durkheim to develop evaluation answers to questions that ask you, for instance, to 'compare and contrast' the work of different sociologists.

Below are a number of evaluative statements about the Marxian concept of ideology. Look at a range of textbooks which discuss this concept and then briefly explain if you agree or disagree with the following comments, stating at least one reason why. The purpose of the exercise is to help you to develop a critique of the Marxian conception of ideology.

- Ideology explains why a revolutionary working class has not emerged within capitalist society.
- The Marxist argument puts too much importance on shared values and beliefs.
- Violence can be used to maintain the capitalist society.
- There is too much emphasis upon class interests; people have other interests related to race, gender and sexuality, for example.
- It is not apparent if the bourgeoisie believe the dominant ideology they are said to produce or simply impose a set of known false beliefs upon the proletariat.

One of the criticisms of the sociologies of Durkheim, Marx and Parsons is that they treat people as 'cultural dopes'. In other words, individuals are simply pushed about by forces outside of their control. As will be suggested below, this is said to be typical of Modernist writers.

Item K

'Mr Trout,' I said. 'I am a novelist, and I created you for use in my books.'
'Pardon me?' he said.
'I'm your Creator,' I said. 'You're in the middle of a book right now – close to the end of it, actually.'
'Um,' he said.
'Are there any questions you'd like to ask?'
'Pardon me?' he said.
'Feel free to ask anything you want – about the past, about the future.' I said. 'There's a Nobel Prize in your future.'
'A what?' he said.
'A Nobel Prize in medicine.'
'Huh,' he said. It was a noncommittal sound.
'I've also arranged for you to have a reputable publisher from now on. No more Beaver Books for you.'
'Um,' he said.
'If I were in your spot, I would certainly have lots of questions,' I said.
'Do you have a gun?' he said.
I laughed there in the dark, tried to turn on the light again, activated the windshield washer again. 'I don't need a gun to control you, Mr Trout. All I have to do is write down something about you, and that's it.'

Source: K. Vonnegut, *Breakfast of Champions*, pp. 266–7, Panther: London 1992

1 Draw up a list of similarities between Mr Trout and the conception of self in the analyses of Durkheim, Marx, and Parsons.

2 How much independence do individuals have in:
- **Durkheim's analysis?**
- **Parsons's analysis?**
- **Marx's analysis?**

It is important for you to build up some arguments about the work of sociologists so that you can develop your own interpretation and evaluation of their work. The responses that you develop can be used in the full practice data-response questions at the end of this chapter. In the questions below we continue to focus on the work of the classic sociological writers.

1 Draw up a list of similarities between Durkheim and Marx, in terms of their understanding of culture and self (human agency).

2 Draw up a list of any differences that you can identify between the work of Durkheim and Marx in general.

3 Write a paragraph which has the following components and which starts as follows:

Although there are many differences between the work of Durkheim and Marx, such as: ...

....

....

....

There are also a number of similarities, in terms of the way in which they view the human agent, e.g.

....

....

....

Either: I find one view more convincing than the other because ...

....

....

or: I find neither the view of Marx nor of Durkheim convincing because ...

....

....

Globalisation and culture

Globalisation is the idea that the whole world is becoming a single place. As a process globalisation directly affects the lives of all the people in the world. Drugs, sex tourism, the nature of the work we do, eating disorders, plastic surgery and more, all have a global dimension to them.

This next exercise will allow you to grasp the nature of the processes that make up what sociologists term globalisation. These processes of globalisation have a significant effect upon the self and upon our sense of identity in that they generate feelings of uncertainty.

Item L

The fact and the perception of ever increasing inter-dependence at the global level, the rising concern about the fate of the world as a whole and of the human species (particularly because of the threats of ecological degradation, nuclear disaster and AIDS), and the colonisation of the local by global life (not least via the mass media) facilitate massive processes of relativization of cultures, doctrines, ideologies and cognitive frames of reference.

Source: R. Robertson, *Globalisation*, p. 87, Sage: London 1992

Item M

What follows is a folk tale, I have no idea as to its validity!

After the completion of the film *Star Trek: Generations*, William Shatner and his wife decided to go on holiday. The Shatners wanted to 'get away from it all' and decided to spend a holiday deep in the jungle of Cambodia. When their plane landed they took a taxi to the river and headed for its source. After changing boats several times because of the river becoming narrower, they eventually made their way up river in a rowing boat. Eventually the Shatners made their way deep into the jungle and their long journey came to an end. As they were taking their luggage out of the boat a figure came out of the jungle to help them. The figure from the jungle stared at William Shatner and said in astonishment, 'Captain Kirk'.

1. **With reference to Item L what is Robertson suggesting about the process of globalisation?** *(4 marks)*
2. **What do you think is the significance of Item M for sociological arguments about the processes of cultural globalisation?** *(7 marks)*
3. **Outline what the significance of Items L and M might be for any sociological theories of identity with which you are familiar.** *(10 marks)*

Commentary

1. Item L is a complex quote and the language used is not easy to follow. However, the message is a thought-provoking one. Robertson is suggesting that:
   - There is increasing inter-dependence between people in the world which is truly global in nature.
   - In addition, part of this inter-dependence is a global concern about the future of the human species itself. Because of ecological degradation, nuclear disaster and AIDS, human beings may become extinct.

- The 'colonisation of the local by global life (not least via the mass media)' means that local cultures are being destroyed by global cultures which are spread all over the globe by the mass media.
- In addition to the destruction of local cultures, we accept global doctrines, ideologies and ways of thinking about the world which Robertson terms 'cognitive frames of reference'.

2 The significance of Item M is that even people deep in the jungle are fans of *Star Trek*. In other words, this is an example of the points that Robertson was raising in Item L.

3 The significance of Items L and M for sociological theories of identity is a complex issue. On the one hand, the process of globalisation can be seen as liberating. These processes enhance the choice of resources available to people in the construction of an identity that they feel both happy and comfortable with. People today know much more about how others lead their lives; this helps to break down traditions and local ignorance.

In contrast, the process of globalisation can be seen to destroy local cultures. This is not only unsettling for individuals but gives their lives an uncertain feel. This is what Robertson called the processes of relativization. Rather than creating tolerance of others who may have very different ways of living, people in communities may attempt to re-invent traditions in an effort to give themselves a sense of identity. The proof of belonging to such new, or what some sociologists have termed 'imagined communities', is the active involvement in acts of great cruelty against others who are seen to be different.

Arjun Appadurai explains that the processes of globalisation are brought about by a number of flows:

- ethnoscapes – the flow of people, tourists, immigrants, refugees, exiles and guest workers;
- technoscapes – the movement of technology;
- finanscapes – the rapid movement of money via money markets and stock exchanges;
- mediascapes – information and images generated and distributed by film, television, newspapers and magazines;
- ideoscapes – the movement of political ideas and ideologies.

The postmodern self

The term postmodernism suggests a radical or 'experiential' break with the past. For Jean-Francois Lyotard, the postmodern condition is a situation in which individuals have lost faith in what he calls 'grand narratives'. These are belief systems which we once accepted and which gave us a feeling of security. We feel therefore as if the 'social glue' is dissolving. The bonds which once held communities together no longer have the same force which they once had. As a social formation postmodernity has no foundations, no shared culture to give us a feeling of security; no grand theory to help us explain or understand the situation we are in. The self is isolated in the postmodern condition without logic, rationality or morality to guide it. The postmodern condition is a world without certainty.

Practice data-response questions

Before you attempt to answer any culture and identity data-response questions, it is important to consider the following list of points:

- Have you identified the 'action' statements or words?
- Do you have a reasoned interpretation of the key arguments or points given in the items?
- Do you have a reasoned interpretation of the questions asked?
- Do you know the appropriate theories, concepts and relevant studies?
- Are you able to take information from one area of the syllabus and use it in the area of culture and identity?

- Do you have up-to-date and relevant examples to make use of?

Question 7.1

The question below is a broad one which covers some of the general issues surrounding the concepts of identity and culture. After the questions we have included two student answers followed by a comment on these answers and on what examiners would expect you to include in order to gain the marks allocated to each part of the question.

Item N

To all intents and purposes a new-born human baby is helpless. Not only is it physically dependent on older members of the species, but it also lacks the behaviour patterns necessary for living in human society. It relies primarily on certain biological drives such as hunger and the charity of its elders to satisfy those drives. The infant has a lot to learn. In order to survive, it must learn the skills, knowledge and accepted ways of behaving in the society into which it is born. It must learn a way of life; in sociological terminology, it must learn the 'culture' of its society.

Source: adapted from M. Haralambos and M. Holborn, *Sociology: Themes and Perspectives*, 4th edition,Collins Educational: London 1995

Item O

As individuals, we are placed in a range of positions which affect our life chances, e.g, British, middle-class, Sikh, adolescent. It is the unique combination of these positions that gives us our individuality and, at the same time, it is the extent to which we experience these positions with others that provides the basis for collective action and change. Here we focus on identity and its implications for social change. In the past one of the most significant bases for individual identity was one's social class position, but with the many social changes that have taken place in Britain during the post-war period, some sociologists now claim that other experiences have replaced social class as the primary source of identity.

Source: adapted from J. Clarke and C. Saunders, 'Who Are You And So What?', *Sociology Review 1(1)*, September 1991

Item P

Ethnicity has been defined in a number of different ways by sociologists and others. Broadly speaking, an ethnic group is a collectivity based on a shared culture which exists within society. This culture is never static, but is dynamic, being both confirmed and continuously changed as it is transmitted from one generation to the next. Although not all ethnic minorities are based on racial groups, a common feature of most ethnic minorities is a sense of racial identity and history which may be passed on to younger generations by their involvement in various cultural institutions and practices.

Item Q

The concept of culture, together with that of society, is one of the most widely used notions in sociology. 'Culture' can be conceptually distinguished from 'society', but there are very close connections between these notions. 'Culture' concerns the way of life of the members of a given society – their habits and customs, together with the material goods they produce. 'Society' refers to the system of inter-relationships which connects together the individuals who share a common culture. No culture could exist without a society. But, equally, no society could exist without culture. However, it is evident that we do not share the same culture. Sociologists have explained such cultural variations (or cultural diversity) in terms of the differences that are to be found in and between societies. Values and norms of behaviour vary widely from culture to culture, often contrasting in a radical way with what people from Western societies consider 'normal' or 'uniform'. Small societies (like hunting and gathering societies), tend to be culturally uniform, but most Western industrialised societies are culturally diverse, often involving numerous subcultures.

Source: adapted from A. Giddens, *Sociology*, Polity: Oxford 1989

1 What is the name of the sociological concept used to describe the process of how children learn the culture of society? (Item N 7)
(1 mark)

2 Apart from social class, indicate four areas of experience from which we draw our identity. (Item O) *(4 marks)*

3 With reference to the items and elsewhere, briefly define and give an example of each of the following concepts:
(a) norm *(2 marks)*
(b) value. *(2 marks)*

4 With reference to Item P and elsewhere, identify and describe three ways in which the culture of an ethnic group may be 'transmitted from one generation to the next'. *(6 marks)*

5 With reference to Item Q and other sources, assess the claim made by some sociologists that each society is characterised by a shared culture. *(10 marks)*

Candidate A's answer

1 Socialisation.

2 Race, religion, age, experience.

3 (a) Norm, e.g. social norm – what we consider normal, e.g. we put on clothes before leaving our houses.

(b) Value – personal belief, view, opinion, e.g. to help someone if they are in need; to be a vegetarian if we don't agree with killing animals.

4 (i) When you are a child you usually want to be like your mum or dad. Certain things they do become your norms, e.g. Chinese people eating with chopsticks. Watching and learning can result in transmitting culture.

(ii) Obeying rules that others obey, e.g. by attending cultural institutions.

(iii) By following cultural practices, e.g. Muslims don't drink alcohol.

5 'Culture can be conceptually distinguished from society but there are v.close connections. Culture concerns the way of life of the members of a given society, habits, customs, together with material goods they produce. No culture could exist without society but society could also exist without culture. The claim that each society is characterised by a shared culture is quite true. As mentioned earlier society cannot survive without culture does show that each culture must be characterised as diff. e.g. in China they eat with chopsticks, in France food like frogs legs, horse and snails are considered delicacies. Each society has traditional stereotypes mainly 'cultures' this is what makes us and allows us all to be different in each society we all follow those certain rules if the British were to start eating sat on cushions off low tables all the time it would probably be considered quite odd.

Candidate B's answer

1 Socialisation is the way in which children are taught their society's culture. The process begins in the home and continues throughout life.

2 Four areas are: our family life; the circles in which we live and move; our hobbies, i.e. the way we spend our leisure time, and a fourth one is the particular form of media we choose to read and watch; in some cases 'The Sun' and Radio One, in other cases 'The Times' and the radio programme 'Classic FM'. These all influence our identity.

3 A norm is an acceptable way of behaving in a particular society, its violation isn't punishable by law but could lead to ridicule, disapproval or, at the extreme, ostracization by other members of society.

A good example is the way we dress in appropriate clothes for particular occasions, i.e. it is the norm to wear sombre and discrete colours for funerals. Someone turning up wearing a scarlet sequinned sexy outfit would be very frowned upon.

A value is a thing we attach importance too, such as, in our own particular society the sanctity of life. For this reason, if we see a home on fire and people screaming for help we would dial 999 immediately to get the fire engine. At the same time we would help in what ever way we could ourselves and perhaps by finding a ladder if to hand or cushioning their fall if they jumped from a height. We wouldn't simply just ignore the situation.

4 The first way would be to ensure that the language was passed on, even if for the greater part of the day, the language of the home country was being spoken. Another important aspect of ethnic minorities culture is the food and this could for the greater number of meals in a week be prepared and eaten as practised by the ethnic minority. A third and final way, is the wearing of traditional dress and even if it is more practical and comfortable to wear the clothes of the home country, ethnic minorities both in their homes and for special occasions continue to wear their own traditional dress.

The above ways not only perpetuate the minorities cultures way of life, but keep the social fabric together by the very fact of sharing; because of this the younger members are encouraged to invite their friends to share in their culture and on inter-marrying outside the culture are encouraged to bring their new partners into the culture.

5 Culture describes all aspects of life which are peculiar to a particular society it includes tangible things such as dress, language, arts and crafts but also it is shared norms, values and beliefs. Without a shared culture human society would not be possible. Life would simply consist of a free-for-all; but having a culture every person becomes aware of her/his identity and role in life and society is better able to function.

However, societies vary, in very simple ones such as that of hunter gathers there is a division of labour between gender only. Thus, as in the Muuiliy pygmy society in Africa. The men hunt and the women gather edible fruits and rear children but otherwise their lives follow much the same patterns and a shared culture is the norm. However, in more complex industrial societies the division of labour becomes more divisive and hence roles ever more numerous and varied, this leads to different levels of income and different ways of life. Then subcultures frequently develop catering for minority groups. Earlier in the century coal miners in the Welsh valleys with their long arduous dirty work underground and their leisure hours filled with choral singing led a much different life to residents in the west end of London passing their time in clubs and wealthy homes and spending their leisure time at parties and going to the theatre.

Young people frequently form their own subcultures in deliberate opposition to the main culture and will have their own form of dress and vocabulary. An example of this is the Mods and Rockers of the fifties. Membership of this type of subculture is often transient and members often will revert to the main culture as they grow older.

Another reason for subcultures within a society is the result of colonisation in the past. In Britain, many ethnic minorities are entitled to hold British passports, hence the large and varied number of ethnic minorities in Britain today: Afro-Caribbean, Jewish, Pakistani and Bangladeshi to name but a few, they live under the aegis of British culture but not unnaturally adhere to their own endeavour to keep this intact. This is demonstrated by them using their own culture (language, diet and dress and is more visible at certain times of the year when they hold their own religious and nationalistic festivals such as the 'Lion dances' at Chinese new year and the famous Notting Hill Carnival held communally by the Afro-Caribbean community. They are all subcultures living within the countries own main culture.

Some sociologists argue that no culture is truly shared within a modern society in as much as there are widely different rewards for the roles played by its members.

Marx more than anyone pointed to what he saw as inequalities in society. He identified two main divisions: the ruling class and the working class, the former always exploit the latter giving rise to oppression and ultimately conflict. Certainly as already mentioned, in the more complex industrial and post-industrial societies there are great inequalities of wealth and power.

Functionalists such as Durkheim and Parsons look at the variety of roles but don't see this as necessarily leading to conflict. People have an innate potential to fulfil a particular role, I believe and since a complex division of labour requires a wide spectrum of ability, those able and willing to train for a long period of time for a particular role deserve a greater reward. Weber like Marx believed that class as such is formed in the market place but he didn't see it as solely economic as Marx did, but also included a notion of status.

However, whatever the derivation of divisions within a culture all modern theories believe that it does exist as an entity per se, where as theories of postmodernists undermine this by saying that a common culture no longer exists. Sociologists such as Baudillard and Lyotard say that there is a fragmentation of traditional groups such as the family and in rejecting these forms and categories say that society is becoming more fluid and dynamic offering much more individual opportunity and choice of roles for the future.

Certainly, with globalisation there are upheavals in the social world 'man' himself does not change. The basic unit of society prefers order to chaos and that there will always be men and women strong enough to strive for all that is good in society, and be able to preserve all the things which help to help to maintain a very real and valuable culture which each one of us, in our own way can enrich our individual participation. So I would argue with those sociologies who claim that each society is characterised by a shared culture, subcultures not withstanding, and that a sharing of all the things we hold dear is the only way to live in an ordered and stable society.

Commentary

1 Socialisation is the expected answer. However, students who mention concepts such as schooling or acculturation should be awarded one mark. Both of the responses above would gain one mark.

2 One mark will be given for the clear indication of four particular areas of experience, such as the ones suggested below:

- national identity groupings;
- ethnic groupings;
- age groupings;
- political groupings;
- feminist groupings;
- citizenship groupings;
- power groupings;
- status groupings (acceptable, but may be illustrated by reference to some of the above groupings);
- religious groupings;
- family groupings.

Candidate A's response would gain three marks and candidate B would gain all four marks.

3 For **norm**, one mark will be given for any clear, acceptable definition, such as 'a specific blueprint for action, defining acceptable/unacceptable action in particular situations', and the second mark will be given for an acceptable example, such as using cutlery when eating, dressing for an occasion, starting a conversation. In our examples, both candidates do what the question asks. Candidate A's response lacks clarity. While the example given is acceptable, the definition of norm as 'normal' would not merit a mark.

For **value**, one mark will be given for any clear, acceptable definition, such as a general guideline for behaviour indicating whether 'it is good, desirable, worthwhile', etc., and the second mark would be given for an acceptable example such as the value of Western materialism, or the value of generosity in Sioux society. As with the definition of norm, candidate A's definition of value would not be regarded as sufficient for a mark although the example given would gain one mark. In contrast, the response from candidate B is full and clear, answers the question accurately and would gain the two marks.

4 Pointing to three sources of identity (drawn from the list below) will gain three marks. In

addition the candidate can receive three additional marks for a brief, accurate description and/or relevant example of each:

- common language;
- sense of belonging;
- an historical past;
- religion;
- mass media;
- forms of dress;
- family;
- identifiable neighbourhood;
- schooling (e.g. 'separate schools);
- regular social interaction;
- clan/group membership;
- lifestyle artistic impressions (e.g. painting, sculpture, films).

Both responses identify three ways in which the culture of an ethnic group may be transmitted, however neither response is very well written. Candidate B does attempt to explain in greater detail how this transmission occurs and this is a better constructed answer which would merit a 'top band' mark of perhaps five. Candidate A's response is rather simplistic and would gain three to four marks.

5 To gain top marks you would need to make full use of interpretation skills, application skills, evaluation skills, knowledge and understanding. The action words make it clear that the candidate must evaluate the arguments put forward by a range of sociologists that within each society there is a 'common culture'. In the first instance you must make clear what you understand by 'culture'. To do this you might make use of Item O. Sociological approaches which suggest a common culture are Durkheim, Parsons, Marx and a range of others. You must outline three of these contributions and evaluate them. Looking at Marxian and non-Marxian contributions allows you to compare and contrast these differing approaches. Finally, you might want to suggest that all three of the approaches suggested are 'modernist' approaches and, as such, are undermined by the emergence of 'postmodern' approaches which suggest that there is no common culture.

Thus to get in the top band of eight to ten marks, your answer should contain evidence that the knowledge presented from the items and elsewhere has been fully understood, with an explicitly theoretical orientation to the question being evident (for example, functionalist, Marxist and feminist views on cultural issues). In addition there should be an excellent expression of these ideas, with spelling and grammar of a very good standard – all of which would facilitate the intelligibility of the answer. The response of Candidate B comes closest to this standard and would gain a top band mark, with Candidate A's response just below that standard.

Question 7.2

Below is an example of a possible examination question and the sort of mark scheme that an examiner would follow in marking the question. Read the items and attempt the question which gives you an opportunity to raise many of the issues that you have explored in the shorter exercises in this chapter.

Item R

Following Durkheim, Parsons considers the value system of a society to be one of its essential characteristics. For both thinkers, common agreement on certain fundamental values among the members of society is an element of the definition of a society. Without such agreement there would be no society.

Source: E. C. Cuff *et al.*, *Perspectives in Sociology*, p. 45, Unwin Hyman: London 1984

Item S

Durkheim argued that society was a reality sui generis. Society is not reducible to the sum of individuals within it, it is exterior to them, but it is nonetheless a social fact since it effects a constraint on their actions. The idea that we live a life determined for us is clear in Durkheim's work ...

Talcott Parsons set out to produce a theory of social action, of how humans act. Parsons (1937) considered human beings to be rational but he wanted to consider the way the choices rational humans made resulted in stable societies rather than anarchy. He argued that an analysis based simply on individual action could not explain the emergence of a society where those activities were regulated.

Source: adapted from M. Kirby *et al.*, *Sociology in Pespective*, pp. 17 and 23, Hainemann: Oxford 1997

Item T

Garfinkel rejects the view that we accomplish everyday activities according to some preset rules or procedures laid down by our culture and socialization. He criticises mainstream sociologists for assuming this, describing them as portraying human beings as 'cultural dopes'. Instead, Garfinkel portrays social actors as highly skilled in accomplishing everyday social activities and creating the appearance of social order.

Source: P. Taylor, *Culture and Identity*, p.198, Collins Educational: London 1997

Item U

Kemalism (the westernising/modernising ideology of the first Turkish leader Mustafa Kemal [Ataturk] in the 1920s) was an ideology imposed on people from above. Its self-declared mission was to revolutionize the society for the good of the people. For the good of a backward and uncivilised people, however, a people whose commitment to progress and civilization could not be relied on – could not be trusted to take part in its own revolution.

Source: adapted from K. Robins, 'Interrupting Identities: Turkey/Europe', in S. Hall and P du Gay, *Questions of Cultural Identity*, p. 70, Sage: London 1996

1 **From the information given in the items, give the name of a sociologist who is primarily concerned with the sociology of social action and an example of a sociologist who is primarily concerned with the sociology of social structure.** *(2 marks)*

2 **Identify and explain two ways in which the social structure can determine the behaviour of human beings.** *(7 marks)*

3 **What do you believe Garfinkel means by the term 'cultural dopes'?** *(2 marks)*

4 **To what extent do you agree with Garfinkel's point that mainstream sociology treats human beings as 'cultural dopes'.** *(4 marks)*

5 **Some sociologies concentrate on social structure while other sociologies concentrate on social action. With reference to the information in the items and elsewhere, outline some of the similarities and differences between these two approaches to sociology.** *(10 marks)*

Mark scheme

1 0 marks — No relevant points.

1–2 marks — One mark for each correct example. For example, for two marks there would be a clear statement that for example, Durkheim or Parsons are sociologists concerned with social structure, while Garfinkel is concerned with social action.

2 0 marks — No relevant points.

1–2 marks — In this band, there is likely to be a commonsensical understanding of how people are pushed about by forces outside of their control. Evaluation will be minimal and not argued.

Answers are likely to be characterised by poor logical expression of ideas and the use of conceptual terms will be limited, imprecise and/or inaccurate.

Spelling, punctuation and grammar may show serious deficiencies and frequent errors.

3–5 marks — Answers in this mark band will be aware of the debate about the relationship between 'agency' and 'structure', and be able to apply relevant information and proof to support the answer. In terms of the explanation, however, there may be some imbalance, with either a deterministic position or a social action position taken for granted.

Sociological terms will be used correctly. In addition, grammar, punctuation and spelling will be of a reasonable standard with few errors.

6–7 marks At the top of the mark band, answers will be more balanced, with a commendable coverage of the arguments and evidence of the relationship between agency and structure. Use of observations which draw upon personal experience or information from books, film and television programmes, where applied, will be rewarded. These arguments and the evidence cited will be directly relevant to the question set. The evaluation will be explicit often within a concluding statement.

Grammar, punctuation and spelling will be of a good to excellent standard. Difficult sociological terms will be used in the appropriate manner.

3 0 marks No relevant points.

1–2 marks Any explicit and appropriate form of words which considers the opinion that individual human agents are pushed about by forces outside of their control.

4 0 marks No relevant points.

1–2 marks Answers in this mark band may tend to be unbalanced and one sided, with either the assumption that sociologists have argued that people are pushed about by forces outside of their control or the assumption that sociologists have assumed that people are not pushed about by such forces. Any evaluation will tend to be of a commonsensical nature.

3–4 marks Answers in this mark band will give a clear outline of what Garfinkel means by the comment 'cultural dopes' together with some evidence and argument that he might draw upon to support this view. The evaluation will be explicit, not simply a juxtaposition, and outline possible alternative views to that stated by Garfinkel.

Grammar, punctuation and spelling will be of a good to excellent standard and should add to the intelligibility of the answer. Difficult sociological terms will be used in the appropriate manner.

5 0 marks No relevant points.

1–3 marks In this mark band the responses from candidates may be little more than presentation of information given in the items. Any evaluation will tend to be of a commonsensical nature.

There will often be mistakes in the use of sociological terms, together with poor spelling, punctuation and grammar.

4–6 marks Though both social action perspectives and social structure perspectives will be looked at, the response may be unbalanced, with a tendency to look at only one perspective in passing and to write a great deal on the other perspective. The evaluation will be by simple juxtaposition rather than by being explicit.

A range of sociological concepts will be used and the expression will be clear and logical. Grammar, punctuation and spelling, including spelling of sociological terms, will be to a reasonable standard.

7–10 marks In this mark band the answers will be well balanced giving a full account of both social action and social structural accounts. Evaluation will be explicit and may be contained with a separate paragraph. Better answers will move beyond the general comparison of the two approaches but will explore the contribution that each perspective has made to our understanding of the human agent.

The ideas and their expression will be excellent. There will be a broad range of concepts used in an appropriate manner. Grammar, punctuation and spelling will be of a good to excellent standard and should add to the intelligibility of the answer. Difficult sociological terms will be spelt correctly and always used in the appropriate manner.